HARD DOWN! HARD DOWN!

HARD DOWN! HARD DOWN!

THE LIFE AND TIMES OF CAPTAIN JOHN ISBESTER FROM SHETLAND

1852-1913

Captain Jack Isbester ExC FNI

Whittles Publishing

Published by
Whittles Publishing Ltd.,
Dunbeath,
Caithness, KW6 6EG,
Scotland, UK

www.whittlespublishing.com

ISBN 978-184995-402-0

HARDDOWN.COM

The author's website contains a wealth of transcripts of the letters and postcards of Captain John Isbester, his family and friends accompanied by spreadsheets recording details of his ships and voyages, of sailing ship casualties of the 1870s to 1910s, a transcript of the Articles of Agreement for *Dalgonar*'s final voyage and a sprinkling of photos which did not make it into the published book.

Readers can leave messages and comments in the Blog.

The Isbester Archive

The Isbester Archive is a considerable collection of letters, postcards, documents and photographs mainly gathered by Allan Isbester, fourth son of Captain John Isbester. They provide much of the source material for Jack Isbester's historical biography of his grandfather.

The Isbester Archive has been accepted in principle by the Shetland Museum and Archive and is to be delivered to the Museum during the Summer of 2019.

CONTENTS

LIST OF ILLUSTRATIONS

FOREWORD BY PROFESSOR TONY LANE

At last a book with an original slant on the men and, yes, the women, of commercial sail's last years. For more than one hundred years, scores of books have been written by seafarers recalling and commenting on their experiences of working and living aboard square-rigged sailing ships. All were written from memory, some helpfully jogged by saved letters and 'telegraphic' diaries/logs. A great deal of this genre, very popular from the early twentieth century and into the 1960s, makes for fascinating and sometimes exciting reading. I've been collecting and reading these books for forty years and I'm persuaded of their essential authenticity by the sheer repetitiveness of accounts telling of deaths, desertions and unrelenting danger; appalling food, low wages, and long hours; brutality not always leavened by solidarities, acts of bravery and skill, and occasional kindnesses. Probably the best of these accounts is David Bone's, *The Brassbounder* first published in 1910 and thereafter more often than not in print. It certainly has literary flair but like the more prosaic authors, Bone has little to say about the family circumstances of either themselves or their shipmates. Now, however, thanks to Jack Isbester, readers have a unique opportunity to see beyond the rigours of daily life in sail (without ever losing sight of them) and find in satisfying detail something of the social origins and familial life of one of the last shipmasters in sail. In this book there is a consistent interrogation of a life at sea intimately interwoven with family relationships despite lengthy separations and scattered, infrequent and unreliable means of 'keeping in touch'.

The story begins in, and often returns to, the Shetlands, the birthplace of Jack's grandfather, Captain John ('Jack') Isbester. His family's daily life and broader social and economic circumstances have been sieved by the author's unremitting diligence in digging down and around in the detail of Shetland's self-supporting agriculture and its fishing industry where Captain 'Jack' learned to be a seaman. All of this has been additionally informed by the author's family's passion for keeping letters and documents. It's an extremely rare thing to be able to read letters passing between a shipmaster, his wife and other family members. Experienced readers of sailing ship days will find themselves in familiar territory when the story goes to sea. A broad reading will have revealed stories of shipwreck through grounding, ships consumed by fire with crews thereafter making lengthy passages in lifeboats, rescues of crews who have experienced the foregoing, a capsized ship drowning its master, its crew saved in a masterpiece of a rescue. But readers won't have found all this in one career as they will here. There is so very much to admire in this book apart from what I see as the real prize – the letters exchanged between Captain 'Jack' and his wife, Susie, and *her* letters home when she's at sea with her husband. Then there's another bonus – photographs which are just plain wonderful as also are the author's explanatory diagrams and 'user friendly' maps. Here is a biography written as a splendidly rounded social history of a late 19th century Shetlander.

Tony Lane

Professor Emeritus

Cardiff University School of Social Science

ACKNOWLEDGEMENTS

My father **Allan Isbester**, eighth child of Captain John Isbester, cherished his parents' history and often expressed the view that the story of his father's life should be written. He saved documents, letters, postcards and newspaper cuttings, and was always ready to reminisce about family, sailing ships and Shetland. Without his compiling and guarding of the Isbester Archives this account would have been much diminished. My mother **Jean Isbester** was an avid and discriminating reader and correspondent who had a big influence on my writing. She would have enjoyed this book.

My wife **Audrey** shared the considerable task of transcribing all the family correspondence – she read while I typed – and welcomed the fact that this book, unlike my previous ones, actually contains human interest. Audrey and my daughter **Claire Isbester** have read every word that I have written and both have helped with constructive suggestions and encouraging comments, for which I am very grateful. Claire also met me regularly in the London Guildhall Library where we spent many hours tracing John Isbester and his ships in the microfiched pages of *Lloyd's Lists*

The late **Captain John P Thomson OBE** of Sandness in Shetland knew John Isbester as a respected elder when he himself was a young officer. On his own retirement in the 1960s he went to considerable trouble to gather together a record of all the ships on which John Isbester sailed and sent it to my father. I have found this record and the commentary with which he accompanied it very helpful.

Useful advice on nautical sources and their interpretation from **Emeritus Professor Tony Lane,** a valued friend for more than 50 years, has been a considerable and welcome help, while **Dr Alston Kennerley** responded to my appeal for information on the loading, stowing and securing of cargo and ballast aboard sailing ships, suggesting a number of helpful and interesting sources.

From Shetland **Davie Smith**, retired fishing skipper, has helped me with his extensive knowledge of Shetland boats and fishing; **John Goodlad PhD** has made his fascinating study of the work of the Faroe smacks available to me; **Marion Hughson**, former Whiteness Registrar, has helped me to sort out details of the Isbester family history; and **Florence Grains** has clarified the story of Maggie Smith of Strome who 'couldna leave the sheep' to marry John Isbester in Liverpool.

A shipmate of mine from the 1950s, the late **Alan Thompson**, found himself sixty years later with the task of sorting through a neighbour's posthumous papers. Recognising that the correspondence included letters from my aunt reminiscing about life at sea with her father, he traced me and sent them to me, for which resourceful and thoughtful act I am most grateful. The aunt in question was the late Kathleen William Margaret Davies, née Isbester, and I am grateful to her son the late **John Davies**, his widow **Aeurona** and their son **Philip** for memories shared and documents loaned.

When needing a second opinion on sailing ship matters I have been fortunate to be able to consult two experienced sailing ship men, **Captain Peter Hamer BEng** and **Bill Dineley ExC**. Bill also explored the resources of the San Francisco Maritime National Historical Park and put me in contact with **Gina Bardi**, librarian, and her colleague **Stephen Canright**, park historian, both of whom were most helpful.

My warm thanks go to my grandsons **Jonah** and **Reuben Privett** who spent many hours searching through 5,000 wreck reports on the internet to identify large sailing ships which had been abandoned or lost between 1876 and 1914. Jonah also redrew and improved my diagrams, while Reuben created a Hard Down! website for me.

I am grateful to my nephew **Andrew Isbester** who discovered the record of John Isbester's sighting of the intra-mercurial planet Vulcan; to **Dr Anna Pegler-Gordon** who provided me with a revealing story about events in Frisco; to **Allen Martin** who translated Captain Jaffré's account of the rescue of the survivors of the *Dalgonar* disaster; and to **Scott Muir** who gave me some simple but effective advice on searching the internet.

Dr Rick Lupton earned my gratitude by honing my computing skills, while **Dr Sean Privett-Main** advised me on medical issues in my manuscript, and **Claire Woodhead ACR** preserved and digitised the 100-year-old *Loire/Dalgonar* trackchart tracing, while **John Theobald** skilfully digitised most of the ancient photos of family and ships. **Alan Hanson** from the Otago Shetland Society in Dunedin provided useful information about Isbester family members in New Zealand.

I am indebted to **Captain Hdjalmar Styra** in Bremen, **Captain Jean-Daniel Troyat** in Brittany, the late **Captain Einar Sjuve** in Tønsberg and **Bjørn Tore Rosendahl PhD** in Kristiansand for help with research in their localities.

Dr Keith Whittles and his publishing team have 'gone the extra mile' to give me a book of which I can be proud and for this I am very grateful.

If with all this help, so willingly and generously given, the book is less than perfect, the fault is mine.

Jack Isbester. Autumn 2018

INTRODUCTION

My grandfather died 21 years before I was born, so the main link between us is that we both spent much of our lives at sea: 47 years in his case and 35 in mine. Even my father's links with his father were diminished by the fact that Captain John was 48 when my father was born, and he died when my father was 13. For me one of the greatest pleasures derived from writing the story of my grandfather's life has been discovering how many of the same ports we visited and how often we carried similar cargoes. Liverpool was his home port throughout almost all of his career: that was where he joined and left most of his ships, and that was where he studied for and passed all his exams. Liverpool was my home port, too, for the first 20-odd years of my seafaring career, but during those years I was completely unaware that I was treading in my grandfather's footsteps. The only surprise is that my grandfather did not marry a Liverpool girl. He found a wife on his doorstep at home in Shetland, and left the privilege of a Liverpool wife to me!

It is a happy circumstance that much of the detail of a merchant seaman's life – when the voyage started and ended, who was aboard, how old they were, where they came from and what disasters befell them – has to be recorded in the ship's official log book (OLB) or Articles of Agreement (AoA), and while many of these records have been lost many survive in archives in the world's seaports. It is an even happier circumstance that in times long before the internet or even the widespread use of the telephone, communication was by letter and my grandfather and his family were committed letter writers.

I have been very fortunate that my father was a hoarder of family documents and that throughout his life he was happy to correspond with anyone interested in my grandparents, the ships and Shetland. I have been fortunate, too, that my unusual name enabled one former shipmate to trace me and provide me with intriguing letters and photos 60 years after we had last spoken.

In this story I have quoted extensively from my grandfather's writings. They vary considerably. His handwriting is always admirably clear, and when writing in the official log book, or composing a letter which he would have considered important, for example a birthday letter to a 13-year-old son or condolences to a friend of his wife's, the punctuation and spelling are good, with few mistakes. When he was writing to my grandmother, however, his punctuation was sometimes missing and the spelling more arbitrary. It may be that when writing his personal letters he was writing colloquially, but it could be that he had a glass of Scotch beside him. With the exception of a couple of lines to be taken away by the pilot or the tug, and once when a trusted sea pilot had the con, he appears never to have written letters while at sea. To remove the distraction which might be caused by the minor errors in his letters I have, throughout the book, usually inserted punctuation and corrected spelling where necessary in the documents I have quoted.

I have usually referred to my grandmother as 'Susie' because that is who she was to her husband and friends, and so that, throughout the book, is how we usually meet her. I do, however, have the clear impression that as the well-bred daughter of a Victorian Shetland landowner and as wife of the captain of large sailing ships she was conscious of her place in society. She died a year before I was born, but I suspect that had we overlapped and had I when a child addressed her as 'Susie' rather than 'Grandmama', it would not have been well received! So I do have a slight feeling of *lèse-majesté* when I use her given name.

Jack Isbester

1 CHILDHOOD IN SHETLAND

On the face of it my grandfather John Isbester could hardly have had a poorer start in life. He was born at Mailand, in South Whiteness, Shetland, on 9 February 1852 to Sarah Anderson, who was illiterate, and John Isbister, a seaman who left for the Antipodes without marrying Sarah and never returned. That my grandfather survived the further blow of his mother's death when he was 15 to become a master in sail at the age of 32, to sail in command for 29 years, and to command for 13 years one of the largest three-masted square-rigged sailing ships flying the red ensign, is a testament to his character, ability and determination, as well as to his good fortune.

John Isbester's first surviving words were not written until he was 32, but there is plenty of information about his family, and about his life and times, to help us to understand his background and early years.

Mailand was the home of the Anderson family, and at the time of the 1851 census the household consisted of Mary Anderson, aged 66, her sister-in-law Elizabeth, 73, and her son's wife Catherine, 22, in addition to a farm servant, Christina Robieson, aged 20, and of course her daughter, Sarah, aged 20, who was to become my great-grandmother. Catherine's husband, Laurence Anderson, was probably away at the fishing at the time of the census. The Andersons were a big family – my great-grandmother Sarah was the last of ten children – most of whom were born in Hogan, South Whiteness, and were by 1851 dispersed through Shetland and overseas. My grandfather's Anderson uncles are variously described in census records as fishermen, seamen and whalers, and family tradition has it that he spent much of his childhood in the household of his uncle Laurence Anderson, a crofter and fisherman of Haggersta, Whiteness. There he was much closer than might be expected to his absent father's side of the family, because his father's younger sister, Catherine Gifford Isbister, had married Laurence Anderson in 1850. The Haggersta home of Laurence and Catherine Anderson seems to have been a real home to John Isbester. In later life he quoted it as his place of birth – perhaps he knew no better – and it was there in 1884 that he shared a bottle of whisky 'with all the town of Haggersta' at seven in the morning of his wedding day![1]

Laurence and Catherine Anderson had moved from Mailand in the 1850s, most of their children being born in Haggersta, and my grandfather would have grown up in a household mainly of women. For Shetland this was very normal: the menfolk worked and often died at sea or overseas. Consequently there was at this time a marked population imbalance, with about nine women for every six men, a circumstance that made Shetland women capable and independent minded.[2] Apart from his mother, Sarah, and his aunt, Catherine, there were her children, his cousins, Ann (a year his senior), Mary (three years his junior), Catherine (four years younger) and Robina (six years behind him). It wasn't until he was ten that male cousins, in the form of Peter, Robert and Laurence, began to arrive. The man of the house, Laurence Anderson, was often away from home, the census only finding him in Whiteness twice in sixty years. The evidence of his children's birth certificates is consistent with his being away from home for most of the summers, suggesting seasonal employment in the Shetland fishing industry, a very familiar pattern at that time.[3]

I rely on my father for the information that my grandfather spent most of his childhood at Haggersta and went to school in Whiteness, but there is confirmation of this from an interesting source. Writing in 1913 my grandfather describes meeting Bella Leask in Melbourne and reports 'Bella minds a whole lot about me when we were at school that I had forgotten'.[4] I think that this must be the Isabella Leask born in 1859, daughter of Arthur Leask, a merchant seaman who in 1871 was living in Hellister, Whiteness.[5] The entire school, comprising the teacher with 59 children aged from 5 to 15 or 16, was housed in a single room[6] but, as is so often the case, the results depended more upon the skill and enthusiasm of the teacher and the interest of the pupils than upon the pleasantness and comfort of the surroundings. John Isbester's future career suggests that his schooling was more than adequate.

In 1857 or thereabouts, when he started school, my grandfather would have been taught by Robert Jamieson, whose letters were published in *Shetland – a love story*.[7] Ten years later, when he left to go to the fishing, his teacher would have been David Hobart (Fig.1.1) who we will meet again as a teller of vivid stories and a friend of my grandmother's family. Between Jamieson and Hobart came James Irvine and possibly other teachers. My father wrote 'Mr Hobart was an excellent teacher of navigation – all the Whiteness boys benefited, my father included – and my mother's Gifford cousins used to come from Busta to stay at Olligarth to get Mr Hobart's teaching.'[8] Shetland teachers who could teach navigation – a day's work and perhaps a meridian altitude[9] – were in demand by seafarers on leave because their prices were lower than those of the navigation teachers in the seaports.[10] Schooling in Whiteness would have been interrupted from time to time for more immediate or, occasionally, more enjoyable matters. Few records from the 1860s remain but they were doubtless similar to later years when attendances were down when the peats were being cut or the crops harvested and when a half day was awarded for the nearby Whiteness and Weisdale regatta.[11]

Figure 1.1 *David Hobart, schoolmaster at Whiteness*

The baptismal register for Tingwall, Whiteness and Weisdale shows that my grandfather was baptised in February 1854 as John Isbuster, son of John Isbuster seaman and of Sarah Anderson.[12] The two-year delay in baptising him may have been partly due to his illegitimacy, although no baptisms were registered between December 1852 and January 1854. It seems unlikely that he suffered any serious prejudice as a child, embedded in a supportive family and with his father well known locally but absent overseas like so many other men from Shetland. Illegitimacy was rare in Shetland at this time, with a frequency of about 4 per cent compared with a frequency of 9 per cent throughout Scotland.[13] It carried a stigma except when the couple were simply anticipating the wedding. John Isbister senior – my great-grandfather – eventually died aged 86 in Hokitika, New Zealand where he had lived, unmarried, for much of the final 50 years of his life.[14]

The 1851 census in Shetland recorded the family name as Isbuster, but the 1861 census adopted the spelling Isbister for the same individuals – and in 1871 the enumerator decided on Isbester! In cases where people were unlettered the enumerators used their own judgement and different enumerators at different times reached different conclusions. My grandfather, at the age of 15, signed his mother's death certificate boldly and clearly in 1867 as 'John Isbester', and that is the spelling of his name which he used for the remainder of his life. A belief within the Isbester family that my grandfather had chosen to change his name from Isbister to Isbester for unknown reasons seems to have been mistaken. While Isbister is by far the most common version of the name in Shetland it is clear that in the 1850s and 1860s the spelling was arbitrary. It seems likely that his schoolmaster decided the spelling to use.

My great-grandmother Sarah Anderson is variously described in official documents as 'a knitter of shawls' and 'an agricultural labourer',[15] which doubtless reflects the life lived by crofters in the 19th century when a skill such as knitting shawls was a means of earning a few pennies to supplement a subsistence diet consisting of what could be grown or caught. She was, at the time of the 1861 census, living in South Hamarsland with her son John Isbister (*sic*) and his two-year-old half-sister Barbara Anderson, later known as Barbara Hunter. Barbara, like John, was illegitimate and her mother signed her birth certificate with a cross, identified by the registrar as 'Sarah Anderson her mark', a reminder that in the days before education became compulsory it was still common for poorer people to be unschooled. South Hamarsland is only 4 miles from Whiteness, but such is the nature of Shetland, with long fingers of sea penetrating the land, that Whiteness is on the West or Atlantic coast of Shetland while South Hamarsland, on the shore of Lax Firth in Tingwall, is on the East or North Sea coast.

Knitting shawls was, for Shetland women in the 19th century a very common activity. Shortly after Sarah Anderson's death the Truck Report[16] provided the results of the investigation into the barter system used in the Shetland shawl and hosiery industries and in the fishing industry during the years when John Isbester was growing up. The report contains some 17,000 questions put to more than 200 men and women about their lives and working conditions, and contains fascinating insights into the lives of Shetland folk in that period. The landlords and merchants who operated the barter system generally claimed that their tenants were treated fairly and reasonably and were not oppressed, while detached observers such as clergymen considered that the crofters were compelled to knit shawls and to go fishing in circumstances where, being usually in debt to the landlords and merchants, they had little alternative.

Women knitting shawls used wool from their own sheep which they spun themselves, or wool obtained from the merchants who bought their finished shawls. These beautiful, intricately patterned creations were about 2.5 yards (2.3 metres) square, and, if the wool had to be spun before the knitting the whole process of making a shawl took about four weeks of hard work. Clementina Greig[17] of Scalloway, a woman with 33 years' experience of knitting shawls, reported 'When I spin the wool myself [making a shawl] it takes me a month, but with clean worsted I will make it in about three weeks,' and when she was asked 'How long will the spinning of half-a-pound [of wool] take?' she replied, 'It will take me a week to spin it sitting very close at it and sleeping very little.'

Euphemia Russell[18] of Scalloway had knitted shawls for 25 years when she could sell them, and when she could not she worked 'Sometimes in the fields and sometimes at the fish' for about three months a year. Working at the fish would have been gutting herring or tending the cod spread to dry on the beaches for subsequent sale overseas.

Shawls usually sold for 17 shillings which would normally be paid entirely in the form of goods from the shop such as tea, sugar, bread, soap and cotton. The knitters preferred payment in cash, but this they say was normally refused except for the odd penny or two. They would accept more tea than they needed and would then exchange it with farmers for produce such as potatoes and meal. The possibility of selling a shawl for £1 cash direct to a summer visitor was a rare but welcome opportunity.

When asked 'Have you often had to barter your goods for less than they were worth? 'Mary Coutts[19] of Scalloway replied:

> Sometimes, if there had been 2½ yards of cotton lying [unused] and a peck of meal came in, we would give it for the meal. The cotton would be worth sixpence a yard, or 15 pence [in total] and the meal would be worth one shilling [12 pence]. I remember doing that about three years ago; but we frequently sold the goods for less than they had cost us in Lerwick.

To explain why spinning the necessary wool would take her more than a week, Mary Coutts said, 'We have to go to the hill for our peats and turf, and that takes up part of our time,' a reminder that the knitting of shawls was no alternative to housework, but just one more task.

It is not clear how long Sarah Anderson lived at South Hamarsland, but six years after the census she was again recorded in the same vicinity. On 4 July 1867 she died in the Garths of Easthouse, a stone-built dwelling with a single room, the ruins of which still stand about 200 metres from the ruins of South Hamarsland. Her death was untimely – she was only 37 – and terrible. The death certificate gives the cause of death as 'Inflammation of the throat and lock-jaw', otherwise known as tetanus. John Isbester was 15 at this time, and had already spent a summer at the herring fishing. He was home between cod-fishing voyages aboard the Faroe smacks. The death certificate records that he was present at her death and that she had no regular medical attendant.

His mother's death and the manner of it must have been a traumatic experience for my grandfather, boy that he still was at the time. My father spoke often of my grandfather – he was proud of both of his parents – but I do not recall him ever mentioning his grandmother's death, and it is possible that he never knew the details of this event, which had occurred more than 30 years before he was born.

So, what was Whiteness like in the 1850s when my grandfather was a boy? The crofters lived their lives at subsistence level:

> It has been calculated that from 1780 to 1850 there was on average one famine year in every four and, although destitution did not reach the level of Ireland or the Western Isles in the 1840s, there were families who lived without oatmeal or bread for months on end. Fish proved to be their salvation.[20]

The census enumerator describes South Whiteness in 1851 as being

> partly pastoral and partly agricultural … Soil mostly thin on limestone rock with a considerable portion of wild moor – precipitous towards sea shore – intersected by the voes [long, narrow arms of the sea] of Binniness and Whiteness … The inhabitants are industrious and chiefly employed in farming and in fishing and in those seasons that out of doors occupations cannot be carried on the men are engaged in repairing their boats, nets and fishing tackle – and the women in knitting hose, gloves, shawls etc.

J. O. Ross, the enumerator for North Whiteness, when describing the district as 'Nearly divided into two distinct parts by a wild barren hill which has to be crossed east and west ere the Census could be taken making it a more difficult task to perform', appears to be trying to justify his claim for expenses, or appealing for sympathy for the privations he had been forced to suffer in performance of his duties. He goes on to observe that

> In the South part of the district agriculture is poorly attended to, in the North end of the district pasturage of sheep and cattle is more attended to than the proper tillage of the soil. The people tho' poor and subjected to inclement weather and other casualties [attempt] by fishing and farming to provide in a measure for their families. For the past two or three seasons the potato failure so prevalent in these islands has reduced the people in circumstances and it will be some time ere they recov'd their position.[21]

It is fortunate that there were almost always fish in the sea. Every croft had its boat, and a few hours on the water would usually bring a catch, perhaps some herring, haddock, ling or cod.[22]

The neighbouring district of Weisdale was in 1851 described as 'Wholly without formed roads, the surface hilly, abounding with marsh and moor, and the houses very widely scattered.'[23] In these conditions in the 1850s and for many years thereafter, most journeys were made on foot or by boat. In Shetland one is never far from water and, particularly when less active people required transportation, the journey was usually by boat. David Hobart, schoolmaster in Whiteness for a number of years in the 1860s and 70s, provides a lively description of a trip mainly by boat from Busta to Whiteness in May 1868. Both boats mentioned would have been double-ended Shetland fourareens, about 23 feet in overall length, rowed by two or four oarsmen, each with one oar. At the helm was my maternal great-grandfather, Magnus Irvine of Strom Bridge,[24] Whiteness, aged 45. The passenger was Margaret Irvine, his wife, aged 41. At the oars were David Hobart, aged 26, and Robbie Tulloch, aged 43, a live-in farm worker with the Irvine family. David Hobart lodged with the Irvine family and was in love with their elder daughter, Mary Jane, for whom this account was written.

> After leaving you at Busta we kept close along the shore [see Fig.1.2] making fair progress, till we came to the opening of St Magnus Bay where, the wind having increased and the sea having more space to gather way, we could with some strokes urge forward the boat scarcely half her length, and with others barely hold our own. [The wind was probably south-west.] Mrs Irvine was for returning. Mr Irvine was for going. This opinion prevailed. There was no danger he said, except

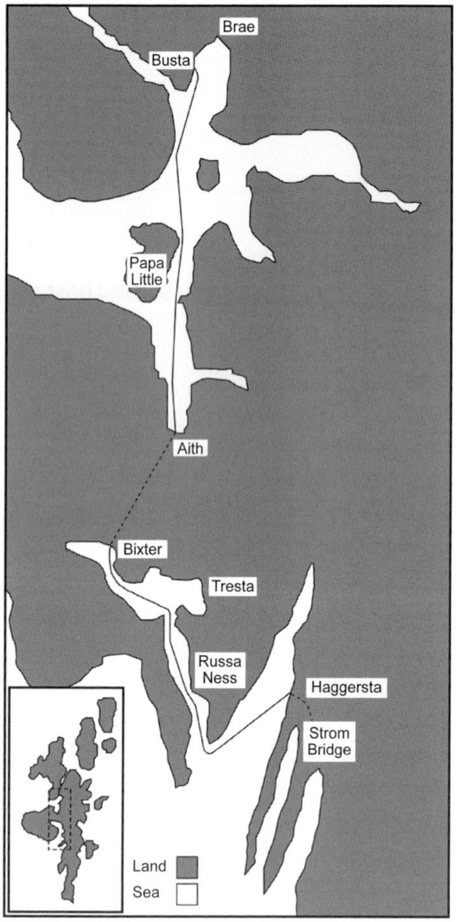

Figure 1.2 Journey by boat and foot from Busta to Strom Bridge

that of a long hard pull, and when the boat had made marked progress across, he further remarked that patience and perseverance – I didn't hear the conclusion of that proverb. Then came a slight lull of which we took due advantage by rowing like galley slaves. This brought us under the lee of the island [Papa Little] and our next difficulty was to get round the point [Selie Ness] on which we nearly went aground last night. We had to go out into the middle of the voe under the full force of both wind and waves and as the wind was still increasing our strength as well as our patience and perseverance was tried to the utmost. The point was slowly passed. To rest was to go backwards. Another point was ahead under the shelter of which we could rest and take in more ballast. Every nerve was strained to reach it which we at last did. A drink of buttermilk, a smoke, a few stones put in [as ballast, to prevent the boat being caught too much by the wind] and we were off, & Busta which had hitherto been in sight and from which we thought you were watching us, was lost to view. The wind and sea were now worse than ever. Robbie sometimes let the head of the boat fall down & the spray would dash over us. [From this I deduce that Robbie and David were each rowing with one oar, with Robbie on the port side.] Once the whole top of the sea came in over the quarter right upon Mrs Irvine which nearly upset her equanimity. A short time after we again got under the lee of the shore and went about as fast as we did at first. Aith was reached about four hours after leaving Busta [a distance of about 7 statute miles]. My hands were the only thing that suffered damage.

A rest at Aith. No thought of another sea voyage. The [second] boat was to be left at Bixter, said Mrs Irvine and likewise Mr Irvine. Not being in command I didn't give any opinion. Little said going over the hill. A little said going down the hill & that little was to take the boat to Tresta – nothing more. [Aith to Bixter had been a walk of 2.5 statute miles.] In to see Mrs Johnson – a biscuit and a dram. The wind had shifted two points to the west – get the boat down – the boat was got down – and

> rowed under the lee of the opposite side – the rudder shipped and down the voe as if running a race. Tresta was never looked at. Now we again met the wind and rowed easily along the lee of the shore till we came opposite the point of Russa Ness – Then along the side of the wind, the boat rolling over the large waves – the skipper was steering, Robbie and I rowing. The point was passed and then right before the wind to old Johnny Abernethy where we landed & drew up the boat. Home at last.

It appears that the boat was headed straight across Weisdale Voe to Haggersta in Whiteness, from where it was a walk of only 0.7 statute miles to home at Strom Bridge. This second boat trip would have been of about 6.5 statute miles.

Writing a few days later,[25] David Hobart remarks that 'The boat has not yet been brought round', which I take as confirmation that the boat had been left at Haggersta or thereabouts and was to be brought down Weisdale Voe and up Stromness Voe, a trip of 7 miles, after which it would be half a mile closer to Strom Bridge.

A further example of a boat trip in the same period is recorded by another schoolmaster, Robert Jamieson, who by coincidence also taught at Whiteness. In November 1860, when he had left Whiteness and moved to Sandness, he visited his beloved in Gulberwick. He was lame and was loaned a horse for the journey home but was forced to leave it at Cova. He records[26] that he went to Clousta and took a boat from there to Sandness, a distance of 12 miles.

> I had to bribe the lazy fellow of a boatman with extra fare before I could make him move. He thought it so cold and a part of the voe was frozen.

When love drove him, David Hobart was prepared to walk as well as to row. One weekend when Mary Jane Irvine was at Busta, he proposed leaving Strom Bridge at 0400 hrs, reaching Busta at 0900 hrs, leaving Busta at 1700 hrs and arriving back at Strom Bridge at 2200 hrs.[27] The distance, over rough open countryside with few tracks, is about 16.5 statute miles each way. In the event he made the return journey to Strom Bridge on Monday morning, leaving Busta at 0310 hrs and reaching Strom Bridge at 0810 hrs, ready for a day in school. When enjoying the simmer dim (twilight) of late June in Shetland this was a practical proposition.

This is his account:[28]

> On leaving you I set out not very fast but gradually my pace quickened till I went at full swing. One hour and three quarters I was passing Voe where I found innumerable fences and dykes the gates of which I never took the trouble of looking for but climbed or vaulted over them as they came in my way. Hunger also made itself felt there & I sat down and ate a piece of bread & took a good draught of water out of a spring. Then into the lee side of a dyke to smoke which detained me about twenty minutes. For the next hour & quarter I was passing between Voe and Setter plunging through mires, over bogs, leaping ditches and vaulting wire fences. Setter was reached at last. Mr M in bed not so much as whiff of tobacco and drink of milk – stingy dogs – said I. Though breakfast was offered – Breakfast took up time & time was everything to me. I found a kinder but less able entertainer in Malley of the Lea – Her tea was not ready – her cow was not calved a cup of cold

> water more of Mr Gs bread and butter & I was on the road again arriving in the dining room or sitting room of Strom Bridge ten minutes past eight, thus being with all my halts five hours exactly on the road.

With the leaping of ditches and the vaulting of wire fences, he sounds like a young man spurred on by love. Tragically Mary Jane Irvine, the object of his affections, died of consumption in 1870 aged 20, but her younger sister, Susie, has a major role to play in this story.

---

1 Isbester, Capt. John, letter J1 of 10.04.1884 (Isbester Collection).
2 Abrams, Lynn. *Myth and Materiality in a Womans World.* Manchester University Press, 2005. p.66.
3 Eight of Laurence Andersons nine children were conceived between September and March and he was at home between September and March to register four of their births. He was also home once in June to conceive a child and three times in June to register the birth of a child. I have found no evidence that he was ever at home in April, May, July or August which fits well with the pattern of summer fishing on the Faroe smacks (See Chapter 3).
4 Isbester, Capt. John, letter J26 of 06.04.1913 (Isbester Collection).
5 Shetland Islands Census 1871, District WW2.
6 Hobart, David, letter H6 of 03.06.1868 (Isbester Collection).
7 Jamieson, Robert. *Shetland – A Love Story,* The Shetland Times Ltd. Lerwick, 2010.
8 Isbester, Allan, letter CAI1 of 07.09.1966 (Isbester Collection).
9 Thomson, Captain J P OBE ExC. *Captain John Isbester's Career at Sea,* Unpublished manuscript. 1971 (Isbester Collection).
10 Smith, Davie, letter DS3 of June 2013 (Isbester Collection).
11 Whiteness School Log Book, 1890–1912, Shetland Archive.
12 Baptismal Register for Tingwall, Whiteness and Weisdale. The Registrar, Shetland Islands Council.
13 Abrams, Lynn. Op.cit. P.154.
14 Isbister, John, Death Certificate, N.Z.No.1911008433, registered 27.10.1911.
15 Anderson, Sarah. Death certificate 04.07.1867 and the 1861 census.
16 The Second Shetland Truck System Report 1872.
17 Truck System Report Paragraph 11,527 et seq.
18 Truck System Report Paragraph 11,562 et seq.
19 Truck System Report Paragraph 11,585 et seq.
20 Thompson, Paul, *Living the Fishing,* Routledge & Kegan Paul, 1981. p.313.
21 Shetland Islands Census 1851, District TWW 8.
22 Hobart, David, letters H8 dated 12.06.1868 and H10 dated 20.06.1868 (Isbester Collection).
23 Shetland Islands Census 1851, District TWW 8.
24 Strom Bridge, Whiteness, my grandmother's family home, later known as Olligarth.
25 Hobart, David, letter H6 dated 03.06.1868 (Isbester Collection).
26 Jamieson, Robert. Op.cit. p.72.
27 Hobart, David, letter H11 dated 23.06.1868 (Isbester Collection).
28 Hobart, David, letter H12 dated 29.06.1868 (Isbester Collection).

2 GOING TO SEA - ARTHUR IRVINE

Starting a career at sea in the 1860s was tough. There are no letters describing John Isbester's early days at sea, but Arthur Irvine, son of Magnus Irvine of Strom Bridge, Whiteness, was aged 15 when he left home in April 1867 to start his life as a seaman. He was my grandmother's elder brother – John Isbester's brother-in-law to be. Magnus Irvine was a farmer and landowner – a laird – his wife's family listing doctors, army officers and clergymen amongst their ancestors, so the choice of a life at sea, starting as a boy or ordinary seaman, is surprising. It may hint at a determination to see the world, a recognition that he was not academic, or that the family did not at that time have the funds to launch him in a professional career.

Travelling from Shetland to Glasgow, where he hoped to find a ship, was in itself a major challenge. David Hobart, the Whiteness schoolmaster, a Scot returning home, described the two-day voyage from Lerwick to Aberdeen via Kirkwall and Wick also in 1867, in the following lively terms.[1]

> We started from Lerwick before one o'clock on Tuesday morning[2] and steamed at an immense rate down past Dunrossness. When we came to the Sumburgh Roost [the area of overfalls and disturbed water south of Shetland] the sea began to be rather rough and the vessel rolled and pitched a good deal but not so much as makes me sick. After that I turned in and had a sleep and awoke about five o'clock in the morning. Going on deck I saw the Fair Isle far astern looking up out of the sea with a helmet with a deep cut across the top of it. The wind was still blowing hard and the sea raging and the weather very cold. So I turned in again and slept a good while and on again going on deck the Orkneys were well in sight. And the way through them very devious. It would indeed require a man who knew them well to guide a vessel through them in the night. We arrived at Kirkwall at about eleven o'clock A.M and started at 1.45 P.M. the wind blowing heavier than ever but being in the lee of the islands we had pretty smooth water. However when the Pentland Firth was opened the vessel rolldt and stachered like a drunken man. This did not last long as we soon got under the lee of Caithness and in due time arrived at Wick where we remained till I got wearied and went to bed. When I awoke next there was a change indeed but very much to the worse. Before this we might be said to have had a tolerably good passage but now the tossing was more than ever I saw it in the Queen [a previous ferry] and the smell around me was quite sickening. So it was not very long till I also gave up what I had put down and then I was all right and went to sleep about five o'clock in the morning and awoke to hear the wind blowing as hard as ever but the vessel having now gained the lee of the shore was in tolerably smooth water and so

> it continued till we reached eleven o'clock A.M. on Wednesday but did not get in on account of the tide till the P.M.

On a small ferryboat, probably the 15-knot paddle steamer *St Magnus*, all aboard were aware of what was going on. The bridge must have been just above the saloon. After a trip in 1869 David Hobart reported[3]

> Friday night was very dark & we nearly ran down a vessel off the coast of Aberdeen. There was an awful roaring & shouting to back the engines & port the helm – helm hard to starboard & so on which were mingled with the shrieks of the ladies in the cabin who thought something terrible had happened or was going to happen. However, we steered clear of her in spite of rain, fog and darkness held on our way till we came to Aberdeen where we landed about two o'clock on Saturday morning.

Arthur Irvine may have been travelling with other Shetland men. In his letter[4] to his mother from Glasgow he mentions A. Tait.

> Dearest Mother,
>
> I arrived here safely today. I went to Moore and he said that if I would wait a week he would get a ship for me. I am very tird and therefore cannot write much but I will write when I get a ship. If I do not get one tomorrow I will perhaps go to Liverpool with A Tait. If I do get a ship it will likely be for eight months and then I will be home. Give my Love all I have not written to Granny but you can tell her that I am finely write immaditely to the Sailors' Home Glasgow.
>
> I remain your loving Boy
>
> A Irvine
>
> Don't put C in the adres

Like many a 15-year-old boy he was concerned about appearances, and didn't want anyone to know that his middle name was Craigie!

A fortnight later he was still awaiting a ship in Glasgow, and resisting the many temptations of a sailor's life.[5]

> My dearest Aunt [probably Elizabeth Gifford of Busta, his mother's 38-year-old sister],
>
> I am sorry that I have not written to you before but I put it off till I should get a ship. I find now that it is all very fine to be at home and speak about the sailor's life but it is different to try it. Dear Aunt I find now that it is all true that I was told about the sailors although I have not yet been at sea The wickedness of a sailor's life on shore here is awful Last night a steward on board a steamer came here paid off with £30. He went out and came in with only £2 & without his coat & that is the way why a sailor can't have money but by God's strength I sall never do that I have

had Many temptations since I came out here, but I have resisted them from the first and now I find that it is easier I have been twice every Sunday at the sailor's chapel since I came.

Kind love to Granny, Uncle, Mrs M and the children and tell them that if I am spared to come home I shall bring them something nice Write next post both you and granny

I remain your loving nephew

Arthur C Irvine

My adress is Mr Burgess Seamens Bordings 34 Brown Street Glasgow

By July 1867 Arthur was well into a voyage aboard the barque *Emerald* and, writing[6] to his sister Mary Jane, a year older than him, was voicing his distress at the failure of his family to write to him and at the heavy demands of the work required of him while in the port of Genoa. The absence of letters from family and friends has for centuries been a problem for seafarers, and on several occasions John Isbester was distressed when letters expected after a long voyage failed to reach him. In Arthur's case the problem was probably caused by his failure through inexperience to provide full addresses or to take account of the time required for mail to travel home and then out to the next destination. But there can be no doubt that he was frequently in the thoughts of his mother, sister, aunt and grandma! If there were any prospects of work to be found ashore he wanted to be informed. He had also decided that his name was Al or Alle.

My Dearest Sister,

What is the reason I have got no letter? I have written twice and received no answer. Is our people angry with me or what? I am sick tired of this place and ship and seeing the Shetland lads geting letters from home and me geting none.

Private Make dear sister would you write to Constantinople and tell me if I should come home in winter or what are people is thinking about me? I know that there is something up, else I would have had a letter. If any of them is dead it is gust [just] as good for me to know it now as after but if I don't get a letter in Constantinople this is the last they shall ever have from me so I must close for want of time tell D to write Love to all I remain your loving brother

Al

Adress to all on board the Barque emerald to the care of Hild & Mathers, ship brokers Constantinople

Private Dearest Sister

I have forgot to tell you something If you see any opening on shore about the time that I come to England for this is hurting me I can agrie fine with the sea work, but this harbour work would kill a horse Write me about 3 weeks and tell me.

Alle

It reads as though he and his fellow sailors were being used to do heavy work, discharging or loading the cargo. One letter which he never received, because it was never sent, was from his mother and sister. It provides a reminder that the laird and his family lived on a working croft, planting potatoes and oats, and were aware of much of the local gossip. In 1867, when Arthur was on his first voyage, his mother writes:[7]

> Strom Bridge Whiteness Shetland 3rd May
>
> My own darling boy,
>
> We were all glad of your letters last week. I hope by this time you are getting on with your voyage & I hope you have fine weather. We have fine dry days now with north wind. We finished our oats on Friday and set some potatoes on Saturday. Andrew Garrick is finished. Annie sends her love to you. That is the only one of them we have seen. Kate writes that she wishes you had come to see her

After giving news of nine family friends and neighbours, she continues:

> Now I think I have told you all the news Mary Jane will finish this to you with much love to your dear self I do hope you are taking care of yourself and not fighting with anyone dear darling boy do write soon. your own Mother WM Irvine Stromebridge

Mary Jane was ready to tell him of the scandals rocking the rural community:

> My dear brother, How are you getting on? We are jugging along the best way we can. Laurie Morrison was bailed out but was no sooner out than Charles Duncan put him in again for £70 which he was owing him as his lawyer when they went to law about Jane Gibbs Rhilo, so he has to sit till he pays it. Peter Jamison Stromness hens are all dead & he has gone to law, for he say Nellies folk have poisoned them. The Police have been out & taken some of the hens in to inspect I doubt it will go hard with them, they are telling so many lies with love your Mary

Arthur was feeling better about life a few weeks later when he wrote[8] from Constantinople to David Hobart, his former schoolmaster and lodger in his parents' home; or perhaps, writing to a man and not a woman, he was looking for admiration rather than sympathy.

> My Dear David,
>
> We are Bound to Odessa to load grain and then I will have more time and write you a long letter Just now I am swearing for the Mate because he wants me to throw a line to the tug & I won't. I shall try and bring home a turk home with me in winter give my love to all I am as fat as a pig and as strong as a lion you can writ to the General Post Office her and I will get it as I come down again [i.e returning south through the Bosphorus] we are Lying under the sultan's Palace

and the Mahomedans is saying their prayers so good bye for the present I remain yours truly

Ale

Figure 2.1 *Arthur Irvine*

In a photo (Fig.2.1) taken about that time, Arthur does indeed look substantially built; but refusing the mate's order after only four months' sea service seems rather reckless. Perhaps he is really admitting that he couldn't, rather than wouldn't, throw the line to the tug – it's a skilled task. What sort of turk he proposed to bring home remains a mystery to me.

Arthur did not return home in the winter of 1867–68 and the next surviving letter[9] was written to his father a year later, in August 1868, from Runcorn.

Dearest Father,

This is to tell you that I have left the *New House* & shipped on board this one which is called the *Norwich Trader* of Sunderland We are going to Peterhead with salt and expect to go from there with salt the Syran left here with salt for Lerwick yesterday I thought it very homely to hear my own native Language among the cockneys Dutch Welch and Scotch as soon as I hear it I was not long of singing out Do you belong to Shetland If I had got 20 or 30 £ I would have come with her You can tell David if he does not rube his Face well with crotin oil I shall have more whiskers than him as I can get hold of it with my Teeth

But I will send my things and then you can judge for yourselves as soon as I get to Peterhead. Give my love to all and write by return of post to peterhead so no more at present I remain your loving son

Arthur C Irvine

Adress Arthur C Irvine Care of Capt Sutherland Schooner Norwich Trader Peterhead Scotland

After 15 months at sea Arthur had grown a bit of a beard, had not saved much money, was aroused by Shetland accents and was thinking of returning home. However he did not do so, and his next surviving letter[10] was, from the context, written in Greenock in April 1869, before he joined the *Ratcliff*.

Dearest Mother and Father,

I have shipped for Quebec and am as happy as lary The wages is £4. No advance but we have all taken £3.15 and £2 advance. She carries all Shetlanders tell Mary that Peter[11] is with me so that he will be comming home neset winter. I won't

> promise to come home neset [next] winter but I will see I am in a hurry as we sail tomorrow and I have got to go up to Glasgow for my things Kind love to all. Write in about a week to Quebec. Your loving boy
>
> Ale Irvine

That was the last his family ever heard from him. In Quebec he died by drowning on Saturday 5 June 1869, aged 17, although the record[12] of his burial in the Hôpital de la Marine on 14 June describes him as aged 22. (In those days seamen in their sixties understated their ages while youngsters evidently did the opposite.) Arthur Irvine was shown in the Ship's Articles as aged 20. The ship's official log book records, in an entry signed by the master, the mate and one of the Shetland ABs:[13]

> June 5th 1869 8PM Arthur Irvine while in the act of taking a rope into the boat fell into the river and sunk [*sic*]. The alarm was immediately given when all hands got onto the booms to use every effort to save him but the man never again rose to the surface. The body was dragged for but [they] did not succeed in finding him.

From his subsequent burial it is clear that his body was later found. Family tradition is that he fell from the ship's gangway. It is likely that *Ratcliff* was at an anchorage and access to the shore was by boat. Saturday evening, after drink has been taken, is a dangerous time, and the access to the ship is often a dangerous place. Whatever the circumstances this was a tragic loss of someone at the very start of adult life and serves well to illustrate the precariousness of life at sea in the 19th century.

Arthur Irvine's effects, after more than two years at sea, are listed in the Official Log Book[14] as:

> Three pair of trousers, two guernsey frocks, two red singlets, two coulered flannel shirts, 3 jumper frocks, 2 pair of drawers, 2 sleeves, 1 waistcoat, 1 black waistcoat, 1 coat, 1 blanket, 1 rug, 5 pairs of socks, 1 towel, 2 caps, 2 comforters, 3 mits, 1 pair of braces, 1 bible, 1 pann, 1 knife, 3 sticks of tobbaco, 2 handkerchiefs, all stored in his chest.

Arthur's wages for six weeks work as an AB were £5 7s 6d, from which were deducted a £2 advance and 5/- for the tobacco, leaving wages of £3 7s 6d due to him. It is likely that his family only learnt of his death from fellow Shetland crew members as the Ship's Articles showed simply that he came from Shetland.

David Hobart, on holiday in Scotland in the autumn of 1869, had apparently been making enquiries on behalf of the family about any outstanding wages due to Arthur Irvine. He wrote:[15]

> James Spence gave the number of the vessel required; it is 15686 and the port she belongs to is London. The only thing wanted now is the amount of wages he received when she sailed. But that might be found out by writing to the owners Hall Brothers, Great Chare, Newcastle-on-Tyne. I shall write and ask them to send

> you word, or if you thought it would be too long to wait you might send in the official number & the port she belongs to at once to Mr Nicolson & he would fill up the shedule & give it to me.

Happily John Isbester, the primary subject of this book, survived and was strengthened by his early years at sea. It was not until 45 years had passed that my grandmother, a little girl when her brother died, was to be exposed to another heart-breaking maritime disaster.

---

1 Hobart, David, letter H3 of 03.10.1867 (Isbester Collection).
2 From the context it is clear that this was 1.00 pm.
3 Hobart, David, letter H16 of 27.09.1869 (Isbester Collection).
4 Irvine, Arthur, letter A1 of 05.04.1867 (Isbester Collection).
5 Irvine, Arthur, letter A2 of 21.04.1867 (Isbester Collection).
6 Irvine, Arthur, letter A3 of 16.07.1867 (Isbester Collection).
7 Irvine, WM & MJ, letter WMI1 of 03.05 1867 (Isbester Collection).
8 Irvine, Arthur, letter A4 of 23.08.1867 (Isbester Collection).
9 Irvine, Arthur, letter A5 of 02.08.1868 (Isbester Collection).
10 Irvine, Arthur, letter A6 of 21.04.1869 (Isbester Collection).
11 *Ratcliff* Articles of Agreement, 1869, The Maritime History Archive, Newfoundland, list Peter Goudie and Peter Anderson, both from Shetland.
12 Quebec, Vital and Church Records (Drouin Collection), 1621–1967 Record for Arthur Irvine.
13 *Ratcliff* Official Log Book, 1869. The Maritime History Archive, Newfoundland.
14 *Ratcliff* Official Log Book, 1869, ibid.
15 Hobart, David, letter H16 of 27.09.1869 (Isbester Collection).

3 EARLY YEARS AT THE FISHING

Family tradition has it that my grandfather started his seafaring career at the Shetland herring fishing in 1866, when he was aged 14. Herring fishing was a summer activity, with the shoals being found to the west of Shetland in May and June before moving east of Shetland in July and August. In Whiteness, as elsewhere in Shetland in the 1860s, fishing was a major activity – there were 363 boats and about 1,500 men and boys employed in the Shetland herring fisheries in 1859, and 17 ship or sloop masters lived in the parishes of Tingwall, Whiteness and Weisdale.[1]

It is not difficult to guess John Isbester's motives for turning to a life at sea. Captain Thomson of Sandness in Shetland was writing about my grandfather, but was drawing on his own experience of growing up in the same vicinity a few years later, when he wrote[2]

> Haggersta was his early lookout station and the mouth of Weisdale Voe with its islands and the great ocean beyond, was the panorama before him. Every croft around the voe had its noost [place where a boat could be drawn out of the water] with one or more boats according to the family requirements, for fishing, travelling and inter island transit. In addition there were schooners, smacks and herring boats making their way to and from distant waters in search of those denizens of the deep, the cod and herring.

In the 1860s much of the Shetland fishing was done from open boats, sixareens, fourareens or quilleys. The sixareens, used in most parts of Shetland were double-ended boats about 10 metres in length overall with a crew of six. They were alternatively known as sixearns, the spelling and pronunciation varying from one part of Shetland to another. The fourareens, about 7 metres long, were used on the southern part of the west coast of Shetland, including Whiteness, where they were better suited to the local harbours and beaches. The sixareens were used for what was known as the 'Haaf' fishing, for cod and ling, up to 40 miles offshore in boats that might be at sea for up to three days. The fourareens were fished up to about 15 miles from land, while the quilleys, about 5 metres in overall length, were used by the old men and boys for inshore fishing for herring, whiting, haddock and shellfish.[3] In 1869, when registration of open fishing boats was first required, there were 15 fourareens spread amongst the various Whiteness crofts, each with a crew of three or four men.[4] The Whiteness boats were owned by the crofters themselves, unlike in some other parts of Shetland where the landlords owned them.[5] However no fourareen was registered for John Isbester's home at Haggersta. This supports the suggestion that his uncle, Laurence Anderson, used to go each summer with the Faroe smacks.

There would be plenty of opportunities for a local boy to find employment fishing in Shetland. In the 1860s herring fishing, like cod fishing, was often done from sixareens. John

Isbester probably sailed with a sixareen from Lerwick. The sixareens were more suitable for cod fishing than for herring. For the former about six miles of line were used. This took up less space in the boat than did the six or eight nets[6] required for herring. Consequently the cod-fishing gear left more room for the catch,[7] a very important consideration. In the 1860s the herring fishermen fished up to about 15 miles from the coast[8] and landed the catch for curing. The relevance of John Isbester's experience of sailing in sixareens will come to mind when reading the account of the loss of the barque *Centaur*, 30 years later and the subsequent eight-day voyage by boat to the Hawaiian Islands.[9]

Figure 3.1 *Sixareen at Unst Boat Haven, Shetland*

The history of the sixareens, their construction, their use and the exploits of their crews are cherished in Shetland, with justified pride in the traditions, skill, ingenuity, courage and endurance with which they were used (Fig. 3.1). There is a Shetland name for every part and fitting of the boat, and the names hark back to their Norwegian roots. The sixareens were usually assembled in Shetland from timber imported from Norway or Scotland.[10] When fishing, they were equipped for trips of up to three days. They were propelled by up to six oars with each man taking one oar, or by an almost square sail set on a yard on a mast stepped just forward of the centre of the boat. They were small – usually 9–11 metres in length overall – and every scrap of space was used. Sixareens were divided into seven working sections by six thwartship rowing benches with vertical gratings beneath them.[11] The aftermost section was for the helmsman with his compass, steering with rudder and tiller when the boat was sailing. The next section could be divided with a broad shifting board, aligned fore and aft, and accommodated the catch of fish or, on the outward journey, part of the ballast – up to a ton of beach boulders – to be thrown overboard when fish were caught. Next came the section devoted to bailing. In heavy weather the boat would ship quantities of spray and quite often breaking seas, and it was the job of the bailer, equipped with a bailing shovel which could contain up to 9 litres of water, to get rid of the water before the next sea broke over the boat!

The next section, in the middle of the sixareen, was used for shooting and hauling the fishing lines when fishing for cod and ling, or the nets when fishing for herring. The mast was stepped through the thwart immediately forward of the mid-section. Forward of the mast was space for most of the ballast and for the fire kettle, the pot and the peat fuel. The fire kettle was a large earthenware jar containing burning peat, kept lit throughout the voyage, over which a pot of food or drink could be heated. The next section contained the sea chest, a heavy box, its lid covered with a tarpaulin, containing provisions and utensils.

Finally, in the bows were stowed two water breakers, or containers, and the sail when not in use.

The sailing of a sixareen in heavy weather has been described in several Shetland books[12,13] with particular reference to the terrible storm of July 1881 in which ten sixareens and 58 men were lost. A survivor[14] published a gripping account[15] of how, when the wind struck from north by east with little warning, three miles of fishing line were cut and abandoned, the close-reefed square sail was set and the helmsman set the boat running south east through heavy-breaking seas for the trip of some 37 miles to sheltered waters or, if they got it wrong, to founder in the stormy seas or to wreck on the unforgiving rocky coastline. The tack of the sail had been set forward, effectively making it a fore and aft sail, and two men took the halyards. What is particularly fascinating about this account is that the boat's speed was varied, to avoid the worst of the breaking crests and, when surfing, to keep on top of the wave, by the combined efforts of the three men who controlled the sail – the helmsman with the sheet and his two companions on the halyards. A version of this technique, called 'pumping the sail' by yachtsmen could be seen on television in use by the Finn class yachtsmen at the 2012 Olympics. Even in the later stages, as they reached more sheltered waters, the sixareen crew had, as the boat pitched forward over a roller, to 'keep the sail low, and ease,' to avoid the bow being forced below the surface. There is no suggestion that John Isbester experienced conditions quite like those described above but he may have done so, and in a season of fishing in the stormy Shetland waters he would undoubtedly have met periods of nasty weather and had the opportunity to improve his boat handling skills by observing his experienced companions.

Following the 1866 season of some four months which John Isbester spent at the herring fishing, he joined the smack *Telegraph* on 1 April 1867.[16] Aged just 15, he joined as ordinary seaman (OS). She was single-masted – a long-boomer – with an enormous sail area for her size, having been built in Barking, Essex, to run fish from the Dogger Bank to the Billingsgate fish market.[17] She was over 70 feet (22 metres) in length and her main boom extended 13 feet (4 metres) over the taffrail.

The 1860s and 70s were a prosperous time for the Shetland cod fisheries in which *Telegraph*, like other Faroe smacks, was employed, and John Isbester had probably signed an agreement earlier in the year which required him to be ready to join on 1 April for the first of three fishing trips of six weeks or thereabouts to Faroe, Iceland or Rockall. Scalloway, the west coast Shetland seaport near Whiteness, remained the main centre where smacks were cleared by Customs, took on crew and loaded provisions.[18] John would have invested in the essential knee-high leather boots, the oilskin trousers and jacket, the personal fishing line and hooks plus meagre provisions, all bought from the owners' store against an advance taken from his anticipated share in the profits of the voyage.[19]

For several days he and his dozen or so shipmates would have been employed in the hectic work of storing the ship, taking aboard perhaps 30 tons of salt for curing the catch, sacks or barrels of yeog (horse mussels) for bait, provisions and fresh water, several tons of coal for the stoves, fishing gear, fish handling gear and spare sails and cordage.[20] John Isbester would have had a good idea of what to expect. About 80 Faroe smacks were in service at that time[21] and hundreds of Shetland men and boys served aboard them. Family, friends and neighbours could recount their experiences, and he would have been in no doubt as to the challenges that could face him in a life that was reputed to sort the men from the boys. The cod fishing was very hard work, and the crews were predominantly young men in their teens, twenties and thirties.

When they put to sea their most likely destination would have been Faroe. Rockall was unpopular, as being an isolated rock it was more difficult to find and because no supplies of fresh water and bait were available there if needed. In addition, when fishing at Rockall, a smack had nowhere to run for shelter. By contrast, at Faroe and Iceland it was usually fairly easy to find shelter in the various fjords and bays if weather conditions became too severe to remain on the fishing grounds.[22] Icelandic waters tended to be ice-infested until later in the year and were, therefore, most likely to be the destination for the final voyage of the season. The Faroe smacks relied entirely upon sail, and the voyage from Shetland to Faroe could take anything from two days to two weeks.

On his first voyage John Isbester would have had to become used to a four-on/four-off watchkeeping system during which he would be trimming sails, steering, keeping lookout, tending the galley stove and doing whatever other tasks were given to the most junior hands, while coping with the cold, the smells and the inevitable violent motions of the ship. All the crew slept in a single cabin, with two tiers of bunks and a central stove. When the fishing grounds were reached the crew changed to a three-watch system with, if fish were found, two watches always on duty and one watch off, so that each man was fishing for 16 hours a day. The only exception was on Sundays when no fishing was done, and the skippers took the opportunity to close with other smacks and get news of what success they had had with the fishing.

Captain Thomson[23] wrote:

> Upon arrival on the fishing banks which were found usually by dead reckoning and the hand lead, sails were balanced to suit the speed required. The fore sheet was hauled hard to windward, the main boom run off and the helm was put hard-down. In this condition the vessel backed and filled, keeping the station fairly well – raching it was called. The hands line the rails, shoot their lines and the vital operation begins, sometimes with little success but the crew toil on, balancing on the slippery deck to the roll and pitch of the vessel.

The cod would be swimming at some level between the surface and the sea bed (at depths up to 165 metres when off Faroe) and would be caught with weighted lines, each armed with two baited hooks. The on-duty crew, including the captain and mate, would be distributed along the weather side of the deck, where leeway would ensure that the ship did not drift over the lines, facing into the wind, each lowering his line into the sea and, when the cod were there, quickly pulling the line back up with one or often two cod hooked on, each weighing something like 14 kg. Once the cod had been brought on deck and unhooked the hooks had to be rebaited and the line with its 3 kg weight lowered back into the sea. If an icy, spume-laced wind was blowing, as it usually was, and the decks were slippery with water and fish, as they usually were, this work became all the more painful, arduous and exhausting. It is difficult to imagine the sheer effort required to haul the heavy weight of struggling fish from the depths time after time and hour after hour with aching and exhausted limbs and with hands chilled, lacerated and stung by salt. Crew members were liable to be fined if they failed to turn-to or if they were considered to be slacking, but they did have an incentive to do their best. Individuals were required to keep a record of the fish they caught, which they did by cutting off and retaining the barbel – the whisker-like organ that hangs below the lower jaw of a cod – to provide the proof. They received a bonus payment, usually sixpence, for each score (20) of fish caught.[24]

When the fishing was really good it was a case of all hands on deck, working round the clock, perhaps catching 1,000 fish a day and only stopping when the shoal disappeared, the weather became foul or there was so much fish on deck that they had to stop fishing and process it.[25]

Processing the fish involved installing the flensing table on deck, then removing the head of each fish, gutting it, splitting it, removing its spine, washing and scrubbing it free of all blood and gut lining, salting it and stowing it in the hold. Junior hands like John Isbester were expected to do the beheading, gutting, washing and scrubbing, salting and stowing, but the splitting and removing of the spine was skilled work usually done by the master, mate, or trusted senior hand.

When the fishing was poor the cold wind seemed even keener, the icy spray more hostile and the slippery, pitching decks more treacherous. As Captain Thomson observed,[26] 'This was indeed an endurance test to make or break, yet many young Shetlanders started their sea career under these conditions.'

To sustain them, the crew were provided with 'biscuit' (actually bread) and with coffee which could be laced with brandy. They could also eat fish. The Shetland practice of eating cod livers, a natural source of vitamins A and D, was a healthy one which helped to prevent illness during long periods at sea. Any other food they had to provide for themselves.

There was one bonus to work on the Faroe smacks – the smuggling of duty free brandy and tobacco from Faroe, and there are reasons to believe that for much of the 19th century 80–90 per cent of the Shetland population was involved in the trade, as either smugglers or their customers. With the Shetland fishermen knowing every inch of the coastline and the Customs officers all coming from England or Scotland, it was common practice for the contraband to be landed at night in some remote spot before the smack made a public arrival in port on the following morning.[27] On his first voyage John Isbester might not have had any money with which to buy contraband, but in the next three years he would have many further opportunities.

John Isbester paid off the *Telegraph* on 10 June 1867 and was at his mother's home, Garths of Easthouse in Tingwall, when she died from tetanus on 4 July that year. We know nothing of her death except for the bald facts recorded in the death certificate.

John Isbester had a half-sister, Barbara Anderson, who like him was illegitimate. At the time of her mother's death she was a few days short of her eighth birthday, and her future must have concerned John and members of his extended family. From census records it appears that his aunt Philophia (or Philadelphia) Sutherland, his mother's eldest sister, took Barbara into her own family. The census of 1871 describes Barbara as a scholar (ie a schoolchild) and annuitant and gives her the surname Hunter, which hints that the previously unadmitted father had played a role in providing for her future. That John Isbester kept in contact with his sister through the years is evidenced by a postcard,[28] couched in affectionate terms, from Barbara's daughter Susan, writing in 1913. She writes 'We were all so glad to see that uncle had arrived safe and well', apparently referring to his final successful passage from Newcastle NSW to Callao, Peru.

With his own career at sea launched, his mother dead, his father incommunicado in New Zealand and his half-sister provided for, John Isbester had every reason to return to sea and he did so by joining the schooner *Novice*, another Faroe smack, on 9 August 1867 for her final trip of the season, ending on 30 September.

---

1 *Zetland Directory & Guide* Second Edition.1861.

2 Thomson, Captain J.P, OBE ExC. *Captain John Isbester's Career at Sea, p.2.* Unpublished manuscript. (Isbester Collection).

3 Smith, Davie. Personal letters Nos.DS5, DS9 (Isbester Collection).

4 *The Shetland Customs and Excise Fishing Boat Register for 1869*, Shetland Archives, Lerwick.
5 Smith, Davie. Personal letters No.DS5 (Isbester Collection).
6 *The Shetland Book*, Zetland Education Committee, 1967, p.89.
7 Halcrow, Captain A. *The Sail Fishermen of Shetland.* The Shetland Times Ltd, Lerwick, 1994. pp.82–83
8 Coull, Dr J.R. *Herring Fishing in Scotland,* A Resources for Learning in Scotland Project.
9 See this book, Chapter 11.
10 Halcrow, Captain A. Op.cit, pp.67–68.
11 Halcrow, Captain A. Ibid, pp. 69–71.
12 Sandison, Charles. *The Sixareen and her Racing Descendants,* pp.16–17. The Shetland Times Ltd, Lerwick. 2005.
13 Halcrow, Captain A. Op.cit, pp.75–80.
14 Johnson, Charles, of Toam, North Roe.
15 *Mansons Shetland Almanac & Directory for 1932.*
16 Thomson, Captain J.P, OBE ExC. Letters JPT9, JPT10 & JPT11 of 1969. (Isbester Collection). For the dates of this and subsequent voyages prior to John Isbester obtaining command I rely upon unpublished research undertaken in the 1960s. Captain Thomson writes that the information on John Isbester's early voyages on the smacks came from Mr Manson of the Shetland News while data for the subsequent voyages was obtained from the Registrar General of Shipping and Seamen at that time.
17 Halcrow, Captain A. Op.cit. p.105.
18 Goodlad, John, PhD. Thesis: *The Shetland Cod Fishery from 1811 to 1908. A study in Historical Geography, Section 5.2.4.*
19 Thomson, Captain J.P, OBE ExC. Op.cit, p.2.
20 Halcrow, Captain A. Op.cit. p.99.
21 *Scottish Fishery Board Records* quoted by Goodlad, John, PhD. Op.cit, Section 5.2.4.
22 Goodlad, John, PhD. Thesis: Op.cit. Section *7.1.3.*
23 Thomson, Captain J.P, OBE ExC. Op.cit, p.2.
24 Goodlad, John, PhD. Thesis: Op.cit. Section 9.1.2.
25 Halcrow, Captain A. Op.cit. p.101.
26 Thomson, Captain J.P, OBE ExC. Op.cit, p.2.
27 Goodlad, John, PhD. Thesis: Op.cit Section 9.1.4.
28 Postcard No.26 to Mrs. Isbester 'from your loving niece Susie'. (Isbester Collection).

4 GOING FOREIGN

The *Novice*, where John Isbester finished the 1867 season, was owned by the well-known Shetland cod fishing firm of Joseph Leask & Co., and in 1868 he signed on the schooner *Anaconda*, another Faero smack owned by Leask, where he was to go to the cod fishing for the next three seasons. These schooners were long, rakish, fine-lined vessels of over 35 metres in length, wet in a seaway and needing to be handled with care – 'Like a glass baby which would as soon drown you as look at you' – as one old salt is reported to have said. Like most of the Faero smacks they had originally been built for other trades. *Anaconda* and her two sister schooners had been luxuriously appointed, and the skipper of the sister ship *Destiny* was reputed to have adopted my lady's boudoir as his cabin.[1] It is unlikely that John Isbester, sailing as ordinary seaman, would have felt much benefit from the luxury.

During the fishing season *Anaconda* carried a crew of 17 of whom 13 were full-shares-men; the three ordinary seamen, of whom John Isbester was one, earned ¾ shares, and a ship's boy earned a ½ share. These were the shares of the earnings from the fishing after the owners had taken a half of the total earnings, plus the costs of fitting out the ship for the fishing.[2]

After the fishing season these vessels made voyages to Spain and the Mediterranean ports with sun-dried Shetland cod (*baccalà*), for which there was a good market, and they made other commercial voyages to British and European ports.[3] This is how the schooner *Anaconda* was employed during the winters of 1868–9 and 1869–70, which must have been frustrating for John Isbester, who as a junior hand was not retained outside the fishing season. His shipmates were visiting new countries, experiencing the adventure of foreign ports, seeing beautiful big sailing ships and enjoying, from time to time the sunshine, blue skies and gentle winds, the flying fish and sporting dolphins of more southern latitudes. From his more experienced shipmates he would be hearing sailors' stories of romantic tropical seaports and great commercial centres. So it is no surprise that after five hard summers of fishing in challenging northern climes amongst his Shetland countrymen he chose to move into big ships, trading worldwide. In the spring of 1871, at the age of 19, he went south to Liverpool, to find employment in square-rigged ships.

In Liverpool he joined the ship *Sealkote,* 1,241 tons gross, as ordinary seaman in April 1871 shortly before she sailed for

> Calcutta and any ports and places in the Indian, Pacific and Atlantic Oceans and the China and Eastern Seas (thence to a port for orders and to the Continent if required) and back to a final port of discharge in the United Kingdom term not to exceed 3 years.[4]

The agreement also provided that:

> The crew shall consist of Mate, Carpr, Bsn, Sails, Std, Cook, 8 Seamen, 1 Ordy and 1 Boy [i.e. mate, carpenter, bosun, sailmaker, steward, cook, 8 seamen, 1 ordinary seaman and 1 boy]. No grog allowed.

Life in the forecastle cannot have been pleasant. James Reddock, another ordinary seaman, fell sick on the third day of the voyage from an unidentified but appalling illness which covered him with a rash, then scabs which rubbed off to leave bare flesh. Despite care which seems to have been well intentioned and kindly, he died 12 days later, by which time he was 'smelling very strong'.[5] Throughout his illness he lay in the forecastle, sharing the space with all the other sailors. After his death, in accordance with tradition, his possessions were sold to his shipmates. This was a way of ensuring that his meagre possessions were not wasted and of providing a little money for the next of kin, when and if known.

Calcutta was reached in mid-September, after about five months at sea. During the passage while *Sealkote* was in the Atlantic, John Isbester would have experienced Westerlies followed by the steady north east trade winds, then the doldrums and the south east trades, mostly pleasant sailing in latitudes far more benign than was offered by the waters around Shetland. Rounding the Cape of Good Hope, probably at a good distance from the land, the westerly winds of the Roaring Forties might have accelerated their passage before they turned northwards into the Indian Ocean and the Bay of Bengal. The final weeks of the voyage would have occurred during the south west monsoon season, providing a fair wind but unpleasant rainy, sweaty conditions when tempers are likely to have been short. Arriving at Sandheads at the mouth of the Hoogly, *Sealkote* would have acquired a pilot and a tug and been towed up the fast-flowing river to Budge Budge or Calcutta. The dense mangrove swamps, the innumerable small boats transporting passengers or stacked high with sacks or bales of farm produce, the fishermen with their nets and the brown-skinned people in lungis and saris would provide fascinating sights for a young man who until that time had seen only the Faeroes, Scotland and northern England.

When berthed at No.5 Hastings Moorings, Calcutta, at 0715 hrs on Monday 17 September, shortly after *Sealkote*'s arrival in the port, Lewis Joseph, ordinary seaman, loosing sails, fell from the mizzen topsail yard onto the poop deck. He was immediately seen by a doctor who happened to be on board at the time and sent to Calcutta hospital where he died at 1015 hrs the same morning of a ruptured spleen. A fall in these circumstances would be unusual – the ship would be steady and the temperature not extreme – but the records show that Joseph had taken a cash advance of 5 shillings on the ship's arrival in port the previous afternoon, in addition to incurring debts of £1 5s with a bumboat man for unspecified goods or services. In Calcutta in 1871, 5 shillings – half a week's wages for an ordinary seaman – would have been a very much more substantial figure than it seems today. Whatever the reason, it is likely that his fall was caused by feeling unwell. When Joseph's effects were sold, John Isbester paid 3 shillings for a pair of boots which Joseph had earlier in the voyage bought for 16 shillings from the captain's slopchest.

Most of the crew deserted soon after the ship arrived in Calcutta, which probably suited both crew and owners well. The latter could use cheap local labour when needed for the two months during which *Sealkote* was in the port, and the former could have a few days ashore enjoying themselves after their five months at sea and then, when their money ran out, ship out to some new destination.

Sealkote remained in Calcutta until mid-November and I like to think that my grandfather wandered around the suburban Kidderpore covered market as I did 90 years later, enjoying the immaculate stalls selling beans and pulses in sacks carefully opened to display their attractive contents, bars of coarse local soap, brilliantly coloured saris and enticing, juicy mangoes, sweet and tasty bananas and delicious papayas. For five months John Isbester had been climbing the lofty masts of *Sealkote* but he may have been surprised at the skill and nonchalance with which Indian men shinned up palm trees to harvest the coconuts.

Calcutta at that period offered plenty of traditional attractions for sailors.

> A great deal of moral latitude, not to say licence, was permitted in Calcutta at that time. Everything was cheap – rum, women and tobacco. The merchant sailor was allowed to do pretty much as he pleased in pursuing his peculiar ideas of personal enjoyment. He might get drunk in the Numbers, riot in the Checkers and then proceed to clean out the German Barracks without fear of serious interference or arrest on the part of the East India police, most of whom were recruited from the maritime contingent themselves.[6]

John Isbester seems to have been an unusually committed and well organised seaman. During nine years of service before the mast he never deserted, adopting a pattern of behaviour more like an established petty officer – a sailmaker or carpenter – than an ordinary or able seaman. Many of his shipmates deserted in Calcutta, but there and on subsequent voyages to inviting places such as Quebec, New York, New Orleans, Buenos Aires, San Francisco, Adelaide and Sydney he appears to have maintained a faultless record, always completing the voyage. This suggests that he was committed to getting on, to earning promotion. He also seems to have made it his purpose to visit all the great seaports of the 19th-century world – and I have to admit to more than a tinge of envy when I read an account of the ports that he visited.

Eight ABs – a typical mixture of Scots, Irish, German, Swedish, Canadian and Channel Islanders – were signed on in early November when the ship was ready to leave Calcutta. One of them, Augustus Jouan, a 30-year-old from Guernsey, had been released from hospital a day before he joined the vessel. After four days at sea and when still in the Bay of Bengal he 'was taken sick with the cholera', and 'despite all possible means being used to save him' he died a few hours later.[7] The homeward voyage around the Cape of Good Hope, through the Atlantic and up through the Channel to Dundee took a bit more than four months, and John Isbester paid off, after a voyage lasting ten and a half months, with £16.17s.3d earned at a rate of £2 per month.

His next four voyages were all quite short ones, being round trips to Quebec, New York, New Orleans and again to Quebec in four different ships, all sailing from Liverpool. The first was the ship *City of Manchester*, 1,116 tons gross, where he signed on as ordinary seaman. The ship's official log book[8] reveals only that on 30 May seven seamen deserted in Quebec, where six replacements were later signed on. It must have been a relief that no-one died.

He then served as able seaman in the iron clipper ship *Strathearn*, 1,784 tons gross, a hard-driven ship credited with making a passage from New York to the United Kingdom in ten days. She carried three mates, a bosun, 26 ABs and four 0Ss, double the size of crew to which John Isbester would become accustomed. She also had an engine driver to look after a boiler and winch, provided to help with heavy hauling. Outward bound to New York, in mid-Atlantic,

Thomas Evan AB fell overboard from the main shear pole, a position low in the main shrouds. The ship hove to and a boat manned by the chief officer and four sailors was launched, but searched for him without success. On the homeward passage from New York at 0300 am John Fillibank OS, taking in the starboard sidelight, 'either overbalanced himself or was washed overboard'. He was presumably taking the light in to top up its oil; the sidelight was probably lost with him, but spares would have been carried.

> There was no possibility of saving him, the ship going 12 knots and the morning very dark. The Chief Officer threw a lifebuoy and put the helm down but he was not seen and we very reluctantly had to give up hope of saving him.

Nine days later misfortune struck this unfortunate crew again. The official log book records:

> At about 5.45am whilst the ship was running 15 knots before a NW gale shipped a sea on the poop and swept Mr Campbell Chief Officer overboard. Blowing very hard with very heavy sea at the time, it was quite impossible to do anything to save him.[9]

At the end of that passage John Isbester must have been relieved to set foot again in the familiar streets of Liverpool.

Next came the barque *John Geddie*, of Halifax, Nova Scotia, 651 tons gross – a small vessel with crew of 13 all told. John Isbester is recorded in the official log book[10] as John Ibister, one of numerous familiar corruptions of the name. *John Geddie* seems to have been a happy ship under the command of George Wellen Smith. The log book records no failures-to-join, no desertions in New Orleans, and no penalties for offences committed, in contrast to her following voyage, a round trip from Liverpool to Halifax under a different master, where each of these misdemeanours were common. By this time, however, John Isbester was aboard the ship *Advice*, 1,261 tons gross, on the last of his four short voyages.

These voyages lasted from three to four and a half months, including a month or so in the destination port, and were separated by no more than a few days of leave – insufficient time for a return to Shetland. That is not surprising. When I was 20, life at sea was fascinating – there were skills to learn, sights to see and adventures to be had – and time away from home was no hardship. John Isbester did not even have parents to whom to return.

He next joined the barque *Beulah*, 746 tons nett, for what was to prove a very different voyage. In the space of 20 months she went from Liverpool to Sydney in Cape Breton Island, thence to Darien in Georgia, USA, next to Pensacola in Florida, and from there to Buenos Aires in Argentina. Following a month or so in Buenos Aires, *Beulah* rounded Cape Horn carrying John Isbester into the Pacific for the first time and working her way north to Portland in Oregon, USA, close to the Canadian border. Her cargo was probably discharged in Portland, and she then moved to Albany, still in Oregon, to load wheat for Europe. As was very common she proceeded via Cape Horn to Queenstown, Ireland, for orders, from where she went immediately to Liverpool to discharge, the passage from Albany having taken four months.

John Isbester paid off on 8 April 1875, at the right time of year for a bit of a holiday and probably with a few pounds in his pocket. He took more than five months' leave at that time and it is likely that he returned to Shetland for some or all of that summer. While there, staying at Haggersta or visiting his aunt and uncle, he may have learnt that his absent father was in Sydney, Australia.

In September he was back in Liverpool to find a ship. He'd done India, he'd done North and South America, east and west: where was new and where would be interesting? Australia sprang to mind – he might meet his father – and John Isbester joined the iron ship *North Riding*, 1,432 tons gross, as able seaman for the voyage to Sydney, which port was reached on 19 December, in comfortable time for Christmas 1875. *North Riding* seems to have spent about five weeks in Sydney before proceeding to Adelaide and then to Port Wakefield in the Spencer Gulf to load wheat, before returning to Adelaide to clear for Queenstown, Ireland, for orders. Seven of the ship's ABs, including two Shetland men,[11] deserted towards the end of the ship's stay in Sydney in late January 1876. John Isbester, however, remained to complete the voyage in Liverpool paying off, in August 1876, with a healthy £30.7s.11d.[12]

My grandfather used to mention that he had met his own father on his own early voyages to Australia.[13] In fact this was the only early voyage that he made to Australia, though he called there regularly during the last 15 years of his life.

He was of course referring to my great-grandfather, John Isbister, who had probably left Shetland in the 1850s, and earned a living intermittently as a gold miner on the west coast of New Zealand's South Island for the better part of 50 years between 1860 and 1911. Like other miners who reached the area in the 1860s he had probably moved to the west coast from gold mining in Victoria in the 1850s and Otago in the early 1860s,[14] having first reached Australia as a seaman. The evidence that he and his younger brother Henry spent their declining years and died on the west coast of New Zealand's South Island is convincing, but there is evidence that he mined for gold in Australia from time to time as well. An item in a New Zealand newspaper describing gold mining in Red Rock, New South Wales, Australia, in 1887 contains an editor's note reading 'John Isbester, late of Kumara [a town on the New Zealand west coast], has a claim next to the aforementioned party'.[15] In view of family tradition it is likely that he had several spells of mining in Australia and was mining in New South Wales in 1876 when my grandfather was there aboard *North Riding*, as well as in 1887. Sydney would be the natural place for a gold miner to go for a break or when travelling to or from New Zealand.

During the five weeks that *North Riding* remained in Sydney there would have been plenty of time for the Shetland network – the informal contacts between people of Shetland origin throughout the world – to bring news of family and friends both near and far. Meeting other Shetland folk in far parts of the world was not at all unusual, but was certainly a matter of interest. A number of encounters of this sort are described in my grandfather's correspondence from his later years. It is tantalising to reflect that we will never know what passed between my goldmining great-grandfather in his fifties and his 25-year-old son, an able seaman with his future before him when they met for the first time. Did my great-grandfather leave Shetland unaware that he was to become a father and only learn the truth years later? Did he intend to return? And if so, was he prevented by some difficulty, or did he decide that Sarah Anderson was not the woman for him?

Some feeling for the special nature of life in the New Zealand goldfields during the gold rush days can be gained from the account[16] of the 1909 annual reunion of the West Coast Old Boys.

> After doing ample justice to the good things provided the toast of The King was duly honoured. [Officers were elected] and the health of Mr Russell the newly-elected president was drunk. The chairman proposed the toast of West Coast and West Coasters and was ably responded to by Messrs J. Keating, J. Jackson and J. Kerr, who paid a high tribute to the pioneer work done by the early arrivals on the Coast. The toast of Departed West Coasters was drunk in silence.
>
> Mr E. Sheedy proposed the toast of Old Sports and held that the West Coast had turned out some excellent athletes. The toast was ably responded to by Messrs D. McKay, J. Evans, L. Broad and C. North. Mr Ashton proposed the toast of Commercial and Professional Interests and [it was] responded to by Messrs Joyce, Kerr and Cunliffe.
>
> Mr Joyce proposed the toast of the Pioneers of the West Coast, those who made our roads and developed our district. Messrs Splaine, Hinkley and Isbester responded.
>
> Several other appropriate toasts were proposed and responded to and an excellent musical programme rendered. The singing of Auld Lang Syne brought a most successful re-union to a close.

By then my great-grandfather was a man of 84. It sounds like a good party!

John arranged his brother Henry's funeral in 1906, though there is nothing to suggest that they actually worked alongside one another over the years. At the time of his death Henry was described as a 'miner, highly respected throughout Westland'.[17] The brothers seem to have mined separately, and there were clearly several other unrelated Isbisters in New Zealand towards the end of the 19th century. Tantalisingly the New Zealand newspapers of that period frequently refer to the activities of Isbester or Isbister[18] without giving a forename. Another younger brother, Robert, also appears to have been in New Zealand for some years until the 1870s, though I have found no evidence that he died there. Like his brother John, he may have decided to move to Australia but, unlike John, decided to stay there. Nowadays there are plenty of Isbesters and Isbisters in Australia!

In John Isbister's will, written three years before his death when he was 83, he describes himself as formerly[19] a miner of Woodstock, Westland. After payment of his debts he specifies that a sum of no more than £30 sterling was to be used for 'paying the costs of my funeral and in erecting a Headstone over my grave and concreting it over and railing it in', instructions that were carried out.[20] The total value of the estate was declared to be less than £100 sterling, and the balance was to be left to Helen Robina Wallace (née Morgan), wife of William Wallace of Kumara, Westland, Bushman.[21] (A bushman was a logger or forestry worker.[22]) It is likely that Helen Wallace was John Isbister's carer before he entered hospital.

---

1 Halcrow, Capt. A. *The Sail Fishermen of Shetland*. The Shetland Times Ltd, Lerwick Ltd. 1994, p.108.

2 *The Second Shetland Truck System Report 1872*. Paragraph 11,279 et seq. By a happy accident the onlyFaroe smack fisherman mentioned by name in the Truck Report is John Isbister (*sic*) OS on the *Anaconda*.

3 Thomson, Captain J.P, OBE ExC. *Captain John Isbesters Career at Sea*. Unpublished manuscript. (IsbesterCollection), p.3.

4 *Sealkote* Agreement, Voy.06.04.1871–21.03.1872, Maritime History Archive, Newfoundland.
5 *Sealkote* Off. Log Book, Voy. 06.04.1871–21.03.1872, Maritime History Archive, Newfoundland.
6 Williams, James H. *Blow the Man Down*. E P Dutton & Co, Inc. New York, 1959, p.115.
7 *Sealkote* Off. Log Book, Op.cit.
8 *City of Manchester* OLB, Voy. 02.04.1872–07.08.1872, Maritime History Archive, Newfoundland.
9 *Strathearn* OLB, Voy.16.08.1872–28.10.1872, Maritime History Archive, Newfoundland.
10 *John Geddie*, Liverpool, England, Crew Lists 1861–1919 on Ancestry.com.
11 Arthur Blunce, aged 23, Gilbert Porteous, aged 26.
12 *North Riding* Agreement, Voyage ending 18.08.1876. Maritime History Archive, Newfoundland.
13 Isbester, C. Allan. Document CAI4, written about 1965 (Isbester Collection).
14 May, Philip Ross. *The West Coast Gold Rushes*, Appendix I, Pegasus, 1967.
15 *Kumara Reef, Red Rock, New South Wales* Grey River Argos. 24 March 1887.
16 *Old Boys Association*. Grey River Argos. 16 December 1909.
17 West Coast Times, NZ 25 November 1906.
18 As seen elsewhere the two spellings were interchangeable. Indeed their death certificates show that John was buried as an Isbister whereas his brother Henry was recorded as Isbester.
19 By this time he was an inmate of the Westland hospital.
20 tony.gott@mac.com by personal email dated 12.11.2011 stating the list of Hokitica NZ gravestones provided by a researcher had been seen by him at the Bayanne Shetland Genealogy website. (Isbester Collection).
21 Isbister, John. Motion for Probate. Archives New Zealand Ref. CH300, HK59/1911.
22 Hansen, Alan. Personal email dated 21.05.2013 (Isbester Collection).

5 SERVICE AS AN OFFICER

At the end of his voyage to Australia John Isbester, Able Seaman, paid off in Liverpool on 18 August 1876 and seven weeks later, on 3 October 1876, aged 24, he was awarded his second mate's certificate of competency, no. 02269. He must have enjoyed an enormous feeling of satisfaction at the achieving of his first ambition. Captain R.S. Cogle, writing nearly 40 years later at the time of John Isbester's untimely death, wrote under the heading *The Loss of the Dalgonar*:

> Sir,- it was with a sad heart that I read the log of the above in the Shetland Times of last week. It has been my privilege to have known the late Captain Isbester for about forty years. He passed all his Board of Trade examinations under my guidance and never failed once.[1]

Captain Cogle was a Shetland man who ran a private navigation school at 35 Pitt Street in Liverpool and, in retirement, lived in Hoylake on the Wirral coast, just a few miles away.

It was not until six months later, in April 1877, that John Isbester returned to sea with an appointment as second mate. It appears that he had taken a voluntary winter holiday in Shetland – in 1884 he was described as having been 'seven years south',[2] i.e. away from Shetland for seven years – which fits with what we know of his movements. Winter in Shetland would seem like a second best when there was an officer's job to be enjoyed, and sunlit seas, gentle breezes and graceful palm trees to be found. It may well be that jobs were hard to come by, as they certainly were two years later, or he may have decided that he had earned a break and wanted to do a bit of courting. This appears to have been the time when John Isbester 'left his watch' (a Shetland expression for an informal betrothal) with Maggie Smith of Strome in Whiteness, the village of his birth. John Isbester eventually joined the wooden ship *Nelson,* of 943 tons gross, in Maryport as second mate. She was bound for Quebec, where she spent a month discharging and loading, and was back in Ayr at the end of June to end a round trip of two and a half months. Ten days later he rejoined the *Nelson* in Greenock for another trip to Quebec, this time under a different master. The fact that he was prepared to travel to Maryport and to Greenock to join the ship hints at an eagerness to grab a berth on a good ship – or perhaps on any ship from a shrinking choice.

A month after leaving the *Nelson* in Gravesend at the end of the second voyage, John Isbester joined the iron barque *Parthia,* 1,063 tons gross, in Liverpool for a voyage to Valparaiso in Chile, where, after discharging they sailed north to visit Iquique and load nitrate in Antofagasta, thence to Falmouth for orders and on to Liverpool. That voyage, with its rounding of Cape Horn in both directions, took 11 months and should have convinced John Isbester, if he needed convincing, that he had a good knowledge of the work of a second mate in square-rigged sail.

Figure 5.1 John Isbester as a young man

Back in Liverpool in October 1878, John Isbester found that there were no second mates' jobs to be found, and on 12 November he took a decision that could have been life changing – he enrolled in the Liverpool Constabulary as a third class constable.[3] Enrolling in the same period were men with such Shetland-sounding names as John Gifford Inkster, Peter Anderson, Hector Bain, John Irvine and Magnus Irvine, so it may have been the 'thing to do' at that time.

Photos of John Isbester (Fig.5.1) suggest that he was a man of good stature, probably a requirement for the police force. It would be good to believe that he enjoyed duty attending the crowds visiting the Walker Art Gallery, where up to four constables were posted, but it is more likely that his main concern was in dealing with the cases of drunkenness in Liverpool, which had in December 1876 risen from 15,763 to 16,859 per annum, leading to protests from prominent members of the public, insisting that the licencing laws be enforced.[4] Other incidents requiring the attention of constables included dealing with the boys troubling Mrs McMillan in Balm Street and the need to apprehend Aaron Lipwitz, charged with stealing Abm. Liebenchutz's cash box. I have found no record of when, why or how John Isbester left the Liverpool Constabulary, but he used to tell his family that he had been a policeman for about six months, which would place his departure from the Force during the summer of 1879. He finally returned to sea on 1 February 1880, joining the iron barque *Cumeria,* 1,336 tons gross, in Liverpool as second mate for a voyage to San Francisco. She had unrecorded problems which caused her to return to Liverpool after a day at sea, but she eventually completed the 11-month voyage with its double wintertime rounding of Cape Horn, returning to Hull to discharge her homeward cargo. That had been John Isbester's first visit to San Francisco, a two-and-a-half-month stay in a port to which he was to return many times in later years. After four weeks' leave John Isbester rejoined the *Cumeria* in North Shields for a voyage to Bombay with a cargo of coal. He must have done well on his first voyage on *Cumeria* because although the new crew signed on in Hull on 14 January his place was kept open for him to rejoin on 29 January.

Bombay would be yet another new destination for him, but the voyage would leave its marks on him for quite a different reason. When he came on watch at 0800 on 7 February *Cumeria* was south of St Catherine's Point on the Isle of Wight and close hauled on the port tack, steering about south-west by west[5] (Fig.5.2). The wind, from the south-south-east or south by east, was getting up, and there was a heavy cross sea from the west. *Cumeria* was carrying courses and upper and lower topsails in addition to jib, foretopmast staysail, maintopmast staysail and crojack, and Captain Evan Williams from Aberdovey ordered all hands on deck to shorten sail (Fig.5.3). John Isbester and his watch were allotted the mainmast, the hands going aloft to reef the main course and upper topsail while the mate and his watch reefed the corresponding sails on the foremast.

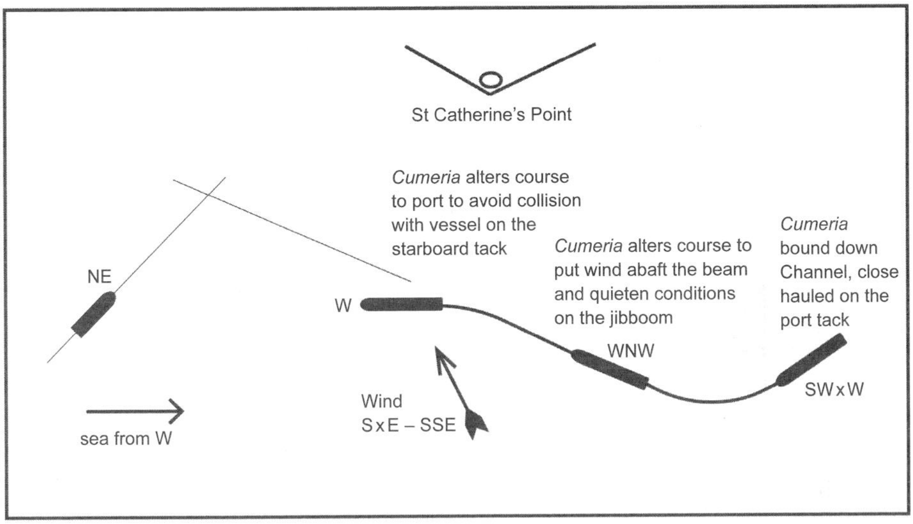

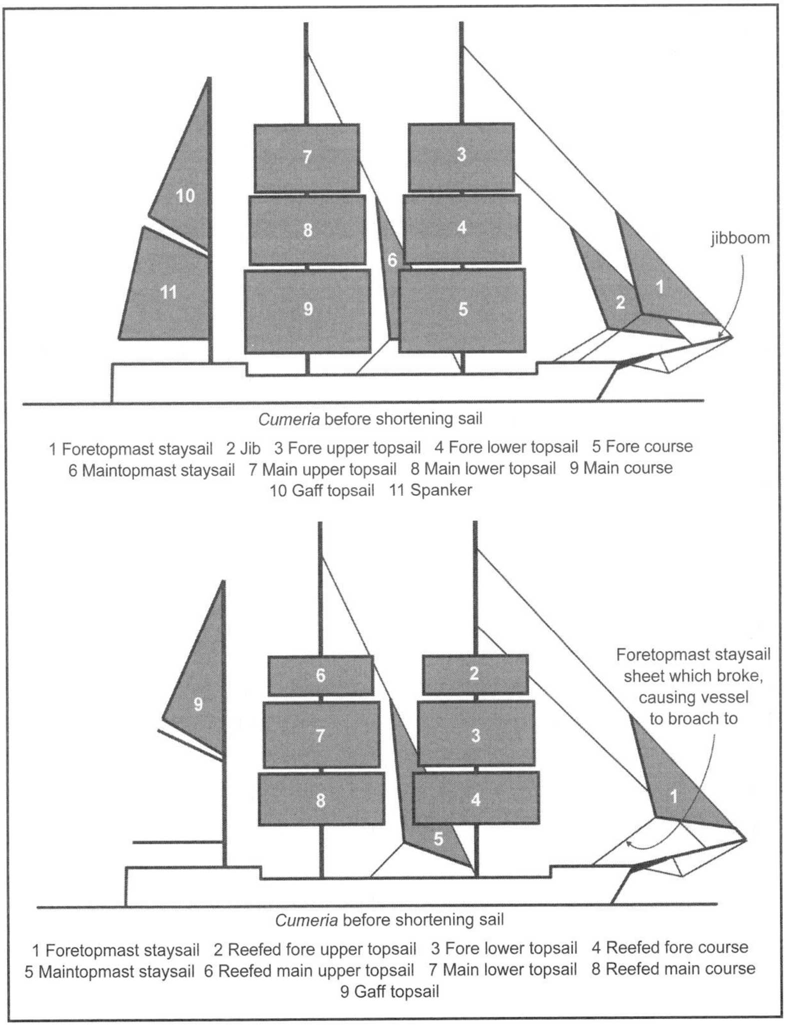

(Above) Figure 5.2 Barque Cumeria *– tragic loss of four men*

(Left) Figure 5.3 Cumeria *before and after shortening sail*

Next John Isbester and his watch commenced furling the crojack on the mizzen mast while chief mate Gilbert Pearson from Shetland, bosun Robert Lloyd from Baltimore and four hands went forward to hand and stow the jib. The men selected were John Dodds from North Shields, John Small from Dundee, John Caygill from Whitby and Konstantine Barintizous from Italy. Captain Williams instructed them to wait for his signal before going on to the jibboom, the light extension to the bowsprit.

He then ordered Able Seaman E.G. (Johnny) Johansson from Sweden, the man at the wheel, to bring the ship's head to starboard to steer WNW, bringing the wind abaft the beam, so that *Cumeria* was running free on the port tack, easing the weight on the jib and reducing the extent to which the vessel was pitching into the heavy seas from the west. This action made it safer for the men to go onto the jibboom, and when *Cumeria* was settled on the new course Captain Williams waved to the men to loose the halyards and go onto the jibboom to hand and stow the jib. When they were so engaged Captain Williams saw for the first time, at a distance of about 1½ miles, a sailing vessel which he judged to be on a collision course crossing on the starboard tack. Captain Williams was required by the Rule of the Road to keep out of the way of the other vessel, and to do this he would have to alter course to port, returning towards the more hazardous course so recently abandoned. Standing at the fore end of the poop, he waved to the men on the jibboom to get back inboard immediately, but they did not notice his signals, the bows being about 60 yards/metres from the poop. He waited as long as he dared, then ordered the helmsman to make a two-point alteration of course, to steer west, in order to avoid collision with the other vessel.

As *Cumeria* came onto the new course the foretopmast staysail sheet carried away (i.e. broke), and the vessel, now with sails unbalanced, broached to (i.e. lurched heavily, in this case with the bow swinging rapidly to port), and a heavy sea struck the port bow and swept over the jibboom, the bowsprit and the forecastle. At that instant the four men were swept from the jibboom into the cold February waters of the Channel, and the chief mate and bosun, on the forecastle, were trapped, reportedly 'under the port tack'.[6] The cry 'Man overboard!' was heard, lifebuoys and ropes were flung overboard and the yards were braced to port, to back the sails and stop the ship. One man in the water managed to catch hold of the mizzen vang, and another clutched the patent log line, but the vessel was at that time still travelling quite fast through the water, perhaps 6 or 7 knots, and agonisingly they were unable to retain their grip.

John Isbester was sent aloft to keep a lookout for the four men in the water, but could see none of them. Captain Williams asked for volunteers to man a boat, but none was prepared to venture, one man saying that if any of the men overboard were still in sight he would have been prepared to go. Captain Williams sailed back and forth through the area of the loss for the next four hours, but then, having seen nothing, resumed the voyage, and called at Falmouth six days later to pay off Johann Baer, AB from Danzig (Gdansk) and Per Rudolf Malmqvist, ship's boy aged 17 from Sweden and to sign six replacements – five ABs and one OS. The leavers were, presumably, unwilling to continue the voyage after the distressing experience of the first ten days.

The official log book was reported to contain an entry, signed by four ABs including Johansson, the man who had been at the wheel, to the effect that the loss of the four men had been an accident and that every effort had been made to save them.

That the foregoing traumatic events are on record is because a letter signed by H.B. Johnson and dated 26 October 1881 was subsequently received by the Board of Trade alleging that the deaths of the four men were the result of 'A piece of wilful carelessness and unseamanlike piece of work amounting to manslaughter.' A formal investigation was held at Westminster in December 1881, the voyage having ended at Gravesend in mid-November following discharge in Rotterdam of a homeward cargo from Bombay. Six witnesses were present at the hearing, one being Captain Williams, and another the cook who confirmed the captain's evidence that another sailing vessel had been nearby. It is likely that John Isbester was present too. He was in the UK at the time, on leave or studying for his first mate's certificate, which he passed in Liverpool on 18 January 1882. One man not present was bosun Robert Lloyd: he had been left behind in jail in Bombay for reasons not recorded.[7] The investigation cleared Captain Williams of any blame, concluding that the broaching-to of the vessel, which increased the severity of the heavy sea striking the port bow, was itself caused by the giving way of the foretopmast staysail sheet and was the cause of the loss of the lives in question. They further concluded that proper and seamanlike measures had been taken to stow the jib and that, *Cumeria* being the give-way vessel, Captain Williams had acted reasonably and safely when altering course two points to port to avoid collision. It was also concluded that every possible effort had been made to save the lives of the men. The tribunal decided that the complainant was the man who had signed Articles as John Johnson (*sic*),[8] the AB at the wheel at the time of the occurrence, now again away at sea in the Mediterranean, and that his motive for making the complaint was that Captain Williams had refused to pay him off in Bombay where he had had the opportunity to obtain a more attractive job as cook and baker on a steam ship. They considered that, as one of the ABs who had signed the log book entry to the effect that the deaths had been accidental and that every effort had been made to save the men in the water he would, if present at the hearing, have found it difficult to justify his accusation.

So what might John Isbester have learnt from these tragic events? That a mariner's life was perilous and could be snatched away in an instant was obvious, and he had seen that previously. He might have wondered why the foretopmast staysail sheet had failed so disastrously and why the master had not sent someone forward to warn the men on the jibboom of the planned manoeuvre. He might have reflected on how easy it is to lose sight of a lifebuoy or a man's head in a rough sea, even at 200 yards/metres. The court hearing could not fail to show him the desirability of having a statement of events entered in the official log book and signed by witnesses who could be assumed to be impartial. It would also have shown him that allegations made but not supported by a witness in court were liable to be given short shrift, and the worst of motives attributed to the absentee.

Within a fortnight of obtaining his first mate's certificate John Isbester was back at sea as chief mate of the iron-hulled ship *West Ridge,* 1,496 tons gross, embarked on a 15-month voyage first to Calcutta, which they reached in May after three and a half months at sea, benefitting from the south-west monsoon in the final Indian Ocean stages of the passage. That same south-west monsoon became their enemy a month later when, having discharged their cargo, they cleared for Liverpool on 20 June. Fighting their way out of the Bay of Bengal against the strength of the monsoon would have been a difficult, perhaps impossible, task, and the master appears to have had second thoughts or new instructions. *West Ridge* remained in Calcutta until the monsoon weakened in September, when they sailed for the lovely Indian Ocean island of Mauritius. Port Louis, the capital city and port of Mauritius, with its benign tropical climate, its gentle winds, blue seas, graceful palm trees and background of spectacular mountains, would have been a welcome contrast to the flatlands of sweaty, monsoon-drenched Calcutta. The Mauritian coconuts, bananas, grapefruit, oranges, limes, papayas, sugarcane, pineapples and guavas, available for the smallest coin would have been very welcome, there were lots of fish to be pulled from the waters of the harbour, and piglets and chickens might also have been available at a price. John Isbester might have noticed an intriguing similarity to his home port of Lerwick. In Port Louis he would see Arab dhows and Chinese junks alongside European square riggers and steamers just as in Lerwick he would see fishing boats from the Netherlands and Poland, from Portugal and St Petersburg as well as from England and Scotland. Both Lerwick and Port Louis are excellent sheltered ports situated at ocean crossroads.

West Ridge remained in Port Louis for two months before returning to Calcutta and finally back to Liverpool after making landfalls at St Helena and Ascension. On their homeward voyage they may have carried sensitive cargoes such as tea, coconut and tobacco. It is more likely that their cargoes were at the contaminating end of the spectrum – hides, horns and hoofs, crushed bones, myrabolams and amotto seed – along with neutral cargoes such as palm fibre, gunnies, hemp, and rope cuttings, as befitted slower and older ships, compelled to round the Cape of Good Hope rather than use the Suez Canal like the steamers.[9]

John Isbester, aged 31, now had the necessary seatime to sit for his Master's Certificate, which he did following a few weeks at Captain Cogle's school. On 7 August 1883 he was awarded Square Rigged Certificate No.02269. He must have felt joyful when he reflected that his years of hardship and sacrifice had earned him the reward for which he had worked with such commitment. All that remained was to obtain a command – and, perhaps, a wife.

But with no commands immediately on offer John Isbester decided that he had no choice but to do another voyage or two as chief mate. Within a month he had joined the wooden barque *Queen of Australia*, 1,328 tons gross, as chief mate for a voyage to Quebec. His experience would doubtless have been enriched by the events of the voyage. A report, by cable, read:

> The Queen of Australia from Quebec for Liverpool went ashore at Cacouna but afterwards came off without assistance, damage if any not yet ascertained.[10]

Cacouna is situated on the east bank of the Saint Lawrence river, about 100 miles seaward of Quebec. A later report gave more bad news:

> The Queen of Australia from Quebec 2nd Inst. and following days had greater part of deck cargo washed overboard.[11]

Coming from Quebec, the deck cargo was very probably timber of some sort, and John Isbester as chief mate, possibly advised by Captain Jardalla or the longshoremen, would have been responsible for the lashings which should have secured it. Loss of deck cargo is not uncommon in the most severe weather, and could be due to ferocious conditions, to poor ship handling and/or to inadequate securing. In any event there were doubtless lessons to be learnt.

---

1 Cogle, Capt. Robert S, Letter to *The Shetland Times Ltd*, Lerwick, undated early 1914 (Isbester Collection).

2 Laing, Robert. Letter to Christina L Jamieson, 17.06.1884 (Isbester Collection).
3 Liverpool Watch Committee Order Book, entry dated 12 November.1878, Liverpool City Archive.
4 Liverpool Watch Committee Order Book, entry dated 17 Dec.1878, ibid.
5 The account which follows is based upon the Report of U.K. Formal Investigation No.1171 *Cumeria.*
6 This phrase from the Report of the Formal Investigation 1171 *Cumeria* is not understood.
7 *Cumeria* Agreement, Voy.14.01.1881–14.11.1881, Maritime History Archive, Newfoundland.
8 The only person signed on with a name like Johnson was E.G Johansson, AB. *Cumeria* Agreement, ibid.
9 Isbester, Jack, HCMM Cadet Log, cargo loaded on *Clan Maclachlan* in Calcutta for Liverpool in 1952 (Isbester Collection).
10 Lloyds List, 24.11.1883.
11 Lloyds List, 17.12.1883.

6 GETTING SPLICED

In 1884 John Isbester returned to Shetland and to Haggersta, where he stayed with his aunt and uncle. My father, Allan, John Isbester's fifth son, was an observant man with an excellent memory and a considerable interest in Shetland and our family history. Although born many years after these events he had often heard the story of how my grandparents met. This is the account that he wrote to Florence Grains, a descendent of one of the participants.[1]

> As a boy my father went to the fishing and as a youth he went South to sea. He left his watch – the equivalent of being engaged – with your grandmother Maggie Smith in Strome.[2] One time there was a slump and he could not get a job at sea so he joined the Liverpool Police and wrote for Maggie to come and join him. She 'couldna leave the sheep' and did not go. Later he got back to sea and later still back to Whiteness – but he did not call at Strome: of course the whole of Whiteness knew that he had not been to see Maggie! Like all the young men returning home he called at Olligarth to tell Magnus Irvine [the laird and the landlord for all the crofts in North Whiteness] all the latest South news. And there he encountered my mother, a very personable, lively young lady of 20 who took it upon herself to scold him for not going to see Maggie. (Father was 32. As a boy of 17/18 he used to call at Olligarth on the way from Haggersta to the school to carry Susie Irvine 5/6 pick-a-back to school).[3] My father was not used to being scolded by young ladies, rather enjoyed it and came back for more. One night after he'd gone, mother went out to the well at the back door and he was waiting to speak to her. He asked her to marry him and said that he'd give her a week to make up her mind. He came the next morning for his answer and they were married within the month! Mother said that night she opened her bible for guidance – and it opened at the passage in Ruth – whither thou goest I will go and thy people shall be my people –
>
> She walked in to Lerwick to buy her wedding needs and to tell her friends who had never even heard of Jack Isbester[4] as in the running (though there were said to be several others). Anyway Maggie's heart was certainly not broken – and the families of Quoyness [where Maggie Smith lived as Maggie Gair after her own marriage] and Olligarth always remained good friends. After we left Scotland aged 12 and 9 Eric and I stayed at Quoyness at your grandmother's for a Summer holiday (we were just about the same age as Agnes and Hettie your aunt and mother).

The *Shetland Times* of 19 April 1884 reported

> At Olligarth, Whiteness, on the 10th April, by the Rev. A McDonald, Weisdale, assisted by the Rev. D Johnstone, Quarff, SUSIE, only surviving daughter of Mr MAGNUS IRVINE to Mr JOHN ISBESTER.

It may be that the two clergymen were in attendance to make clear to everybody that although John Isbester was illegitimate he had a Master's Certificate and, therefore, the full approval of the church!

Early on the wedding day John Isbester had written his first surviving letter to his bride-to-be.[5] After suggesting that he would meet her at the schoolhouse where the wedding was to take place and expressing his pleasure that it was such a lovely day, John continued:

> This morning about 7am I took a bottle of whiskey and treated all the town of Haggersta and they all drunk hartily to our long life and happiness and the remainder of what took place I will tell you again I have no paper so you must excuse this scrap I am Your Loving Johnie X

In the 1880s the 'town of Haggersta' consisted of four households – the Davidsons, the Mansons and the Smiths as well as the Andersons – so John Isbester's hospitality was not on quite the scale that his words would seem to suggest.[6]

Captain Thomson,[7] a local man who knew Whiteness well, points out that the schoolhouse used for the wedding was the place where bride and groom both received their early education, and suggests that after the wedding the guests all walked in couples along the banks of Brugarth (where the absent John Isbister, gold miner, had lived as a child) to Olligarth House (Fig.6.1) for the wedding breakfast and reception for the happy couple.

Figure 6.1 *Olligarth House in 1916 (Courtesy of the Shetland Museum and Archives)*

John's bride, Susan Elizabeth Irvine (Fig.6.2), was born and brought up in Whiteness, and in her early years had attended the Whiteness school, but as the daughter of the laird she had had opportunities not given to most of the Whiteness community. My father says that his mother 'Was spoiled, but not spoilt', as her parents only surviving child. He continues:

> My mother who was known to be delicate, – she had valvular disease of the heart – had been taken gt. care of during her girlhood & had several years wintered with relations or friends in the Scottish Lowlands where the climate was less severe than in Shetland.[8]

Figure 6.2 *Susie Irvine, about the time of her wedding to John Isbester*

Miss Urquart, a live-in governess from Scotland, was found for her, and seems to have coached her well because she became a talented singer and pianist and a fluent and entertaining letter writer. Her Sinclair ancestors on her mother's side included doctors, clergymen and army officers in their number, and it was from that side of the family that her parents had inherited ownership of a number of crofts in Whiteness. Her father, Magnus Irvine, was a farmer and, by virtue of his wife's inheritance, a landowner. That he was actively involved in farming can be seen in a photo (Fig.6.3) which shows him ploughing with two oxen. He is the man guiding the plough. The large black-bearded man with the oxen is probably Robbie Tullock, the general farm servant who remained with the family for many years.

An elderly acquaintance of the Irvine family visited Olligarth a few months before the wedding and, writing to his own granddaughter, explained that Mrs Irvine had not been at home but reported that they had been given dinner and that 'Miss Irvine of Strom Bridge is a sprightly young lady and did the honours of the table well'.[9] In the weeks after the wedding, clearly charmed, he wrote:

Figure 6.3 *Magnus Irvine, on the left, ploughing with oxen*

> The husband of the young lady of Olligarth is a grandson of Peter o'Brugarth and his mother was Sarah Anderson. The young man had been seven years south and he and the young lady fell in love at first sight. She was just the age for that, full of life.[10]

If we take that literally, as I think we should, this was John Isbester's first return to Shetland in seven years.

John Isbester (Fig.6.4) and Susie Irvine had made a very happy and rewarding choice. Allan Isbester writes:

From my Father's first letters – written when he was Master of the *Ann Mactavish*, – it is apparent that my Mother and he when they married did not know each other at all – what they had in common was temperament. They were both lively and spirited, they were both entertaining talkers and good listeners, they were both responsive to, interested in and fond of other people. Each was proud of the other, each took responsibility for the other's relations, and when they were together on the *Centaur* or the *Dalgonar*, their ship immediately became the host ship of the other ships of whatever port they were in. And they each had a serious side to their natures.[11]

Figure 6.4 *John Isbester in his early years in command*

John Isbester clearly believed that one reason to get married was to have babies. When his own daughter married and after a year of marriage was still not admitting to being pregnant, he expressed his anxiety: 'Kathleen writes bright enough but surely she is not well if there is no sign yet'.[12] His own marriage gave scope to no such concerns: Susie gave birth to their first child on 4 January 1885 and must have known that she was pregnant within weeks of the wedding. John Isbester needed to earn some money but did not want to risk a deep sea voyage which might put him on the other side of the world when their first child was born. Instead he was fortunate to obtain a short-term appointment as master of a schooner sailing from Lerwick to the Baltic.

The law required that when a British ship travelled outside Home Trade Limits a master with a full foreign going master's certificate must be carried. Captain Mactavish, owner and master of the schooner *Ann Mactavish* had no foreign going certificate, so when his ship was offered a cargo from Lerwick to Danzig he needed a master for the voyage.; John Isbester took the job, sailing from Lerwick on 22 August 1884. Being in love's grip and on his best behaviour and having little experience of writing love letters his communication usefully reads very much like a voyage report.

> About 9 o'clock we took our departure by bearings of Bressay and Sumbrugh Head lights, course SE with a light breeze NE and we ran 140 miles. When the wind changed to about South we tacked ship and made another 70 miles SSE [*sic*][13] when we sighted an Island, Utsira, on the coast of Norway on the Friday after I left you. But we had moderate weather tacking along the coast up to Sunday afternoon when the wind commenced to freshen and we had a strong breeze the remaining part of Sunday and Monday and we have had two or three breezes since but nothing to hurt us but head winds all the time.[14]

Arriving at Hornbæk at the northern entrance to The Sound, the waterway between Denmark and Sweden, he wrote:

> we have arrived all safe as far as Hornbek that is about 30 miles from Copenhagen and I expect to be a week or two yet before we get to Danzic as the weather here is very fine light airs of headwinds and calms and the glass up to the top branches. It is so calm today that we have had to drop anchor to stop us from going back with the current what we have already come and the village ashore here looks most beautiful.[15]

John Isbester was visiting the Baltic for his first and only time, and it is no surprise that he was enraptured by the Danish village, with its clean and brightly painted houses set in a verdant countryside basking in still, clear summer weather. He continued:

> I wish you were here with us until we lift anchor again. We have had a bumboat alongside and old Mactavish has bought a bag of potatoes, a fresh cod and a lb of potatoes. I have bought 20 eggs for 1/6 and a lb of tobacco for 2/- so we have had fresh cod for dinner and eggs for tea. Now we are ready for another passage a week of light fair winds or a fortnight light airs and calms but I would rather have the fair wind. I am thinking long as I never did before it is very wearing making so little headway but I can keep my mind easy as the owner is on board and can see that I am doing all I can to get ahead. I daresay now I could count 50 vessels in the same condition as ourselves beating with the light air and at anchor with the calms.[16]

Later, when in The Sound, he wrote:

> Now we have got into a beautiful narrow sound only about six miles across and fine calm weather. We have about 70 miles of this narrows then out to free sea again about 300 miles more so you can reckon the time we will be going with light airs and calms and the time we would take with a fair wind as I have no doubt you will. So I am afraid that Sept. will be done before I get back and where we will come back to I can give you no idea of. So Dear Susie I suppose you will be tired of reading of all the different courses and distances.[17]

After explaining that he hoped to land his letter when passing Copenhagen, John Isbester enquired about the farm work and visitors to Olligarth, then continued with some intriguing domestic details.

> I forgot when my changing week was so to make sure did not change until Wednesday 10th except stockings. I had five pair wet all at the same time. I shaved off the chin Thursday week. After I left I had a long look for your photo as I knew you gave me the one saying it was the only one you had and it was only last Sunday I found it when I took a good turn and started to read the bible it dropped out but before that I consoled myself with the one in the locket. I have read old Daniel's religious Notions and a few pieces of the other. I don't know if it was Daniel's Notions I was to read on Sunday or was it the bible you put in my trunk?

> I find everything I require and thanks to you for them it shows me how careful you have been to mind on everything Now My Dear Susie with kind love to your Mama and Papa, Dolly, Mip, Meek and Mr H M and remain yours faithfully John Isbester with a X-X.[18]

It reads as though Susie was laying down some rules about when a change of clothing or a spot of religion was needed, and John was prepared to go along with that provided he could remember what he had been told. In their correspondence throughout their marriage there are hints that Susie, using tact and charm, exercised her influence on him to make the best of himself.

Writing from Danzig, John Isbester noted that there were a number of Scots and Shetland schooners all carrying certificated masters just for the voyage with the old masters signed on as purser, so now in port there were two separate gangs – the certificated masters and the pursers/owners. Old Mactavish was the best of the latter: 'he's a good old sort, very easy minded and content and I am very comfortable'.[19]

On 24 September the *Ann Mactavish* was discharging in Danzig but with no news of a homeward cargo. Captain John wanted to buy a pair of slippers for Susie but it was difficult:

> There is scarcely a shop you go into that they can speak a word of English. You have just to go and take a hold of anything you want, then they tell you how many Marks it costs. So it's very difficult to get anything you want. I went into a shop last night to buy a pair of slippers for you. I came in and pointed to them, got a lot on the counter and was looking through them and every pair I took hold of he would tell me how many Mark they cost, which I said nothing about. At last I tried to ask him the size of them – but he could not understand me but thought I was going to bid him down of the price, so he got hot and I got hot. He was going ahead in Prussian and me in English and I believe that the girls that was in the shop nearly turned red headed, and at last a Prussian soldier officer came in that could speak some English so he cleared the dispute up for us. The dispute was I was asking for size 5 and he was saying 5 Mark and every time he said 5 Mark I gave a roar at him and he thought I was thinking it too much and wanting to get the slippers out of my hand and I would not give them so I bought them such as they are and there were nothing but girls crowing and laughing in every corner of the shop before I left with the slippers bidding them all good night.[20]

In 1884 Danzig was part of Prussia, part of the German Empire. In the 19th century, when the British merchant navy comprised half of world shipping, British merchant seamen expected the whole world to speak English.

Later in the letter John tells Susie that the pipe she had bought him 'turned out to be good. I have used it ever since we left. It is now getting nicely coloured'. He adds that he has bought a snuff box for the old man (i.e. his father-in-law) 'with a compass on the top so that if he is at Scalloway and fog comes on he will be able to steer by the compass'[21] – an interesting reminder that from Whiteness to Scalloway was 7 miles by land and only 6 miles by sea. Making the trip by sea, when you had your own boat and people to row or sail it, was more convenient that hiring a pony and trap.

Writing again from Danzig while the crew, assisted by three local men, were loading a timber cargo, John Isbester responded to Susie's questions about drink.

> You were asking me if old Mactavish took much and all that I can tell you is that he takes more I think than does him good but he don't trouble anybody with it for he's always in such good humour with it. But you did not ask me if I was taking much so I am going to tell you Susie, Dear Wife, that I really don't take much. I think you are afraid of me in that way but you need not Dear. Old Mactavish tells me that ever since his wife died he does not appear to care how things goes and I think myself that he does not care much for his family.[22]

Turning to the way the schooner was sailed, he reports:

> The men that are with us are very steady sober men. At sea I don't keep any regular watch but just on deck when I am wanted. Sometimes I have a long watch and sometimes a short one. The man that was Mate and the boy are in the one watch and Mactavish and the other man in the other so that very seldom I have anything to do with regards to work at sea. When they go off to reef or make sail I do the steering for them. The schooner is so handy to anything I have been used to that it's only a pleasure to work with her, she is as easy tacked as a boat and never misses stays.[23]

To reassure Susie he writes:

> I am trying to take as much care of myself as I can. I don't go with wet stockings. I have had a change of clothes and five pairs of stockings ashore at the wash and have just got them back so all we want now is a Good SE wind and we'll soon be home, so ta ta for this night Susie Dear and all the kisses as soon as we can get them and a cuddle you know what I mean don't you …[24]

Clearly the sports page[25] was not a recent invention, but gentle jokes were also worth trying. He may have been complaining of midges rather than flies when he wrote:

> The flies are so thick here that they even disturbed me, but if I was beside you I would have peace for I know they like you better than me.[26]

As he was going to bed another thought struck him and he took up his pen again:

> You were asking me if ever I made my bed since you did. I thought I would do it tonight. There has been a turn in my blanket now for some time and I could not find out how it was, so tonight I have taken it out. I'm off now, ta ta.[27]

By this time John Isbester was some six weeks away from Lerwick. It is clear that bed making was not a frequent activity.

He remarks that the timber loading in Danzig had taken nine days and that he had never previously loaded in less than ten days – though mostly, it must be remembered, on larger ships. This is a gentle pace of work that contrasts strongly with fast turn rounds experienced by most shipping nowadays, when nine days in port would be viewed as luxury. The timber cargo was destined for Hartlepool, where John Isbester paid off on arrival, to be back in Shetland with his bride a few days later.

---

1 Isbester, Charles Allan, letter CAI1, 17.09.1966 (Isbester Collection).
2 By the time my father knew her, long after these events, the lady in question had married and become Maggie Gair of Quoyness. Before her wedding she was Maggie Smith of Strome and not as my father had it. His letter has here been amended to correct this.
3 This implies that John Isbester still visited the Whiteness school when aged 18. He may have done so to study navigation during the winter months when he was not fishing, or this may simply have been a joke between my grandparents.
4 My grandmother always called my grandfather Jack. I was named after him.
5 Isbester, Capt. John, Letter J1, 10.04.1884 (Isbester Collection).
6 Shetland Island Census 1881.
7 Thomson, Captain J.P, OBE ExC. *Captain John Isbester's Career at Sea*. Unpublished manuscript, p.6. (Isbester Collection).
8 Isbester, Charles Allan, Note CAI4 written about 1965 (Isbester Collection).
9 Laing, Robert. Letter to Christina L Jamieson, 19.01.1884 (Isbester Collection).
10 Laing, Robert. Letter to Christina L Jamieson, 17.06.1884 (Isbester Collection).
11 Isbester, Charles Allan, Note CAI4 written about 1965 for Captain J P Thomson (Isbester Collection).
12 Isbester, Capt. John, Letter J32, 27.07.1913 (Isbester Collection).
13 From a plot of the courses and from the wind direction it is evident that ESE not SSE is meant.
14 Isbester, Capt. John, Letter J2, 11.09.1884 (Isbester Collection).
15 Isbester, Capt. John, Letter J2, ibid.
16 Isbester, Capt. John, Letter J2, ibid.
17 Isbester, Capt. John, Letter J2, ibid.
18 Isbester, Capt. John, Letter J2, ibid.
19 Isbester, Capt. John, Letter J3, 21.09.1884 (Isbester Collection).
20 Isbester, Capt. John, Letter J4, 24.09.1884 (Isbester Collection).
21 Isbester, Capt. John, Letter J4, ibid.
22 Isbester, Capt. John, Letter J5, 30.09.1884 (Isbester Collection).
23 Isbester, Capt. John, Letter J5, ibid.
24 Isbester, Capt. John, Letter J5, ibid.
25 *Sports Page* – sailors' term for that part of a letter devoted to sexual matters.
26 Isbester, Capt. John, Letter J5, op.cit.
27 Isbester, Capt. John, Letter J5, ibid.

7 IN SEARCH OF COMMAND

John and Susie's first child, Arthur Craigie Isbester, was born on 4 January 1885 and was named after Susie's brother, drowned in Quebec 15 years previously. Tragically he died less than three weeks later, on the 22nd of the month. John was still at home when this devastating occurrence took place – he had registered the birth the previous day. Over the years four of their children were to die as infants, but five survived to live full lives. I am aware of no official explanation for the deaths, but my father speculated that the water in the Olligarth well had been contaminated by liver fluke from sheep and was the cause.

My father, Charles Allan Isbester, was in later life an early user of the drug warfarin to thin his blood and, because this was of interest to the medical profession, a 'routine hospital post mortem' was performed when he died, aged 74. This found the immediate cause of death and also found 'hepatic cirrhosis [i.e. cirrhosis of the liver] a morbid condition contributing to death but not related to the immediate cause'.[1] My father was a lifelong teetotaller. Could he also have been a liver fluke survivor?

By the beginning of April John Isbester was back in Liverpool, staying in lodgings at 25 Chester Street and looking for the chance of a command. A possible temporary command was taken by a man prepared to accept £3 a week in port and £6 a week at sea, the superintendent telling John Isbester that he knew that John would not agree to such a low rate. The superintendent was not necessarily right on that: John Isbester's pay as chief mate of the *Queen of Australia* had been £7 10s a month[2] and this would have been significantly better, but he probably knew what a competent master could expect to be paid. A big barque was expected shortly from Queenstown, a ship on which Captain Arthurson of the *West Ridge* had served as mate, and John Isbester could probably get the mate's job there. It was frustrating to not have promotion but when he reflected on how other men fared, he was doing no worse than they were.[3] Addressing his wife affectionately once or twice during the course of the letter as 'Susie pusie' he ended with news of one or two other Shetland men in Liverpool and with good wishes for all those at Olligarth.

His wait came to an end on 22 June 1885 when he joined the barque *Centaur* in Hull as chief mate for a voyage to San Francisco. He may have been told that this was to be Captain Thomson's last voyage and that if he found favour the command would be his the following voyage, as actually happened.

The *Centaur*, in which John Isbester was to spend the next 11 years making annual voyages from the UK to San Francisco, was a three-masted barque of 1,645 tons gross, 1,599 tons nett (Fig.7.1). A barque is a sailing ship which is square rigged on the fore and main masts and fore-and-aft rigged on the mizzen mast. She was iron-hulled, 232 feet in length, 37 feet in beam and 25 feet in depth. With a freeboard of 5 feet she had a deepest even keel draught of 20 feet. Built at Millwall in London in 1864, she was owned by Johnstone & Spurle of Liverpool and operated by

Figure 7.1 *Barque* Centaur *at anchor with men working aloft*

Gracie Beasley of Liverpool, who were to employ John Isbester for the next 28 years. Her official number was 51419 and her identifying signal letters NMVD.

Few official documents for the first nine years of John Isbester's life aboard *Centaur* survive, but the Articles of Agreement (AoA) for the voyage immediately before his first voyage, also a voyage to San Francisco from Hull, survive in the National Archive and provide a lot of detail about the ship, her crew and the conditions under which she sailed.[4]

She had a ship's company of 27, consisting of master, chief mate, second mate, cook, steward, sailmaker, carpenter, sixteen ABs, one OS and three apprentices, one aged 19 and two aged 14. It was normal for such vessels to carry no boatswain: the chief mate directed the work of one watch, the second mate the other. The ship's company were from an absolutely typical mixture of places: the master, a 52-year-old Scot from Arbroath, was the oldest man aboard, the chief mate was an Englishman from Workington, and second mate was from St Vincent in the West Indies. The carpenter was from Stavanger in Norway, the steward from Glasgow, the cook from Bristol, the sailmaker from Hull and the sailmaker's mate from Oskarshamn in Sweden. The ABs came from Rotterdam, Brixham, Stralsund, Leeds, Bremerhaven, Rostock, Weunersberg. Hamburg, Minnesota, Haverhill Massachusetts, Boston, Norway and Finland. Typically, only six members of the ship's company remained from the previous voyage: the master, the chief mate, the steward and the three apprentices. Once appointed to a ship, a master remained in post permanently, snatching a few days or weeks of home leave while his ship remained in a UK port, or having his family visit him aboard ship. The apprentices were bound to the managers, Gracie Beasley, and usually remained with the same master for the entirety of their four-year indentures, but they did take leave when the ship was in home ports. The chief mate, particularly if he had a master's certificate and was ambitious for a command, would find a berth wherever it best suited him and his employers. The steward, if competent and trustworthy, could provide the master with valuable support, and the master might encourage him to remain in the ship.

The chief mate's wages were £8 a month, the next best paid man aboard being, perhaps unexpectedly, the carpenter on £6 a month, a measure of his importance. The second mate was paid £5 a month. The remaining petty officers earned £4–£5 a month. The ABs were paid £3 a month and the Ordinary Seaman came bottom of the scale with £2 a month. The apprentices were paid £5 per annum in their first year, £6 in the second, £7 in the third and £12 in the fourth year. Should they be in the middle of a voyage when their four-year apprenticeship ended, they would be paid at the same rate as an ordinary seaman signed on in a UK port for the balance of the voyage.[5]

The ship's company signed the Articles of Agreement on Saturday 19 April 1884 in Hull and were instructed to be on board ready to commence work at 0600 on Tuesday 22 April, at which time five of the ABs failed to appear. Five replacement ABs were immediately found and signed on, with instructions to join the following day. When signing on, the officers and petty officers received one month's pay in advance but the sailors (the ABs and the OS) received no advance of wages. San Francisco was clearly a very attractive destination for seamen, and it was well understood by all parties that many of the sailors were likely to jump ship, to desert, when that port was reached. Inserted into the *Centaur*'s Articles for the voyage, signed by every crew member, was the handwritten notice 'and it is also agreed that any of the crew deserting at Frisco shall be paid at the rate of one shilling per month'. Without this clause, the wages due to deserting seamen would have had to be landed to the British Consul in San Francisco for subsequent payment to the deserting seamen. With the clause included in the agreement the wages could be kept by the master for the benefit of the shipowner. They would be some compensation for the cost of hiring replacement seamen, who would command a higher rate of pay in San Francisco. In fact the sailors signed on in San Francisco that voyage were paid one shilling a month for the first two months and £5 a month thereafter. None of the sailors required the owners to send money home by an arrangement called an allotment, so the only reason I can guess for the one shilling a month payment is that the sailors may have insisted on getting a £10 advance on joining.

John Isbester used similar wording about one shilling a month for those deserting in San Francisco when opening Articles in Cardiff in October 1888[6] but had abandoned them, perhaps reluctantly, by July 1894 in Gravesend for a voyage during which six of the ABs deserted in San Francisco.[7]

An indication of how seamen, fresh off a ship after four months at sea, were exploited in San Francisco, and elsewhere, can be gained from a casual item in the *Wharf and Wave* column of the *San Francisco Chronicle* which reported:

> The British ship *Slieve Bawn* arrived in port on Friday night, 123 days from South Shields. There was a scramble for her by runners and boarding house men to secure her crew. Sailors are so scarce that competition between this class of people is very keen. Edward Mordaunt and John Rogers, ex Chief Jailor, had a wrangle over several men, each claiming them. The result was a free fight and Mordaunt got the men.[8]

Returning to our consideration of the *Centaur* voyage which preceded John Isbester's joining one AB died during the six-month voyage from Hull round Cape Horn to San Francisco and, as expected, 13 of the remaining 16 seamen deserted in San Francisco, where *Centaur* appears to have spent a little over two months from 16 October to 27 December. The steward was paid off sick on 24 December. During that period and similar periods in future voyages, a cargo of coal was discharged, the holds were cleaned and a cargo of grain was loaded.

On completion of his voyage as chief mate John Isbester was able to take a month's leave before rejoining in Dublin in early July where, aged 34 and after 20 years at sea, he took command of *Centaur* on what must have been one of the most satisfying days of his life. Those years of study, of staying aboard and saving his money when his shipmates were partying ashore, of putting up with drudgery and boredom, with freezing winds and soaking seas, had all been worthwhile. His dedication, determination and commitment had earned its reward and he finally had the command for which he had longed.

With discharge of the cargo of grain completed he took his command to Cardiff and loaded coal for San Francisco. Departing on 29 July 1886 he reached San Francisco exactly five months later, on 29 December. On 9 January 1887 Lloyds List reported

> British ship *Centaur* at San Francisco December 29th reports had gales off Cape Horn for 26 days carrying away rigging, steering gear and several sails, breaking two boats.

It must have been a very testing first voyage in command, with plenty to show why carpenters were valued almost as highly as chief mates. Were the conditions exceptional, or was John Isbester guilty of the recklessness of an inexperienced master? He had, after all, previously rounded Cape Horn westbound in four different ships, *Beulah*, *Parthia*, *Cumeria* and *Centaur*. His good record during 26 further years in command suggests that if there were lessons to be learnt he was a quick learner.

The coal was unloaded and a cargo of grain was loaded in the space of two months, *Centaur* departing for Queenstown on 1 March 1887 with John Isbester, knowing that Susie was eight months pregnant, eager to reach his destination as soon as possible and hoping for a passage of about 130 days. In the days before departure he had written at length to his mother-in-law and to Susie, exhorting them both to have every care for Susie during the final stages of the pregnancy. Amongst many other assurances are the words:

> Do not fear about money, Susie, or me not being able to pay off my debts. Mind that you have everything you want. Don't hesitate for any expense. If anything was to happen to you what would be the good of money then?[9]

He added a later note:

> I have left in the office here 80 Dollars to be sent to you through the bank. That is about £16. I hope you get it all right. I will give you the clerk's name I have left it with. I expect it will come about the time you will be in need of money

On reaching Queenstown on 8 July 1887 he would have received the happy news that Susie had given birth three months earlier to a son, John Magnus St Clair Isbester. During the two months that *Centaur* was discharging grain in Dublin and loading coal in Cardiff, it is clear from correspondence[10] that Susie left the infant with his grandmother in Shetland and travelled south to stay with John aboard ship or somewhere nearby. During those few weeks their third child was conceived.

The relentless demands of ships and their cargoes parted them early in September when John Isbester sailed once again for San Francisco, arriving late in January 1888. Three months later, just before he sailed once again with a cargo of wheat for Queenstown for orders, he received the welcome news of the birth of their daughter, Kathleen William Margaret Isbester. Kathleen was to live to a good age.

Arriving at Queenstown was a distressing experience for John Isbester. This, it appears, was one of the three occasions in his 29-year married life when he arrived in a port of which ample notice had been given but no letters awaited him. He came to fear these experiences because he learnt that they were the precursor of very bad news. The news when it eventually came was devastating. Their son John had died in June aged 14 months, but Kathleen was flourishing.

During the usual two months spent discharging wheat in Bristol and loading coal in Cardiff *Centaur* was reported 'in entering Roath Basin struck quay making a hole in her starboard bow'.[11] The damage appears to have been readily repairable as the barque was able to sail, for San Francisco as always, on 17 October. In those days when sailing ships met others they often took the opportunity, by exchange of International Code flag signals, to report their details for the benefit of their owners and other interested parties such as charterers and underwriters. In November Lloyds List reported

> Centaur barque of Liverpool (NMDV) Cardiff to San Francisco 40 days November 25th 19S 35W. By the August Offler at Bahia.[12]

Thus in compact form Lloyds List reported the ship's name, type, port of registry, signal letters, ports of departure and destination, number of days into passage, date of report, position in latitude and longitude, name of reporting ship and port in which the report was delivered to Lloyds List. It took a full month for the *August Offler* to reach her destination and the report to be transmitted to Lloyds List, but even then *Centaur* was only two months into a voyage that was to take her a little over four months in total, and the news of her safe progress would be welcome.

Leaving San Francisco with wheat for the UK on 30 April, John Isbester must have been filled with anxiety. Susie was once again eight months pregnant, and he could expect no news until he reached Queenstown in September. This time the news was good and Kathleen had been joined by a brother, Arthur Gifford St Clair Isbester. Both were doing well.

By the end of October 1889 *Centaur* was bound for San Francisco from Barry, and John Isbester was embarking upon the last voyage for several years during which he would not be accompanied by his wife (Fig.7.2). In San Francisco he managed to get himself some embarrassing publicity, the *San Francisco Chronicle* reporting:

Figure 7.2 Captain Isbester, on steps, with officers, petty officers and apprentices of the barque Centaur

> A British Captain's bluster
>
> Captain Isbester of the British ship [*sic*] *Centaur* attempted to interpret the harbour laws to his own satisfaction yesterday afternoon but was very promptly called down by Wharfinger McGinney. His ship was lying at Mission 2, and the brig *Percy Edward* came off the drydock to go into her berth at Mission 1. The schooner *Gem* was there, however, and the *Percy* attempted to make fast by getting her lines on the *Centaur*, which is the custom. Captain Isbester cast the lines off and sent the vessel adrift. Wharfinger McGinney was appealed to and he showed the captain the law. Isbester said he would be — if any American vessel should be tied up at his ship. The wharfinger went aboard the ship and saw that the lines were made fast. The captain, however, said that he would cast them off again, when he was informed that he would be arrested if he did so. A large crowd assembled, anxious to assist the wharfinger. Captain Isbester at last descended from his high horse and let the lines alone.[13]

No shipmaster welcomes other ships tied up alongside his. They are a potential source of thieving, accidents and rubbish, but it is a wise shipmaster who knows when he is outgunned. I suspect that the news item would have been well received by the locals on the Frisco waterfront!

(Far left) ***Figure 7.3*** *Magnus Irvine with granddaughter Kathleen*

(Left) ***Figure 7.4*** *Margaret Irvine with grandson Arthur*

During these difficult years of long separations, lack of news and the births and deaths of babies, my grandparents had been sustained by thoughts of when a family had been established and they could all join Captain Isbester aboard the *Centaur.* The matter having been seriously discussed, the owners gave their permission for Susie to accompany her husband on the next voyage, but it appears that the children could not make the voyage ,though it is not clear whether it was the owners or the doctor who forbade it.[14] But, with willing grandparents at home (Figs.7.3 & 7.4), Kathleen and Arthur could be left in Olligarth while Susie joined John to head for the high seas - and adventure!

---

1 Isbester, Jack. Note taken when viewing the Post Mortem report. (Isbester Collection).
2 *Queen of Australia* Articles of Agreement closed 17.12.83, National Archive.
3 Isbester, Captain John, Letter J6, 06.04.1885. (Isbester Collection).
4 *Centaur* Articles of Agreement closed 02.05.1885, National Maritime Museum.
5 Simpkin, E. S. Indentures dated 06.03.1900. (Isbester Collection).
6 *Centaur* Articles of Agreement closed 11.09.1889, National Archive.
7 *Centaur* Articles of Agreement closed 29.07.1895, National Maritime Museum.
8 *San Francisco Chronicle,* 09.03.1890, Wharf and Wave column.
9 Isbester, Captain John, Letter J7, 01.03.1887. (Isbester Collection).
10 Isbester, Captain John, Letter J8. Illegible date in 1887. (Isbester Collection).
11 Lloyds List 06.10.1888 Column 21.
12 Lloyds List 27.12.1888 Column 24.
13 *San Francisco Chronicle,* 09.03.1890, Wharf and Wave column.
14 Isbester, Captain John, Letter J9, 24.07.1889. (Isbester Collection).

8 MRS ISBESTER GOES TO SEA

In order to go to sea with John Isbester, Susie had left the two-year-old Kathleen and her one-year-old brother, Arthur, in the care of her elderly parents. In her first surviving letter, this one from the tropical Atlantic in lat 7.50 N, long 25.30 W, having sailed from Liverpool in early December 1890 and expecting to reach San Francisco four months later, Susie Isbester writes:[1]

My own Dear Mother,

Won't you be surprised to get this letter, but there is a Danish barque near us bound for Rio Janeiro and as the day is fine Jack has proposed sending out a boat with a letter. I can just imagine your joy in getting it. We are now 21 days out and I am quite an experienced sailor. The first week was rather rough and I was in bed all the time – not at all sick while I lay still – and Jack so good to me, doctoring me up with wine and beef tea; the next week I was up most of the time and now am up every day and feel all right and able to eat all that's going. I have got my [sewing] machine started up in the deck house and have got one pair of Jack's drawers made. The weather is most gorgeous. Xmas Day was a holiday with all hands and so warm and I had on Maggie's skirt and my white blouse. One man, a Dane, is very ill, a heavy cold evidently, but we are all hoping he will get better. Jimmie is not repenting coming yet but he has a bealing [*sic*] finger; I think it is not going to be very bad.

Wasn't it silly of me to forget to write to Meggie about those little things for you all at Xmas, but I think she would understand what to do with them. I do trust all is well with you. Oh if I could just hear I would be perfectly happy. We always look at the time with you and picture what you are doing. I often dream about my darlings.

The mate has turned out very nice and attentive to his work. The flying fish are thick here and they sometimes fly on board – little things just like sillocks [young coalfish[2]] – the mate had one fried to my breakfast the other day. We sighted this ship yesterday and have caught her up today; it's just lovely getting this home, I feel too excited almost to write. Do take care of yourselves. I can never realise it is winter with you and so warm here. We wonder if old Margaret is living yet. Give our love everywhere, Haggersta, Cova, Strome, Quoyness, Bruchs, Pund, Taylors, Hobarts, and everybody. Kathleen will have her dear Willie Garriock home. I hope Andrew got better. Mind not to worry dearest Mother, if anything should happen to the bairns I know that they are safe with you as though I was there. If spared to go another voyage sometime after this I'll take my little Kathleen. Dear son, I wish I could see him walking, tell him always about his father and me, do not let them forget us. The sailors are shouting away, getting the boat over the side – we are quite close to the ship. Do not mention at the office that you have got this letter.

I had a washing today of nine pocket handkerchiefs and I bet I had a better drying day than you. We have had every sail set now for over a week and sometimes a fine breeze, doing over 200 miles a day. The only land we have sighted was San Antonia [possibly Santo Antão in the Cape Verde Islands] and it just looked like Foula [the westernmost of the Shetland Islands] in the distance. We have breakfast at 8 and I take porridge and sugar, dinner at ½ past 12, tea at 5 and I get beef tea at 8 and then, if the night is fine we are on deck a while and then turn in. Jack is so good to me and it must make a great difference to him my being here.

Love to the Baynes and Sunnyside, also Dattie and Nell, and fond best love to all at Busta. I wonder if it was an 1890 or 91 almanac I sent Papa. Tell Doll I always think of her on the Saturdays and hope she is being good and diligent. We always know by the chronometer your exact time. I wonder if you are in the kitchen and if it vents well. I did a crewel work comb and brush bag for Jack and gave him such a surprise.

Love to all Lerwick friends. I hope Hattie Leisk got better – I meant to wire and ask for her but never got a chance. I find the flannelette clothes nice and better for the heat than cotton, but I am going to turn Jack out of the bed till we get to colder climes. I find the organ a great companion and play on it often – sometimes nearly rolling off my seat. I generally lie down a lot if we are doing a big roll but it's often, and I am always at the table to meals. I wonder if Lewie had a boy. I couldn't tell you all we wonder but we think and talk about <u>everybody</u>. I hope Christina and Maggie are well – tell Maggie she mustn't leave Kathleen till I come back, even for a husband. I hope Maggie liked the concertina, she is to play to Kathleen and Sonnie Boy on it. I hope Papa is not coughing but taking care of himself and that you also keep well. Mind us to the Manse and Setter and the Dr. Let Dolly have some bairns to tea now and again to keep herself and the bairns cheery. Now I must close up Jack says – a thousand kisses to each one of you and don't neglect writing. Have no fear for us. Oh I do feel so glad to be able to send you this. Jack sends love and kisses with me to Mama and Papa, Dolly, Kathleen and son.

Ever your very, very loving bairn,

Susie Isbester

There can be no doubt that my grandmother was enjoying all her new experiences enormously, and welcoming the chance to show off a bit to friends and family at home. At last she was living the life that she had anticipated during the years when she had been separated from John for much of the time, and finally seeing the world from a quite privileged position.

Mrs Irvine was indeed surprised to receive her daughter's letter, months before she had expected it. Before opening it she jumped to the conclusion that something terrible must have happened and, as my father has recorded, suffered a severe heart attack.[3] Happily, she recovered and Susie's seagoing career was able to continue.

Centaur arrived in San Francisco after a voyage of nearly five months, to spend May and June in the port. It must have been an idyllic time for the young couple. John knew the port well and doubtless had numerous friends there and Susie, there for the first time, would have been fascinated by much that she saw. It would have been with mixed feelings that they set sail for the familiar 'Queenstown for Orders' at the end of June, to reach Queenstown, and thence Dublin, in November 1891, 11 months since they had sailed from Liverpool.

There was no question of Susie rejoining for the following voyage. Their daughter Violet Susan Isbester was born in Olligarth on 17 January 1892, a few days before John Isbester sailed from Barry, bound as usual for San Francisco. Tragically, Violet Susan died aged 15 days, only four days after her father had put to sea – news that he would not receive for another five and a half months, after a rather slow passage.

It could have been on this visit to San Francisco that John Isbester had an experience which he described many years later to a passenger he carried on his final ship, the *Dalgonar*. Arnold Franz McJannet was a Scots solicitor in his thirties who, in 1908, travelled as a passenger on the three-and-a-half-month passage from Liverpool to Sydney, for health reasons. His parents had paid for the voyage and, as repayment, he kept for them a detailed and usually interesting log book of the events of the voyage covered in some detail in Chapters 16 and 17 hereafter. This is his record of Captain Isbester's experience in San Francisco.

> The Captain was seated on a Frisco Street Car, when an affable stranger courteous, well dressed, seats himself beside him and enters into conversation. Affable stranger points out places of note and interest, and nudges the Captain repeatedly attracting his attention to fellow passengers. Captain smiles at humorous pleasantry of affable stranger, and in turn relates some sea yarn or other, being constantly interrupted by a jab of affable stranger's elbow when the radiant vision of a well-dressed woman enters or leaves the car, or affable stranger otherwise distracts Captain's keen vision. At length affable stranger smilingly rises, having reached his destination, and with a final nudge, smirk and bow takes his departure and passes out of Captain's horizon. Captain, thereafter, notes with consternation that his fine gold watch and chain have also gone. Captain is now cautious with affable strangers in Frisco Street Cars.[4]

On this voyage *Centaur*, returning from San Francisco, was sent from Queenstown to Shields where she spent the next 11 weeks, mid-March to 29 May 1893. Susie was with John for some and probably most of this period and he may have managed some time home in Shetland to see Kathleen and Arthur.

In Shields the cargo of wheat had to be discharged and a cargo of coal loaded. These tasks were routine but not easy, with difficulties to which the master and his crew had to be alert. A vessel with all her masts and spars – her top hamper – in place aloft and with empty holds would capsize. As the wheat was discharged it was necessary in the later stages to load ballast, consisting of sand, rubble or some other suitable material, to replace the discharged cargo, counteracting the unstabilising weight of the top hamper. If on completion of discharge the vessel was to load a cargo in the same port but at a different berth, like *Centaur* in Shields, the quantity of ballast required would be less than needed for a sea passage and would be known as 'stiffening'. But if going to another port the vessel would have to carry more ballast, perhaps equivalent to 25 per cent of a full cargo.

The next factor to juggle resulted from the vessel's hold being a single large space, like a warehouse, stretching almost the full length of the ship, usually with only three relatively small hatchways through which to load or discharge cargo and ballast. How could the stiffening be placed separate from the cargo, and how could mixing of ballast and cargo be avoided? Before loading a cargo, particularly a sensitive cargo like wheat, the holds had to be swept and washed to ensure that they were scrupulously clean, and the steelwork at the vessel's sides had to be covered. Weights within the ship had to be distributed to avoid concentrating too much in any one area and to keep the ship reasonably close to an even keel and not down by the head. When a vessel went to sea and started pitching and rolling heavily, the cargo or ballast, if not well secured, could shift to one side, causing the vessel to capsize and sink. The shipowners, of course, wanted all these problems to be solved with minimum delay and no extra cost. The only factors helping to reduce these problems were that units of cargo or ballast were usually quite small, that work proceeded slowly by present-day standards and that solutions to most of these problems existed. A discussion of some of these matters can be found in Appendix 1.

Leaving once again for Frisco, John took the chance for a final letter to Susie while sailing from Shields to the Channel at a time when the pilot 'had the con' (i.e. was guiding the ship). He provides a useful account of the ship's business routine once the lovey-dovey 'as we parted I waved to you here and you waved to me there' is stripped out.

> My Own Dear Susie
>
> We are getting along fine and have a nice fair wind. The pilot if this breeze stands will be leaving us in the morning …
>
> When I came on board (after bidding you farewell) Brown was waiting for me so we squared up accounts then came the pilot Capt. Blanch, the Capt. of Tug and river pilot all in a heap. About 10 o'clock [probably 1000 on Sunday 28th] the doctor & consul. In the first place the doctor went round and saw all places of accommodation. Then examined several stores then the crew was mustered and supposed to be examined, all except 3 which came before the Dr left. Everything pronounced good and the crew healthy. (Such a sham)
>
> Then aft and the Dr, a young man, enjoyed a glass of whiskey. Got a clean bill of health simply endorsed that the men had not been vaccinated. Capt. Blanch was disappointed not seeing you at the time but I told him where you had gone so he would send that wonderful alarm home to his long lost love. [Susie seems to have made a conquest of the sea pilot.]
>
> Next we were unmoored. I think it was about one o'clock and had two tugs tugging at us till we got clear of all the ships. Then one. Next was I saw you sitting on a seat on the pier with a pair of glasses looking at us I dipped the flag and waved my red handkerchief which you answered … [Susie must have waited more than three hours for that final wave!] Well the tug towed us out well over the bar and left us in a calm which almost lasted till the Monday Morning. Since then we have had nice fair winds 5, 6 & 7 knots. Tomorrow morning we expect to pass through the Straits of Dover and the pilot will leave. Our men all came on board perfectly

sober and even raised a song on the halyards. Our green horns are all steering and doing fairly well. Andrew came off the other night to report to the Mate who had relieved him on the Lookout

He said so-and-so relieved him on the outlook and the light was burning brawly, him and Jamie are both in the Mate's watch. [It seems there were some young Shetland first-trippers known to Susie amongst the crew.] Eanson is the principal man to show them around, so it's a blessing to have some help in that way, his new fiddle is getting lots of attention, Sankie & Moodie all day on Sunday. Now you must confess that you never knew me to write such string in my life and all at once. My bottom is getting hot to get on deck we should be seeing a light ship by this. So tata for tonight. Just a line more before the pilot leaves, it's now half past 9PM.

Wednesday 2PM. Pilot just leaving, all well. Off Beachy Head just now, the wind light and baffly. ByBy Susie Dear. Love to all and a Kiss to the children. Your own Jack.[5]

That letter, posted on 31 May, reached Aberdeen on 3 June and Lerwick on 4 June 1893,[6] and would have been the last that Susie heard from her Jack until the following November, five months later, when he arrived once again in San Francisco to discharge, then load for Queenstown and thence to Middlesbrough, returning after 15 months away from the UK. For John and for Susie the time apart must have seemed hard to bear, but for both of them life was about to become rather better.

1 Isbester, Susie, Letter S17, 29.12.1890 (Isbester Collection).
2 www.thefreedictionary.com/Sillock.
3 Isbester, Allan, Note CAI2, 1960s (Isbester Collection).
4 McJannet, A F. *The Log of the Dalgonar*. 09.07.1908 (Isbester Collection).
5 Isbester, Captain John. Letter J10, 31.05.1893. (Isbester Collection).
6 Details from the envelope of Letter J10, ibid.

9 SUSIE ISBESTER'S SECOND VOYAGE

In 1894 *Centaur* discharged in Middlesbrough and then loaded in Northfleet on the Thames, sailing from Gravesend as always for San Francisco. Kathleen, now aged six and Arthur, five, were both healthy, and Susie felt able to leave them in Olligarth with their grandparents and to put to sea again. There is no mention of Susie in the Ship's Articles[1] because John Isbester had an informal agreement with Gracie Beasley that his wife could accompany him provided that she was not listed as being aboard. This appears to have caused no problems with officials in foreign ports, and the practice was probably widespread at that period, as letters contain regular references to the wives of captains accompanying them.

Besides John Isbester and his wife, one other Shetlander was aboard. A.J. Anderson, aged 22, was signed on as AB, and the record shows that he had also been aboard for the previous voyage, so he was obviously a steady man. He was probably the 'greenhorn' Andrew who had reported at the start of the previous voyage that the lights were burning 'brawly'. He paid off at the voyage end with £24 17s 8d, a healthy sum on wages of £2.15s[2] per month for 11 months, and having taken a month's wages in advance. He can have spent no more than a pound or two during the voyage.

Also rejoining from the previous voyage was James Neil, the steward, a 37-year-old from Peebles, and the four apprentices: George Wainwright from Barry, aged 17, Christopher George Sweeting from London, aged 16, and two 15-year-olds, Robert John Johnstone from Liverpool and Edward William Bland from London. They could have had no idea of the adventures to which they would be exposed during the next two years, with experiences they would remember for the rest of their lives.

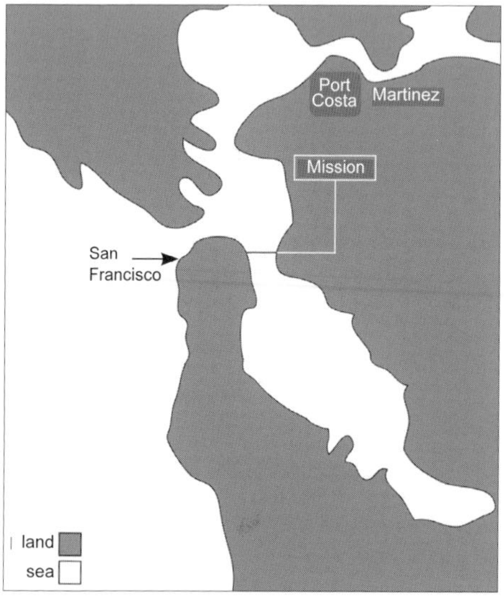

Figure 9.1 San Francisco Harbour with Port Costa, Martinez and Mission 1

San Francisco port (Fig.9.1) is situated in an outstanding natural harbour which has been called 'One of the three great natural harbors in the world ... A port, as was said in its early days, in which all the fleets of the world could find anchorage'.[3] In practice when visiting San Francisco *Centaur* would be berthed or anchored in various parts of the vast waterway. Wheat, for example, was usually loaded at Port Costa, a full 40 miles from the city of San Francisco, while on at least one occasion *Centaur* was berthed on the fringes of the city, at the Mission 1 jetty.

Figure 9.2 *Susie, with the family who stayed in Olligarth (1. Magnus Irvine, 2.Arthur Isbester, 3.Dolly Irvine, 4.Mary Meek, 5.Susie Isbester, 6. Margaret Irvine, 7.Kathleen Isbester)*

Shortly after reaching San Francisco on 28 December 1894, Susie received the devastating news that her mother had died on 7 January. Living in Olligarth with her parents were Dolly Irvine, Susie's adopted sister, and her dear Scottish friend Mary Meek, later to marry and become Mary Nicolson (Fig.9.2), both helping to look after the children. But Susie realised that her father, now aged 72, would be devastated with grief and sick with worry, and that she must return home as quickly as possible. Arrangements were made for her to travel by rail from San Francisco to Chicago, then on to New York and by steamer to Liverpool.

She left San Francisco on Saturday 9 February 1895. John Isbester, who saw her off, fretted in his next letter[4] that she would have been cold in a compartment that had frost on the windows and when, by Sacramento, she would be 'in the snow'. He wished he had given her a cigar to keep her warm! (At that period he was smoking cigars in addition to, or instead of, his normal pipe.) She reached Chicago on Wednesday 13th and New York on Saturday 16th, in time to board the Cunard Line RMS *Umbria*, travelling second cabin class and bound for Boston and Liverpool.[5] By the time she reached Olligarth towards the end of February her mother would have been dead for well over a month.

John Isbester was devastated by Susie's hurried departure, and he feared she would have some disastrous misfortune on the way back to Shetland. I suspect that he underestimated her, and that she was well able to use the natural authority of a well-bred woman or, when more appropriate, the wiles and charms of a lively and attractive 30-year-old. In any event she reached home safely.

Returning aboard the ship in San Francisco after waving farewell to Susie, John found his cabin in darkness and the fire unlit, circumstances that matched his downcast mood, but the steward appeared, lit the fire and served him some tea and biscuits. Then the ship's agent, Nicholson, arrived on board, laughed at John's sombre mood, suggested he needed a run ashore and offered to treat him to one. They went ashore at about eight o'clock and visited the Wig Wam Theater where the show, tumbling and wrestling, was 'not bad'. After this they dined on oyster stew and curry. John had an unsettled night followed by an unsettled Sunday which he attributed to his loneliness.

In his first letter to Susie after her departure[6] John Isbester mentioned that he was enclosing a letter for her from Mrs. Bland, obviously the mother of apprentice Bland. That does not surprise me. From what I have heard about my grandmother, I think it likely that when aboard she wrote to the parents of the apprentices, doubtless telling them that their sons were doing well and probably recounting a story or two to reassure them that life on board was tolerable and at times enjoyable. Sadly, I am not aware that any such letters survive.

In his letter[7] John confided that the ship had loaded more than 600 tons of stiffening: sand, gravel or similar ballast. They were to remain at No.1 Longbridge for another day to load more stiffening, 'but of course we are willing for that'. Longbridge must have been a convenient berth, preferable to being placed in the anchorage. Keeping Susie fully up to date with the things that preoccupied him John reported:

> Yesterday when the men were painting the yards they discovered that the yardarms of our lower topsail yards were both bad. This morning I went up to look and found them far gone. So down both topsail yards have to come to be repaired. That will likely cost from $150–200. Won't the owners be surprised.

In his next letter,[8] written after receipt of a cable from Susie to tell him that she was home in Shetland and that Kathleen and Arthur both had whooping cough, he replied at length, fussing about his concern for the health of wife and children and obviously distressed at his inability to help. He turned next to crew matters, reporting:

> I cleared the sailors all out last Monday except Andrew, that is I paid them off. They continued to be a complete nuisance, shamming sick etc. So we will have a whole fresh crowd for the passage home. I think I told you about the five that deserted the night before we came here so I only had 5 to pay off. Martin told me when I gave him his money that he was very sorry that he had left. Hamilton came to say goodbye and I told him to go to heaven. What led to the conclusion to pay them off was on the Sunday they growled about the fresh meat not being good enough so on Monday I told them to pack up, I would give them their money, so every man shouldered his bag and left about 9AM Monday. Of course I gave them no breakfast. Tuesday I went down with the 8 o'clock train and paid them off and back with the 4 o'clock so before I got through with all their growls I had time to see nobody.

When I first read that John Isbester allowed the men he was sacking no breakfast my reaction was that that was a vindictive way to treat them. Perhaps it was a family joke? 'A malicious captain once sacked me without any breakfast but, as I've told you Susie, I would never do that to anyone.'

On reflection I think that the words mean exactly what they say. John Isbester had served before the mast as a sailor for seven years. Men from such a background often have the reputation for being stricter disciplinarians because they have a better understanding of the motives of the men who are trying to take advantage of them. The men had been deliberately unco-operative and troublesome, and John Isbester showed them that 'two could play at that'.

To judge from the contents of his surviving letters John Isbester's favourite recreational activity was conversation. He makes frequent references to hours spent in the company of friends or business contacts visiting the ship or in their homes. In his loneliness after the departure of Susie he wrote more fully than usual about what he had been doing.

> James [the steward] has got a bad cold in the head and chest. I have given him a stiff grog and honey, hot, and had his feet in hot water and he is in bed and I expect will be better tomorrow. Today both the Norwegian ships had left so we are all alone at the wharf.
>
> Today Captain Green, wife & baby & nurse came alongside in their boat. They climbed on a lighter alongside of us then up a stepladder and over our high rails. She of course very big in front. She is a big brown, skinny, common-looking woman, and I would say pretends to be something more than she really is. They sat a few minutes. The Capt had come to ask for some cement sweepings which I gave him.

The reference to cement sweepings is interesting. Sweepings are normally the residues of the cargo after completion of discharge, which suggests that *Centaur*'s cargo that voyage from England had been cement, not the usual coal. This is consistent with having loaded in Northfleet on the Thames, not a usual coal-loading port. Minor repairs aboard ship were often made with cement, and Captain Green would welcome the opportunity to obtain a supply free of charge. John Isbester's letter continues:

> As the tide was ahead of them they all started to walk to Martinez, you know that's a long walk but I have no doubt that she would make it. She certainly does not look as though she had been wheeled about in a bathchair all or any part of her life. I am not much troubled with the asma [asthma] now. Still I burn the paper when I mind.

John Isbester refers to asthma from time to time in his letter; it obviously troubled him occasionally. The mention of burning the paper appears to be a reference to potassium nitrate or saltpetre paper, now an obsolete treatment for asthma in which potassium nitrate-impregnated paper was ignited and the smoke inhaled by the patient.[9]

> All our yards are fixed and aloft now. The new Royal Yard set. All the light sails are bent so we won't have much to do when we come down [from Port Costa to San Francisco and the open ocean]. This forenoon Capt. Gilmore came here and him and I went up the valleys. I shot a squirrel with the first shot. I gave him more shots but he hurt nothing. He went back to his ship and I came on board about half past

> one. Jem had dinner keeping for me. Tell Kathleen and Arthur that I was very glad to get their letters and give them an XX each for me and here is one . yourself … Love to you all, your own loving Husband Jack.

In a final note to be landed with the tug[10] John Isbester tells Susie that they have been at sea for 24 hours off San Francisco but with hardly a breath of air and, drifting dangerously close to shore, he has had reluctantly to hire a tug for $60 to tow them 10 miles off shore. It had been necessary to do a lot of 'box hauling' (backing the yards to benefit from any random zephyr), but, he reports with satisfaction, there had not been a mumble from the new crew.

---

1 *Centaur* Agreement, Voyage ending 10.09.1889. National Archive.
2 In the eight years from 1886 the monthly pay for an AB on *Centaur* had been reduced by 5s, indicative of the hard times through which sail shipping was passing.
3 Morphy, Edward; Board of State Harbor Commissioners (1923). *The Port of San Francisco*. Sacramento OCLC 2220209. Quoted by Wikipedia.
4 Isbester, Captain John. Letter J44, 13.02.1895. (Isbester Collection).
5 Second Cabin Passenger List. RMS Umbria.16.02.1895, (Isbester Collection).
6 Isbester, Captain John. Letter J44, op.cit
7 Isbester, Captain John. Letter J44, ibid.
8 Isbester, Captain John. Letter J11, 27.02.1895 (Isbester Collection).
9 Farlex Partner Medical Dictionary © Farlex 2012 & Segens Medical Dictionary. © 2012 Farlex, Inc.
10 Isbester, Captain John. Letter J12, 08.03.1895 (Isbester Collection).

10 THE NORWEGIAN SHIP *FJELD*

On 24 February 1895 the Norwegian three-masted full-rigged ship *Fjeld*, bound for San Diego, California, from Grimsby, UK, with about 3,500 tons of coal, had rounded Cape Horn and was making her way north through the tropical Pacific when it was discovered that the cargo was on fire. Following good practice all ventilation was closed and the hatches were completely battened down, and at one time it was thought that the fire had been smothered. Hopes were dashed when 'A tremendous explosion of gas occurred in the hold, blowing the hatches open and giving the coal plenty of air for combustion. There was no longer any possibility of smothering the flames, and with the fire taking a firmer grip Captain Nielsen had no choice but to abandon ship. The weather was calm, making it possible by 28 February to transfer two months' rations and the 25-man ship's company plus their one passenger to three boats. Sailing in line ahead and linked by painters, they set sail from position 12°11 S, 108°37 W for an unstated destination.[1] It was reported[2] that they took advantage of the steady south west [*sic* – actually south east] trade winds to steer almost due north. 'It was evidently the intention of Captain Nielsen to keep to the track of the Australian and coastwise vessels rather than make for land.'

Centaur left San Francisco on 9 March and encountered the three boats on 21 March.

> The Norwegians presented a truly pitiable appearance. During the 21 days they were in the boats they suffered terribly from the tropical sun. Their faces and other parts of their bodies were scorched and sunburnt.

Captain Nielsen came aboard *Centaur* and explained their circumstances to Captain Isbester, who calculated that with his own ship's company of 31 plus the 26 from the *Fjeld* he would need to provide accommodation for 57 souls aboard a ship only certified to carry 34. 'Hot bedding' (the process by which one man climbs out of his bunk to go on watch, and the man he has relieved then climbs in) would be required. He also calculated that there was sufficient food for all hands for only 110 days when the voyage was likely to take another 150. He assembled the crew, explained the circumstances to them and told them that he hoped to land the castaways on the Falkland Islands once they had rounded Cape Horn. When he asked his crew for their acceptance of these proposals it was readily given – they were compassionate men, and the need was obvious. Once all hands and the three boats had been taken aboard, *Centaur* resumed her voyage and, when passing Pitcairn Island on 5 April the opportunity was taken to trade 'flour, bread, soap, calico and ladies' drapery for 2 cwt of oranges and various other fruit'.[3] This detail comes from the account of events which John Isbester gave to the passenger who travelled with him 13 years later. He also mentioned in that conversation that the Pitcairn Islanders 'were exceedingly religious, and said grace before a supper which he gave 18 of them who came on board. They had their Hymn Books with them and were well behaved and decorous'. In addition, the islanders were given the smallest of the three Norwegian boats and 43 letters to be put on a ship bound for a nearby port, for onward transmission to various anxious relatives of those aboard. This they did, catching the attention of the passing British ship *Marion Frazer*, Captain Wall, bound from Newcastle NSW to San Diego, California.

John Isbester knew that Susie was only too well aware of the hazards of life at sea and he appears to have been presenting a particularly optimistic interpretation of the situation when he wrote reassuringly to her:

> My Dear Susie Just a line to tell you that I am all well.
>
> Wonders will never cease I have onboard the whole crew of a Norwegian ship. I picked them up in Lat 8^{0}N They had been 21 days in the boats. Still they were all well and brought a lot of provisions with them so that we have plenty for the whole passage if I don't get them landed somewhere on the east side of the Horn. Everybody on board is well. Captain Nelson [Nielsen] and I dine together in the after cabin, on the best, of course. Jem attends us and his steward attends the mates. Everything all right … Love to all XXX to My Susie. From your Loving Husband Jack.[4]

The after cabin was a private sitting room for the captain abaft the saloon. Susie preferred it to the arrangements on the *Dalgonar*, where she sailed subsequently and which had only the saloon and adjoining cabins for captain and officers. It reads as though John Isbester, dining in the after cabin – 'on the best, of course' – was 'putting on the style' to show that he was equal to Captain Nielsen from the larger ship.

Adverse weather prevented Captain Isbester from putting his extra hands ashore on the Falkland Islands, a circumstance that may have dismayed them less than it did him, because they might have been isolated there for a long time. However, the food was running out.

In this desperate situation the fellowship of the sea provided a heart-warming remedy. On 24 May, two months after they had boarded the *Centaur*, five of the Norwegians were accepted by the German barque *Marco Polo* bound from Australia for Rotterdam. Four days later Captain Nielsen and six sailors were transferred to the Norwegian barque *Ringhorne* from the Friendly Islands bound for the Azores. Finally, on 28 June, a further five hands were taken aboard the Danish barque *Herthe* from Chile bound for Falmouth. When they arrived in Queenstown on 22 July, the only Norwegians remaining were the chief mate, Mr Hansen, and eight men.

For the Queenstown newspaper, Captain Isbester stated that:

> Great credit is due to Captain Nielsen for being able to keep under control so large a number of men in such trying circumstances, also for the able management of the boats for 21 days which was a very difficult job owing to the rather boisterous weather having being occasionally experienced.

Mr Hansen and the other castaways were equally gracious:

> speaking in the highest manner of the treatment received aboard the *Centaur* and of the courtesy of her captain, officers and crew. Captain Isbester deserved the highest commendation for his entire actions in the matter. He has the satisfaction of having saved, perhaps from a watery grave, 26 fellow human beings.[5]

Clearly everyone was very, very relieved to be safe in port.

---

1 The account of this incident is assembled from the two newspaper cuttings listed below, with some amendment to suspect dates.
Unidentified Queenstown, Ireland, newspaper dated 23.07.1895 (Isbester Collection).
Unidentified San Diego, California, newspaper dated 05.07.1895 (Isbester Collection).
2 'Fate of the *Fjeld*'. *The San Francisco Call.* Saturday 6 July 1895
3 McJannet, A F. *The Log of the Dalgonar*. 1908 (Isbester Collection).
4 Isbester, Captain John. Letter J13, 05.04.1895. (Isbester Collection).
5 Unidentified Queenstown, Ireland, Newspaper, op cit

11 THE LOSS OF THE BARQUE *CENTAUR* BY FIRE

From Queenstown, *Centaur* moved to Liverpool where during August and September she discharged and then loaded as usual for Frisco. John Isbester undoubtedly would have taken the opportunity to spend time with Susie, Kathleen and Arthur in Shetland, a time that he would have cherished. His warm affection for his wife and children is clear from his letters. When he left Liverpool again, Susie was not with him. She no longer had a mother to whom to entrust the children and she would have been aware of her father's failing health. He died on 4 January 1896, while John was still on his way to Frisco. She may well also have been aware that she was pregnant once more.

The four apprentices, Wainwright, Johnstone, Bland and Sweeting, would have still been aboard, and another memorable voyage awaited them. For the following detailed account we are again indebted to passenger Arnold McJannet, who recorded the story in 1908.[1]

> Captain Isbester, while on a voyage in the Sailing Ship *Centaur* from Liverpool to San Francisco in the last days of the year 1898,[2] sighted Easter Island, and on approaching closer he observed houses on it. Thinking it, therefore, to be inhabited he hoisted the British Flag, which was immediately answered by the inhabitants with the Chilian colours. The wind being light, and fresh meat being very desirable if procurable, the Captain decided to shorten sail and land on the Island. A whale boat set out from the shore containing sixteen inclusive of the preposterously elected King and a Chilian Governor. The King was simply and inexpensively clothed in an old dilapidated pair of dungarees. He was a young man under thirty years of age, slightly built and of an amiable disposition. The Governor was dressed in an ordinary suit of Tweeds. He appeared to be a Chilian and to be the Governor over this Island and under the Chilian Government. The other men wore either a loin cloth or a pair of old tattered trousers. The boat was a good strong whale boat, of which the Islanders have two. Speech was an impossibility as neither the King nor the Governor spoke English, but it was eventually arranged that the Captain and four of his men should go ashore with the Governor while the King and eight of his Subjects should remain on board the Centaur as hostages for the good faith and friendliness of the remainder. The native crew pulled with right good will, and taking advantage of a breaker, ran the boat high up the beach, and then carried the Captain and the Governor through shallow water to land. The Captain was received with much rejoicing as his was

the first Ship to near the Island for three years. He found the King's horse awaiting, caparisoned with a beautifully mounted Chilian saddle and bridle. The Islanders crowded around, the women with a long cloth crossing over their bosoms and hips and the children — even boys and girls up to fourteen years of age — completely naked. The adult females were handsome, carried themselves erect and were well proportioned. The population in 1902 was not more than 100. The procession made its way to the Governor's house, after the Captain had distributed biscuits and plug tobacco.

It was amusing to watch even the little children eagerly seize the Tobacco, tear off a leaf with their sharp finger nails, roll it up and stick it in their cheek. While on the way Captain Isbester noticed an exceedingly decrepit old man, evidently in the last throes of exhaustion, lying by the wayside and painfully moaning. Reining in his fiery Pegasus he enquired why the poor creature was not being taken care of, and was given to understand in reply that the old man was now no good to the community and that they thrust him, and any others — male or female — like him, out of the fold and deprived them of any sustenance so that they might die all the quicker. One native who appeared to be a sort of Minister, Teacher and Fidus Achates all in one, created a more imposing appearance that the others as he had donned a discarded royal Navy Frock Coat Uniform with glittering buttons and gold epaulettes, and as he seemed more intelligent and civilised. An old half caste sailor was found who had picked up a few words of English and he acted as interpreter.

The houses of the islanders are underground and dug out in circular form, with an entrance from the top down a stairway, the entrance being protected by a round dome. The dwellings of the King and Governor were, however, rough wooden shantys, the furniture consisting of a rough table and benches. The Captain was entertained in the Governor's house to a dinner of stewed mutton and sweet potatoes which he did not much relish, but to which he did as much Justice as he could so as not to offend his hosts' ideas of hospitality. Having obtained some fresh meat such as 6 sheep, 2 young pigs, fowls, fresh eggs, a hundred weight of bananas and a sack of potatoes, a return was made to the Ship, and the King and Governor royally entertained in the Cabin. A bottle of brandy was placed before the Guests, and to the Captain's astonishment the King calmly proceeded to fill his tumbler – a large thick tumbler – about three quarters full of the liquor, notwithstanding the Captain's protests that it was Brandy! Cognac!! Strong Drink!!! They evidently knew the tipple and smiled and nodded in response, and without the slightest hesitation or tremor swallowed the full contents at one gulp with a great smacking of lips. Some amusement was now anticipated, and the anticipation was speedily verified for both King and governor became so royally tipsy that neither of them could lift an eyelash. The King being clad in an old white suit, and his subjects having received various provisions in exchange for the goods they bought, the King and his Governor were hoisted overboard and tenderly deposited in the stern sheets of the boat along with some bottles of the fiery liquor which would serve them as a thirst quencher on the following day. A sharp eye had to be kept on the natives while on board, as they prowled around and tried to steal the Sailors' knives. The crew also bartered with them and obtained fowls in exchange for an old shirt or pair of trousers etc. The fowls were carefully kept each with a different coloured ribbon on them to denote to which sailor they belonged, and who was the owner of the eggs they laid: but on reaching San Francisco the poultry had to be destroyed and eaten, and the delicacy of a fresh egg foregone. Amid cries of vive l'Angleterre the Ship dipped her flag, and made all sail on her voyage.

This lively, observant and convincing account tells us, I suggest, a lot about John Isbester's accurate and detailed memories and his abilities to tell a story, very much in the Shetland tradition. Our debt to Arnold McJannet's training as a solicitor and readiness to keep a record is also obvious.

Centaur reached San Francisco in mid-February and discharged as usual before an unprecedented change in routine found them loading wheat for a voyage across the Pacific to Maryborough and Brisbane in Queensland, Australia. They sailed on 5 April 1896, with John by this time undoubtedly well aware that Susie was about eight months pregnant.

When 12 days out from San Francisco Captain Isbester and his crew found themselves confronted with the terrifying challenge of fire aboard. The facts are set out very clearly in Captain Isbester's abstract of official log.[3]

ABSTRACT OF OFFICIAL LOG BOOK OF THE BQE CENTAUR

Friday 17th April 1896 – Lat 14°41N, Long 142°14W at Noon. Wind East Strong breeze, squally with passing showers. Sea choppy and confused with considerable swell.

About 3.30 PM the acting third mate and acting lamp trimmer were sent down to draw paraffin oil from barrel kept in an empty space in the after tween decks. Before leaving the deck Mr Neilson cautioned third mate to be very careful with the light. However a few minutes afterwards the third mate rushed on deck and told Mr Neilson [chief mate] that the ship was on fire. He at once called my attention and called all hands. Started both pumps and threw water as near as possible to the seat of the fire from the after hatch. This proving ineffective, we closed down all hatches and cut and bored holes in the sail locker deck over the seat of the fire and flooded the same. This appeared to bring the fire somewhat under control. However water was kept on incessantly by all hands until about 10 PM when I thought the fire was about out. It appeared to be only hot steam and allowed one watch to rest, the other watch continuing pouring on water. This appeared to prove sufficient until about 8 AM on Saturday morning 18th inst. when on opening the hatch in the cabin over the lower sail locker we found the fire had extended aft along the port side into the sail locker and the sails and the hemp rope stored there was then in flames. All hands were again called and poured water on the fire, all to no effect. We were [approximately eight words indecipherable]. We then closed cabin doors and went on the poop deck and continued water down the skylight. About 10 AM the whole cabin was then in flames. We then saw that the fire was beyond control. I ordered one watch to get the boats ready, having previously secured provisions from the cabin, the other watch continuing the water on the fire. About noon backed the main yard and put out the two after boats. While doing so the main brace was burned off and the whole poop was then in flames. The first two boats lowered had to be manned and sent from the ships side as the seas was so rough they were in great danger of being stove in and in danger of mizzen mast falling as the rigging was then all burned off. The remainder of the crew launched the forward lifeboat[4] from the fore and main yardarms and additional water and provisions and transferred to the other boats.

About 2 PM the fire broke through the front of the poop to the main deck. About 2.30 PM the remainder of the crew, the first mate and myself left the ship and joined the other boats and stood by at some little distance. About twenty minutes after we left the side the mizzen mast fell to starboard, breaking down the half round and sheer strake plates. In the mean time we were getting provisions to the three different boats, having arranged that the second mate should take the pinnace with five hands, the first mate and myself the other two boats with eight hands each. About 7 PM we decided to all sail up to the ship and stand by till morning. While sailing up to the ship the second mate's boat was struck by a sea and split, and so rendered unseaworthy.[5] We then divided into the two boats and remained by the ship till 8.30 PM. The ship was then almost in full blaze fore and aft, the main rigging mostly burnt off. We then decided to steer for Hilo [in the Hawaiian or Sandwich Islands] as we considered it useless to stand by the ship any longer on the chance of being picked up as we were so far out of the usual track of vessels and the sea was rough and weather squally. We decided to keep together and to do so I had to tow the second boat as one was faster than the other. The first four days after leaving the ship we had strong Easterly winds and high breaking sea. Used considerable quantity of oil to some advantage during the last four days of our passage. Weather moderate sea also moderate. At 9 AM Sunday April 26th we arrived at Hilo where we were very hospitably received.

On questioning the Third Mate and Maurice Turley as to the cause of the fire Third Mate informs me that he was ahead of Turley and on coming to the barrel found some burlap around the same and was lifting it clear when Turley, coming behind with the lamp, made a stumble towards the barrel so that the lamp came in contact with the burlap and the whole thing instantly went on fire. They rushed to the wheat and threw some sacks on the fire, thinking to choke it. This proved insufficient – they rushed on deck and gave the alarm.[6]

A third mate was not part of the ship's normal complement, so he would almost certainly have been one of the apprentices, probably the 18-year-old senior apprentice, George Wainwright. It was Captain Isbester's practice to promote apprentices to third mate when he considered that their ability and diligence warranted it. He made every effort over the years to give the apprentices a really thorough training, efforts that they surely appreciated.

A San Francisco newspaper[7] of the time reported the loss of *Centaur*, commanded by 'Captain Isbester, who is well known in San Francisco, having been running into this port for many years' and added that 'Upon arriving at Hilo they entered a church and offered up prayers for an hour.'

After describing the fire, the newspaper reports approvingly that

> The voyage of 800 miles was completed in a little over eight days, remarkably fast sailing for such small craft. Every member of the crew was almost completely exhausted when the shores of Hilo were reached, but their condition did not prevent them from offering thanksgiving before attending to their physical needs.

A local newspaper report[8] mentions that during their passage the castaways were drenched through and suffered greatly from the heat by day and the cold by night. In Hilo, where the two lifeboats were auctioned, they remained for five days and before departing for Honolulu Captain Isbester, first mate John Neilson and second mate Edward Roberts named a long list of leaders of the community plus many natives, names not known, and expressed their thanks for special kindnesses shown.

> During their stay in Hilo the wrecked crew were invited to a social at the residence of Mrs. F.S. Lyman. They accepted the invitation and were given a very pleasant reception. Mr Henry West representing a large number of natives, called upon the party and presented them with nearly a thousand pounds of island fruit. An Hawaiian send-off, with music and leis, was planned but was spoiled by a rain storm which prevailed at the time of departure.

His crew must have thanked Captain Isbester's navigation skills, which seem to have been substantial, for bringing them safely to the Hawaiian Islands, possibly one of the best places in the world to be a wrecked crew member – far, far better than going to sea!

In Honolulu, Captain Isbester would have been relieved and probably a little proud when the British Vice Consul issued the following communication.

Barque CENTAUR Letter from British Vice Consul, Honolulu

British Vice Consul

Honolulu

May 6th 1896

Sir,

It has not appeared necessary to produce any formal enquiry by means of a naval court into the circumstances attending the loss by fire of the British barque Centaur under your command as the statements made in the protest signed by yourself, two mates and a seaman, are entirely substantiated by those entered in the official Log-book and attested by the whole of the crew except two who are absent; and no statements have been made to me which do not fully corroborate those to which I have alluded.

I have much pleasure in expressing my satisfaction with the excellent discipline and conduct which appear to have prevailed throughout your crew under the very trying conditions which you and they have had to encounter.

I remain, Sir,

Your obedient servant,

(S) Thomas Rain Walker

Br Vice Consul

Captain Isbester

Late commanding British barque *Centaur*

Off. No. 51419

Unsurprisingly Captain Isbester had his own informal version of events and, happily, passenger Arnold McJannet made notes.[9]

> In the month of October twelve years ago the Sailing Ship *Centaur*, Isbester Master, on a voyage with a cargo of wheat from San Francisco for Maryborough and Brisbane, Australia, took fire when twelve days out and was burnt to the water's edge … The crew combated the raging flames for twenty four hours, and had, eventually, to take to the boats. There was a strong breeze and a heavy sea, and they [*Centaur*] had sailed 210 miles that day. Captain Isbester taking with him, he tells me, the Apprentices — four — and some of the crew in one boat, the Mate and the rest being in the other. Their chances of life were small, but the Captain did not lose heart and shaped his course for the Sandwich Islands, the nearest point of land – 800 miles off. He described, in a modest way, the perils they encountered in their 8 days and nights in the boats before they reached safety. How when an enormous sea was approaching oil was poured on the waters to let the boat glide over it! How the men began to be discouraged, and the biggest blackguards on board Ship to pray, and how he had to cheer them up though he was downhearted himself! How he had to sit at the helm for days and nights until he could hardly open his eyes, and when he tried to look at the Compass it swam round and round before him! How he had to be relieved for half an hour occasionally to try and get some sleep, and how during a half hour's respite the boat was nearly swamped owing to the Second Mate being afraid of the frightful seas, and not steering it right over the wave! How glad they were, and how thankful to sight Hilo, or Bryon Bay, on the windward side of the Island Hawaii of the Sandwich Islands. Hilo is the second town in population and commercial importance in the Hawaiian

> Islands. The surrounding scenery being the most beautiful in the Islands, but the climate is wet, showers occurring daily. The Captain describes a huge wave formed by the rain rushing down a slight declivity as sufficient to overwhelm and drown a horse … Sufficient be it to say that they were five days on the Island, being most hospitably entertained, and being decorated with flowers when they left by a Steam Boat to Honolulu, seeing a burning mountain over 7000 feet high on their way. The Consul at Honolulu was very attentive, giving the men two changes of clothes and assisting the Captain. After waiting six days they embarked on a China Steamer, which called at Honolulu, and sailed back to San Francisco.

In San Francisco the crew would have dispersed. All hands bar the captain, the mates and the apprentices could have returned to Liverpool as DBSs (Distressed British Seamen) travelling by the cheapest and therefore most uncomfortable and probably slowest route. However, ships or shore jobs could be found in San Francisco and 'They would have been daft not to have taken the opportunities. In season, ships in SF were at this time always desperate for crews and the local wage rates far in excess of UK rates.'[10] Captain Isbester very probably travelled by exactly the same route as Susie the previous year – Chicago, New York, then steamer to Liverpool, and the apprentices may have been transferred to other Gracie Beasley ships, either those in the port or expected to arrive. Their parting from Captain Isbester would have been a sad one after such exceptional adventures over the last two years. McJannet ends by saying that 'The freight and ship being well insured, there was no pecuniary loss, indeed the freighters [charterers] saved money through the loss of the ship.' They had omitted to take note that the Charter Party, the document governing the conduct of the voyage, permitted the captain to visit Maryborough, north of Brisbane, first. This he would naturally want to do as it was nearer. However, the depth of water available at Maryborough was less than at Brisbane, and if *Centaur* had visited Maryborough first the charterers would have incurred a considerable sum in lighterage costs to tranship the cargo from the mouth of the estuary leading to Maryborough, a factor they had overlooked. They would have wanted *Centaur* to visit Brisbane first because after discharge of the Brisbane cargo the reduction of her draught would have allowed her to enter Maryborough, eliminating the need to hire lighters.

---

1 McJannet, A F. *The Log of the Dalgonar*. 18.06.1908 (Isbester Collection).

2 At year end 1898 Captain Isbester was ashore following the loss of the barque *Rossdhu*. These eventsprobably took place in 1895.

3 *Centaur*, Abstract of Official Log, undated. (Isbester Collection).

4 Strictly speaking this was not a lifeboat, but a pinnace.

5 The pinnace was probably intended for ferrying people between ship and shore, not specifically for lifesaving.

6 The clarity of this document is typical of other reports written by John Isbester but it is likely that he received help from the staff of the British Vice Consulate in Honolulu with spelling and punctuation which is better than his normal, and the typing is certainly not his.

7 Unidentified and undated San Francisco newspaper (Isbester Collection).

8 The Hawaiian Star, 04.05.1896.

9 McJannet, A F. op.cit. 13.07.1908.

10 Lane, Professor A. Personal correspondence, November 2015.

12 THE UNTIMELY END OF THE BARQUE *ROSSDHU*

John Isbester would undoubtedly have been in contact with Susie by cable from Hilo to assure her that all was well, in advance of possible alarmist newspaper reports, and letters would surely have followed. After the sea passage from Hawaii to San Francisco, then by rail from Frisco to New York and on by sea to the UK, Captain Isbester probably arrived back in Liverpool early in June 1896 when he would have been overjoyed to learn of the birth of his son, John Eric Isbester, always known as Eric, on 27 May. Eric was to join Kathleen and Arthur as a surviving child of the family. John Isbester's reports to his Liverpool owners could have been completed within a couple of days, and if he had been treated with a bit of sympathy and understanding he could have been home in Shetland with his family by the middle of June. He was certainly there on 29 June to register Eric's birth.

Gracie Beasley wasted little time in finding a replacement for *Centaur*. On 25 August the barque *Rossdhu* was reregistered in London with John Isbester as master. She was a three-masted barque of 1,371 tons gross, 1,321 tons nett, but with a little less cargo capacity than *Centaur* 'because of her shallower depth'. She was iron-hulled, 232 feet in length, 38 feet in beam but only 21 feet 9 inches in depth – 3 feet 3 inches less than *Centaur*. Her mean draught was probably about 18 feet. Built by James E Scott of Greenock in 1874 she was owned by William Montgomery of London and operated by Gracie Beasley of Liverpool. Her official number was 67943.

Rossdhu left Cardiff on 4 September 1896 for Zanzibar on the east coast of Africa, which port she reached on 8 December. While in Zanzibar John Isbester would probably have learnt that Magnus Irvine, his father-in-law, had died in November, leaving the grieving Susie with the responsibility of farming Olligarth with the assistance of farm servants and managing the adjoining crofts that her mother had owned.

This visit to Zanzibar was John Isbester's only visit to an African port, and it would have been difficult to pick a more colourful one, with the harbour packed with Arab dhows –beautiful craft to a seaman's eye – carried there by the gentle winds of the north-east monsoon. He would have found the town a fascinating, intricate network of narrow streets and alleys lined with shops packed with an enticing assortment of spices and ivory.

I have found no record of the cargo that *Rossdhu* carried from Cardiff, but it might have been coal to replenish a bunkering station; by the 1890s there were plenty of steamships, both commercial and military, burning coal and requiring bunkers. After about a month in Zanzibar *Rossdhu* sailed, probably in ballast, for Newcastle NSW, arriving on 1 March 1897 and spending about six weeks in the port, presumably loading coal for Tocopilla in Chile, where she arrived in mid-June. During the next two months the coal cargo was discharged and a cargo for Europe, possibly saltpetre, was loaded. Captain Isbester rounded Cape Horn and while in the Atlantic,

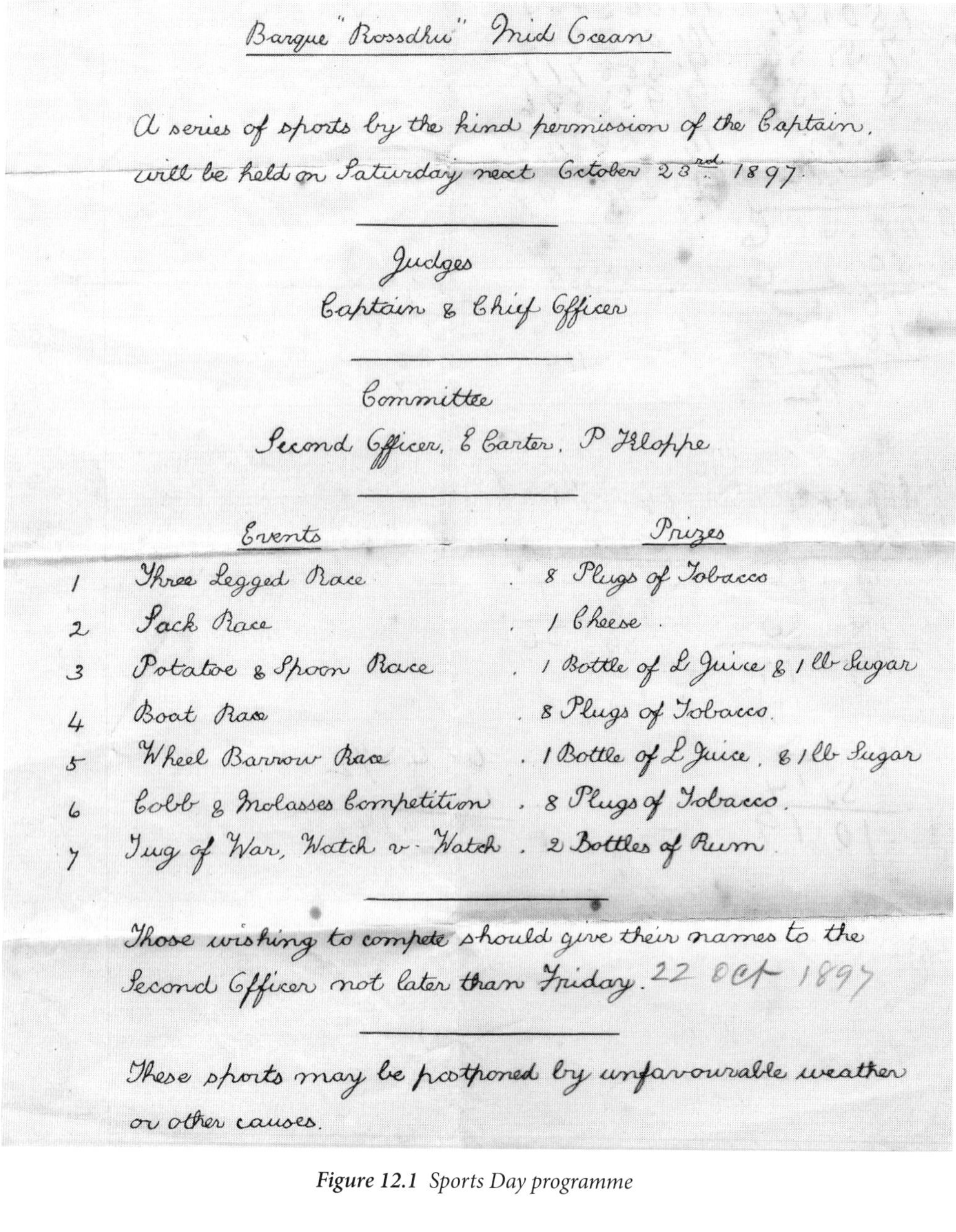

Barque "Rossdhu" Mid Ocean

A series of sports by the kind permission of the Captain, will be held on Saturday next October 23rd. 1897.

Judges
Captain & Chief Officer

Committee
Second Officer, E Carter, P Kloppe

	Events	Prizes
1	Three Legged Race	8 Plugs of Tobacco
2	Sack Race	1 Cheese.
3	Potatoe & Spoon Race	1 Bottle of L Juice & 1 lb Sugar
4	Boat Race	8 Plugs of Tobacco.
5	Wheel Barrow Race	1 Bottle of L Juice. & 1 lb Sugar
6	Cobb & Molasses Competition	8 Plugs of Tobacco.
7	Tug of War, Watch v. Watch	2 Bottles of Rum.

Those wishing to compete should give their names to the Second Officer not later than Friday. 22 Oct 1897

These sports may be postponed by unfavourable weather or other causes.

Figure 12.1 Sports Day programme

sailing north towards Europe or, perhaps more likely when becalmed in the tropics, a sports day was held. (Figs.12.1 & 12.2) The holding of the sports day suggests a happy ship with a sympathetic and generous captain prepared to provide substantial prizes and supported by a lively and well organised second officer. (I had no idea that I was following in a family tradition when, as second mate of the *Clan Graham* off the port of Morombé, Madagascar, for Christmas 1962 I persuaded Captain Dalley to agree to a similar event.) The programme of events for *Rossdhu* prompts one question: what was a Cobb and Molasses Competition?

Rossdhu, on arrival at Falmouth in November, was ordered up-Channel to unload. The past 15-month voyage had been John Isbester's first circumnavigation of the globe, a programme that was to become more common for him in the following years. After discharging at an unidentified port *Rossdhu* was reported on 5 January 1898 passing the Lizard, bound for Sharpness, in the Severn Estuary, under tow – this would have been for lack of a favourable wind. In the Bristol Channel she loaded a cargo for Melbourne. During these weeks spent in home waters John was able to spend some time in Shetland, or Susie joined him aboard the ship, the evidence for this being the subsequent arrival on 12 August 1898 of a daughter, Thyra William Isbester. *Rossdhu* discharged in Melbourne in May 1898, then went in ballast to Newcastle, NSW, to load a full cargo of coal for Gatico (Copper Cove) in Chile. In a rough draft of a letter to the owners[1] (Fig.12.3). John Isbester describes what happened when they reached Chile on 7 September 1898:

Figure 12.2 *Tug of war, watch v. watch*

Messers William Montgomery & Co.

Gatico

1 Sept (sic) 1898

Dear Sirs

The wreck of the *Rossdhu* must have come to you with a great shock. I grieve for your heavy loss. All went well with us throughout the passage. No mishaps whatever. Before arriving here we had two or three days light winds and calms. At 6 AM on the Morning of the 7th inst. we were about 7 miles south of Gatico with a light air of wind from the southward. We squared away for Cabaja [Cobija] point – three miles south of Gatico Pt. When off Cabaja pt [Fig.12.4] hoisted the jack for a pilot – and boat came off to us and said they were from the capt. of the port, and told me that there was no pilots but that he could take the ship to anchorage at Gatico as he had often done so before. I accepted his assistance for $10. Nearing the anchorage sail was reduced and when the ship was hauled up for Gatico Pt a hand was set on the bow with the lead and up to the time of dropping anchor there was no bottom with the 22 fathom line. When in position the Starboard anchor

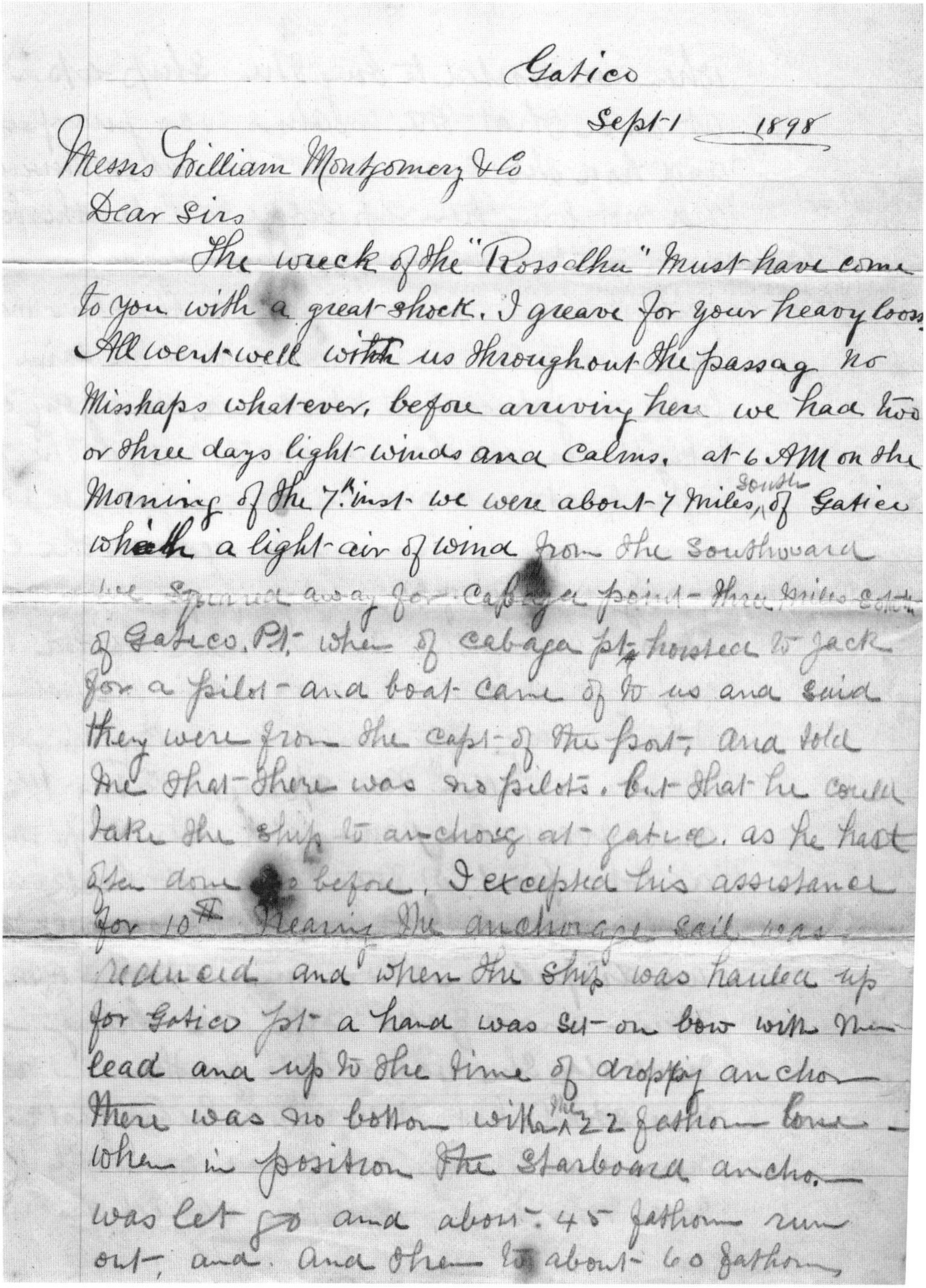

Gatico

Sept 1 1898

Messrs William Montgomery & Co

Dear Sirs

The wreck of the "Rossdhu" must have come to you with a great shock. I greave for your heavy loss All went well with us throughout the passag no Misshaps whatever, before arriving here we had two or three days light winds and calms. at 6 AM on the Morning of the 7th inst we were about 7 miles south of Gatico which a light air of wind from the southward we squared away for Cabaga point three miles South of Gatico Pt. when of cabaga pt hoisted to jack for a pilot and a boat came of to us and said they were from the capt of the port, and told me that there was no pilots. but that he could take the ship to anchorage at gatico. as he hast often done so before. I excepted his assistance for 10£ Nearing the anchorage sail was reduced and when the ship was hauled up for Gatico pt a hand was set on bow with the lead and up to the time of dropping anchor there was no bottom with the 22 fathom line. when in position the Starboard anchor was let go and about 45 fathom run out, and. and then to about 60 fathom

Figure 12.3 Page 1 of a draft of Captain Isbester's letter to owners reporting the loss of Rossdhu was let go and about 45 fathoms run out, and then to about 60 fathoms when we started to bring the ship up. I noticed at once that the anchor was jumping home and had the second anchor let go. However this did not bring her up before too late. She bomped on a rock amidships, at first slight and in a few minutes later very heavily, so that the masts were likely to come down and at the same time listed very heavily to starboard as if going over taking the sea on the main deck. We got the port after boat out and all hands got into it almost saving none of their effects. I got into the cabin and got hold of the ship's papers and the old chro. when the Second Mate called to me saying that the ship was over. The water was then rushing into the cabin taking every thing before it, all in the space of about ½ an hour and about an hour later the ship [came] up right a lot [and] part of the crew got back and saved the three head sails. About 10 AM we dropped anchor and about 3 PM the main mast fell with all belonging.

Next day she was a little further in and more steady but still with a heavy list. The men and officers went and saved the fore top sails and fore sails. Aft we could do nothing the sea breaking right over the poop and the crew ashore drunk of course – I have sent the First Mate and crew all to Tocopilla keeping the Second Mate with me. I could get no one here to salvage, but the Capt of a Chilean bark lying at a little place came and wanted to buy a boat, so I got him with part of his crew to go on salvage paying him with boats and sails equal to one [half?] the estimated value of what he saves. We have grappled the most of the sails, but our ropes are below the main deck and I am afraid we won't get them without a diver and I doubt that would only be throwing more money away. I don't think we will get any sale for what we have saved. This Capt leaves here tomorrow so I will be utterly helpless. Today we advertised for offers for the ship and cargo. The capt of the port of Cobico attends here daily along with me to value the salvage.

This report makes absolutely no reference to any information provided or assistance given by the volunteer pilot. So, how did this disaster occur? It appears that an Inquiry was held in the weeks following the shipwreck but, tantalisingly, I have been unable to trace the Wreck Report. However, Captain James Peter Thomson OBE of Sandsound in Shetland did see it and wrote to my father in the 1960s, saying

> An enquiry was held by the Chilean Maritime Authorities at Valparaiso and I think that Captain Isbester may have been present. In brief the findings were that the master was overconfident and that he should have had a pilot. There was no pilot station at the port and pilotage at the port was non compulsory. In my opinion Captain Isbester was the best pilot under the circumstances.[2]

The sea bed at Gatico Cove shelved fairly evenly from the shore (zero fathoms) to the 20-fathom contour which lay about 800 metres to seaward, beyond which the sea bed dropped away rapidly. The 1894 chart (Fig.12.5) shows an anchorage position about 1.3 cables (240 metres)

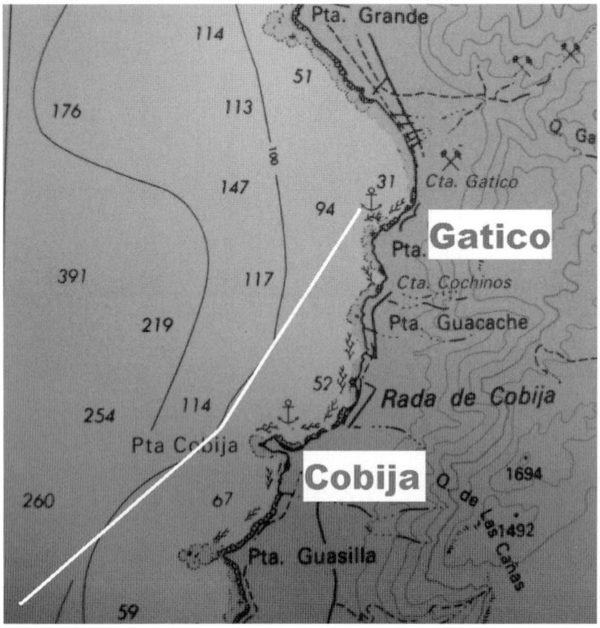

Figure 12.4 The approach of the barque *Rossdhu* to Gatico on 7 September 1898 superimposed on BA chart 1301(large corrections June 1894) Cobija Bay. Source: from the UK Hydrographic Office (www.ukho.gov.uk)

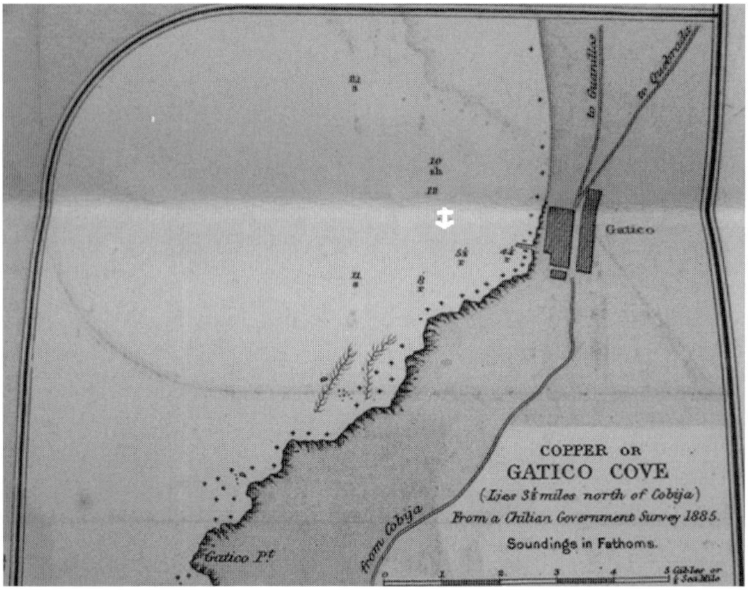

Figure 12.5 Gatico Cove, from BA chart 1301 with large corrections to June 1894 with the recommended anchorage position highlighted in white. Source: the UK Hydrographic Office (www.ukho.gov.uk)

from the jetty end in depths between 5½ and 12 fathoms, while on the 1912 chart (Fig.12.6) the anchorage position is marked much further from the shore, about 3 cables (555 metres) from the jetty end, in depths of 18 to 20 fathoms. This probably reflects the increase in the size of ships visiting the port over the years, and their increased draughts.

Sailing shipmasters rarely knew much in advance what ports they would be instructed to visit, but were required to keep their vessel provided with charts and publications that were

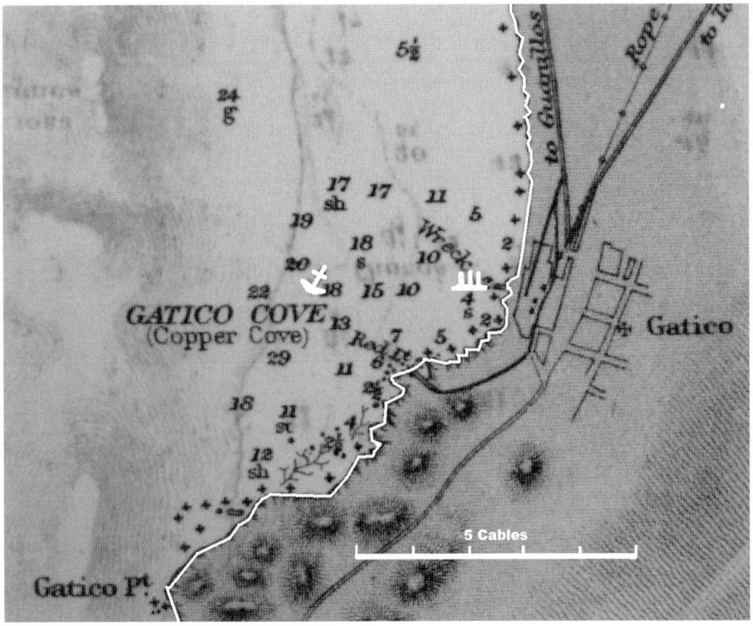

Figure 12.6 Gatico Cove, from BA chart 1301 (New edition 19th June 1912) with the recommended anchorage position and the position of the wreck of the barque *Rossdhu* both highlighted in white. Source: the UK Hydrographic Office (www.ukho.gov.uk)

'proper for the voyage'.[3] It is quite likely that Captain Isbester had no large-scale chart of Gatico Cove and relied on a published *South American Pilot*, either commercial or Admiralty. The 1884 edition of *Findlays Pilot*[4] states of Copper Cove:

> The coast is easy of access and free from danger within a short distance from the beach. The best anchorage is … in 18 to 15 fathoms, (not less than 15 fathoms), fine dark sand.
>
> There are no good leading marks for making Copper Cove, the hills being constantly covered with mist, halfway from the summit to base. The white church at Cobija is, however, a conspicuous object, and in clear weather will be a good guide … A heavy swell sets into this cove and with the constant light S.W. winds and calms, renders it difficult for heavily laden sailing vessels to get out. They should never attempt it without the aid of boats to tow, for before they could attempt to claw off the land under sail alone, the swell would very probably set them ashore.

Even if provided with the 1894 chart, its scanty soundings and lack of depth contours would have given Captain Isbester poor information about the approaches to the anchorage. If he had actually done what is claimed in the draft of his letter to the owners, and dropped anchor when the sounding was still greater than 22 fathoms, a process shown in Fig.12.7, his vessel should have brought up safely to two anchors well short of the wreck position. There may have been problems in letting go the anchor, or the soundings with the hand lead line may have been reported inaccurately, but the most likely reason for the stranding is that the order to let go the

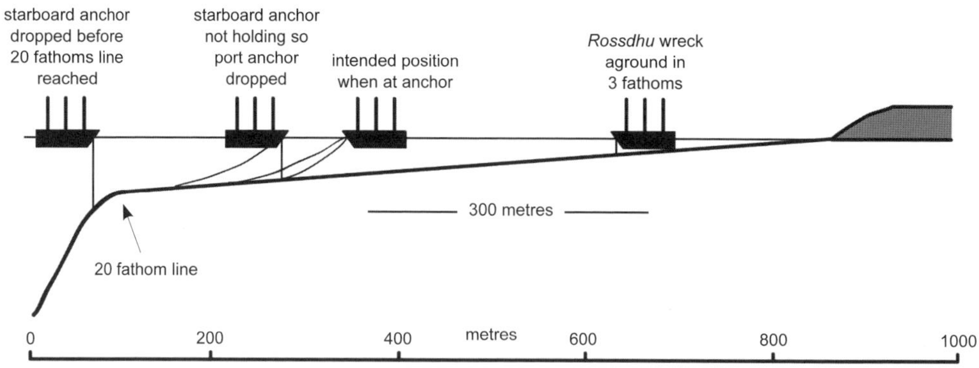

Figure 12.7 Rossdhu *anchoring at Gatico Cove*

starboard anchor was delayed. Captain Isbester may have made that decision on the basis of what he knew and could see, or he may have relied on faulty advice from the pilot. There would have been commercial benefits to be gained from anchoring closer inshore. The small boats employed in carrying the coal cargo ashore would have had a shorter distance to travel and could have made more trips in a day, resulting in a quicker discharge.

Whatever the circumstances it is clear that this disaster was one that John Isbester would have regretted bitterly: it would have been with a heavy heart that he turned his attention to efforts to salvage what could be salvaged to minimise the loss. Constantly in his mind would have been the thought that he might never obtain another command, that Gracie Beasley might decide that they were better off without his services. From his letter to the owners, which was probably copied to Gracie Beasley, it appears that he was diligent and sensible in pursuing the salvage work, and this must have counted in his favour. In any event John Isbester was unemployed for 18 months, after which Captain Kitchen of 'the Mighty *Dalgonar*'[5] (so called by marine writer Basil Lubbock), retired, and in March 1900 Captain Isbester replaced him as master.

---

1 Isbester, Captain John. Letter J14, 01.09.98(*sic*) (Isbester Collection).

2 Thomson, Captain J.P, OBE ExC. Letter JPT13, 16.09.1969 (Isbester Collection).

3 Blue Backed Charts, Maritime Notes & Queries Volume IX, 1896, Spottiswood & Co.

4 Findlay, A.G. FRGS, *Directory for the Navigation of the South Pacific Ocean.* Fifth Edn. Richard Holmes Laurie. 1884

5 Lubbock, Basil. *The Last of the Windjammers* Vol.II, Brown, Son & Ferguson. 1929. P.163.

13 'THE MIGHTY *DALGONAR*'

In 1900 the Gracie Beasley fleet consisted of six sailing ships:

Name	Gross tons
Dalgonar	2,665
Glenlui	1,847
Westgate	1,814
M E Watson	1,670
British Princess	1,480
Tennaserim	1,419

Dalgonar (Fig.13.1), by virtue of her size and the seniority of her master, was Gracie Beasley's commodore ship, and by his appointment as master John Isbester became Commodore of the Australasian Line, entitled to fly a swallow-tailed version of the house flag. [1]

Dalgonar had been built for Gracie Beasley in the Southampton shipyard of Oswald & Maurdant in 1892. She has been described, though never by my grandfather, as 'One of those clumsy unhandy ships which was built by the mile and sawn off into lengths'.[2] More sympathetically, Commander Woollard of the Society of Cape Horners called her 'the beautiful full rigged ship'[3] while to Gerald Burton, who sailed in her as an apprentice from 1895, she was a 'beautiful vessel to look at with painted ports and a white and gold painted lady as her figurehead'.[4] She was one of the largest three-masted ships in existence, and John Isbester used with good reason to say that she should have had four masts. She was 296 feet in length overall, and 42.3 feet in breadth; her

Figure 13.1 *Ship* Dalgonar *at anchor off Seattle in 1895. (Courtesy San Francisco Maritime NHP)*

Figure 13.2 *The forecastle, looking aft, with windlass and a rather dirty port anchor*

Figure 13.3 *The* Dalgonar *saloon: Captain and Mrs Isbester with friend in foreground*

Figure 13.4 *The steering position*

Figure 13.5 *Mrs Isbester knitting on the poop, the chartroom in the background*

Figure 13.6 *The figurehead*

Figure 13.7 Dalgonar*'s bows and bowsprit*

depth of hold was 25.2 feet and her registered tonnage was 2,565.15. She was able to carry about 4,000 tons of coal, which in the early years of the 20th century continued to make her attractive to shippers. She had a single hold occupying almost the full length of the ship and accessed through three hatches. She had a forecastle (Fig.13.2) and poop, the master and officers being berthed in the latter (Fig.13.3). The seamen and petty officers were berthed in a large steel deckhouse abaft the foremast, which also contained the galley and donkey boiler.[5] The apprentices were housed in the 'halfdeck', a deckhouse between the mainmast and the after hatch.

Dalgonar had steel pole masts with wooden topgallants and royals. Her sail plan was normal with upper and lower topsails but, unusually, on the mainmast, the topgallants were also split, a modification introduced some time after 1895.[6] The steering position (Fig.13.4) was aft on a whaleback stern, a stern which curved downwards towards aft to assist drainage; and at the forward end of the poop deck there was a chartroom (Fig.13.5). *Dalgonar* had a light grey hull, black topsides and 15 painted gunports port and starboard on a broad white band to complement her red boottopping. Beneath her steel bowsprit she had a white and gold painted lady as her figurehead[7] (Figs 13.6 and 13.7).

Dalgonar was owned by a one-ship company, The Sailing Ship Dalgonar Co. Ltd.[8] When first commissioned, the ship was given a nominal value of £22,500 and 225 shares were issued, each valued at £100. By the early 1900s, when John Isbester was given command, 132 shares were registered, with most people owning one share but a sprinkling of people with five or ten shares. Most of the shareholders came from Merseyside, but there were also some from London,

Glasgow, Arbroath and Truro. Shareholders described themselves variously as 'Shipowner, Clerk, Lady, Registrar, Merchant, Spinster, Manufacturer, Solicitor, Widow, Master Mariner, Gentleman, Insurance Agent, Salt Distributor, Sugar Merchant, Farmer and Engineer'. Neither John Isbester nor the two masters who preceded him aboard *Dalgonar* owned any shares in the ship.

There had been eventful times aboard *Dalgonar* in the years before John Isbester joined, as the following account from an anonymous Liverpool sailor illustrates:

> I signed on the *Dalgonar* on 27th June 1896 and we were loaded for Sydney with a general cargo. This consisted of barbed wire, crockery, paint, sheep dip, oakum and various other articles for the colonies. To liven things up a bit we also had twenty tons of gunpowder in the tweendecks beneath the after hatch. I was in the second mate's watch, and when we were fifteen days out, I was watch below when things really livened up.
>
> One of the men in the mate's watch was working up aloft and whilst at the main crosstrees he suddenly noticed a thin wisp of smoke coming from the top of the steel pole mast ... fire! Instead of coming down the ratlines to raise the alarm he slid down the topgallant backstay. Then, with his excellent vocal chords, excitedly let everyone on board know that there was a fire in the hold.
>
> Everyone in the ship knew there was gunpowder amongst the cargo and indeed, the crowd's [the crew] response to the alarm was lightning quick. In a very short space of time and without waiting to be ordered by captain or mate, the after hatch was stripped to reveal thick black smoke pouring out. Without any telling some of the crew went below. A chain gang was formed and the twenty tons of explosives were jettisoned over the wall [into the sea] in record time.
>
> Ships of sail like *Dalgonar* were without bulkheads and only had one big hold. With the wind being on the quarter, the fore hatch was then opened to allow the smoke to be blown right through and escape at the other end. Whilst the explosives were being thrown overboard a boat towing astern was made ready fully laden with provisions; then, just in case, the other boats were swung out on their davits.
>
> When the last case of the gunpowder had gone over, the hatches were battened down and the donkey engine started. The ship had a two and a half inch pipe that ran under the top rail, and on this couplings were spaced twenty feet apart. On these couplings, or fire hydrants, hoses to fight a fire could be connected. The chippy [carpenter] was then given the job of cutting through the wooden deck to allow a steam hose to be inserted into the hold, however he could not get through the steel deck below the wooden decking. Old Captain Kitchen said he thought he could make St Vincent [Cape Verde Islands] that night, but on seeing the palls of smoke from our ship, a steamer came to the rescue; I think she was one of Houston's of Liverpool. Standing by us all night the steamer's captain offered to take us all off and let the ship burn; but when morning broke the Old Man thanked him and away he went.
>
> The following day we started getting the [anchor] cable up from the [chain] locker [in preparation for anchoring]. A sailor went down to hitch a rope onto the cable, but just as he'd made it fast he dropped unconscious.

> Another sailor went down with a bowline round himself to rescue him but as soon as he had secured his fallen shipmate he dropped as well.
>
> With lines already around both men they were hauled up and laid out on the deck where after some time they both recovered. The fumes from the sheep dip in the cargo had turned into a poisonous gas, and almost finished the pair of them off.[9] Two days later the ship made St Vincent with the fire in the hold still burning. We then started the donkey boiler to force steam into the hold. The captain hired lighters and barges, and as soon as they were alongside we started discharging cargo into them. However the locals who worked the barges wouldn't go into the hold. With the fire still going on, we had to go down below in the smoke-filled hold where we worked for about an hour at a time, but as soon as we came back up and climbed over the hatch coaming each man went down in a fit when the fresh air hit him.

After about three weeks the fire was eventually extinguished, and the tug *Blazer* arrived from Liverpool with a couple of fire pumps on board. In restowing the cargo from the lighters, much of the tweendeck cargo was stowed in the lower hold to stiffen her up a bit (i.e. to make the ship more stable). The topgallants and their yards were sent down from each mast, then with the tug *Blazer* in charge the long haul back to Liverpool began. The tow started on 11 August 1896.

> After six days we made Funchal in Madeira then left the next day. Unfortunately we had a lot of head winds from there, and due to that, *Dalgonar* could only assist the tow with a staysail from time to time. Reaching Liverpool on 7th September we went through the Wapping then into the Albert Dock – otherwise known as the pawn shop.[10]

Also aboard on that voyage was apprentice Gerald Burton, who tells the story of a visit to Philadelphia with John Healey as first mate.

> John Healey was a top line seaman but he did like the bottle. Reminds me how he sent me ashore for a bucket of beer … and as he wasn't watching for me the seven of us in the halfdeck all had a pannikin of the brew and then topped the bucket with water. He never complained but neither did he send me for beer again.[11]

Healey remained aboard as mate when John Isbester took command.

Captain Isbester's first voyage on *Dalgonar* took him from London to Sydney, a port he was to visit many times in the coming years. In Sydney he would have received the glad tidings of the birth of his eighth child – my father, Charles Allan Isbester, always known as Allan – on 21 March 1900.

Sydney was a place where a Shetland captain could find many friends. Foremost amongst those who became valued friends was Captain Charles Hay Linklater of Tingwall, close to Whiteness. He was from a very normal Shetland family for those times, being one of ten children and with two of his brothers being master mariners. After time spent in the Shetland coastal trade, Captain Linklater had moved to Australia in 1862 and become mate of *The Watch Dog*, a sailing vessel commanded by one of his brothers and trading between Australia and New

Caledonia. After three years he was given command of this vessel and subsequently commanded other sailing ships trading in the same area, including the barque *Camila* employed in carrying live cattle from Queensland to New Caledonia, doubtless the excuse for a few interesting stories. In 1872, aged 33, he returned to Shetland and in 1873 married the 27-year-old Mary Hunter of Strome, a close neighbour to Haggersta and Olligarth, who probably overlapped with John Isbester when at Whiteness school. Indeed, David Hobart, the schoolmaster, was a witness to their wedding. The Linklaters returned to Sydney where, after further seafaring, the captain retired in 1882 at the early age of 43 – clearly the live cattle trade could be lucrative. One remarkable fact mentioned in his obituary[12] is that Captain Linklater had survived being washed overboard on three occasions! This is tantalising information – it would be much more interesting to be told how he got back aboard. Charles and Mary Linklater had seven children, several of whom were to play an active part in visits of the Isbester family to Sydney aboard *Dalgonar*.

After a doubtless enjoyable two and a half months spent in and between Sydney and Newcastle, NSW, cementing friendships and promising to return, John Isbester and *Dalgonar* continued to Tocopilla in Chile to discharge coal, load saltpetre and receive the painful news that his daughter Thyra, aged two, had died. In a letter to Susie's closest friend Mary Nicolson who had written with condolences, John Isbester poured out his concerns that Susie had not given him any details of Thyra's death and must be ill. He had got the news from the *Shetland Times*. He continued: 'Every day I think I care less what happens now since my Thyra is taken. I did so look forward to coming back to see her. She is better [in heaven] than being with us.'[13] Turning to prospects of getting home, he wrote:

> The cargo is now almost discharged but our lay days for loading don't commence before the 7th Janry. We have 30 working days after that date so that if we are kept all our time as I doubt we will it will be in Feb before we leave here. And by that time the ships bottom will be grown over with shell so that she won't be able to sail enough to get out of her own way and we are likely to be four months coming home.[14]

His prediction, probably reflecting his mood, was unduly pessimistic. *Dalgonar* sailed from Tocopilla on 12 January and reached Falmouth three and a half months later.

From there she continued, under tow, to Hamburg to complete a second circumnavigation of the globe in a voyage taking some 15 months.

During the two months spent in Hamburg, John Isbester was finally allowed by the owners to realise an ambition he had nurtured for years, to bring his wife and children aboard for a voyage. He was joined by Susie, accompanied by the younger boys – Eric, aged five, and Allan, one. Kathleen, now thirteen, remained in Shetland, at school in Lerwick, boarding with family friends during the week and returning to Olligarth at the weekends. Arthur, aged twelve, may have been at boarding school. It may be that Susie, too, realised her dearest ambition. During the time they were in Hamburg a new upright piano was delivered to the ship. It had actually been purchased from James MacBeth of 184 Union Street, Aberdeen, but as it was manufactured by G Klingmann & Co of Berlin it is likely that MacBeth had arranged for it to be delivered direct to the ship in Hamburg.[15] Klingmann started making pianos in 1869 and my grandmother's instrument was No.8935. Susie Isbester was certainly a competent and confident pianist, and she may have been a gifted one. Four bound volumes of her often dogeared sheet music remain.[16]

They were bought in the 1870s and 80s for prices between 2 shillings and 4 shillings a copy, at a time when a sailor's weekly wage was £3 (60 shillings). Their dilapidated condition testifies to the regularity with which they were used, and from the fact that they are all marked with Susie's name I deduce that sheets would have been passed around amongst the assembled company to be eventually returned to their owners. Susie had been taught to play the piano by her Scottish governess, Netta Urquart, who later married the Whiteness schoolmaster, David Hobart, and several of the pieces of music have notes to show that they were from her. 'Gruss dem Walde' ('To the Woods'), a song for contralto by F. Warner, was a gift from one Madlanch Gard, who may have been frustrated by the total absence of woods in Shetland, and other pieces of music were gifts from D. Lenam, M. Caedler and 'Aggie with love'.

The music ranges from piano pieces such as Handel's 'Where E'er You Walk' and Mendelssohn's 'Wedding March' to a quadrille called 'Les Rats', a ballad entitled 'Could I But Relive the Past 'and 'Oh Dem Golden Slippers', a popular song with chorus for four voices. The collection includes sentimental Scottish songs such as 'The Bonnie Braes o' Airlie' and 'Thule my Fatherland', but no Shetland music. My grandmother lived before the revival of Shetland folk music, and may never have heard such hauntingly beautiful songs as 'Da Sang o da Papa Men'.

It is unlikely that Susie played the piano at sea except in unusually calm weather, but the time in port often stretched to a couple of months. In the days before radios I am sure that her piano music drifting from the saloon skylight, like that from a guitar, a mouth organ or an accordion on deck, would have lifted the heart and would have been welcome aboard.

Figure 13.8 A gathering in Sydney including Captain and Mrs Isbester, sons Eric (aged 5) and Allan (aged 1) accompanied by officers, petty officers, apprentices and friends from ashore

Susie Isbester's gifts were not limited to the piano: at home she played the church organ too. Ruby Hunter, a child in Whiteness at the start of the 20th century, told her family that

> Mrs Isbester was ... the organist at the Sunday School. She liked Ruby's voice and always wanted her to sit next to the organ. According to Ruby, Mrs Isbester used to wear long dresses and the choir had to be careful when they walked into the church behind her not to tread on the edge of her long dress.[17]

My father, Allan, used to claim that he boarded *Dalgonar* as a babe in arms and first walked in the Botanical Gardens in Sydney aged 18 months. During the passage from Hamburg the ship was too unsteady to allow an infant to walk. This claim is supported by a postcard showing The Pond, Botanical Gardens, Sydney, which John Isbester send to Allan some years later, with the words 'this is the Gardens where you first commenced to walk'.[18]

I like to think that *Dalgonar* may have berthed at Browns Wharf, Woolloomooloo, quite close to the Botanical Gardens, a berth used by the Clan Line ships in which I served 60 years later. Even in the 1950s and 1960s Browns Wharf remained a charming part of the old Sydney, where jetties, still constructed of timber, were located immediately alongside parks, pubs and residential housing.

My father didn't get much respite when they left Sydney. Exceptionally, *Dalgonar* was given a cargo, perhaps grain, for the UK and from Sydney she went directly across the Pacific, round Cape Horn and back to Liverpool by way of Falmouth. In Sydney the Linklaters remained good friends (Fig.13.8). When I met their daughter, Maggie Linklater, in Sydney 50 years later, she told me, 'Your grandfather used to take us for picnics in Sydney Harbour, in the ship's gig rowed by the eight apprentices.'[19] That would have been a very special experience in beautiful surroundings, a treat for all involved. In 1902 Maggie was aged 26, and of her sisters, Grace was 24 and Aggie 17. Her married sister, Ellie, was 28, and may also have been one of the party.

---

1 McJannet, Arnold Franz. *The Log of the Dalgonar.* 26.07.1908 (Isbester Collection).
2 Richardson, John. *Dalgonar* Shipping Today & Yesterday. January 2009, p.12.
3 Woollard, Commander C. L. A., R.N.(Ed.) *The Last of the Cape Horners.* Arthur H. Stockwell, Ltd. Ilfracombe. 1967. p.238.
4 Burton, Captain Gerald D. J., quoted in *The Last of the Cape Horners*, p.240, ibid.
5 Richardson, John. Op cit.p.12.
6 The photo taken in 1895 (Fig. 13.1) shows the topgallants were not split at that time.
7 Burton, Captain Gerald D. J. Op cit. p.240.
8 *Dalgonar's* Register, National Archive.
9 120 years later, accidents of this sort on merchant ships remain far too common.
10 Richardson, John, Op cit. pp.13–15. Extensive quotation from an unnamed Liverpool seaman.
11 Burton, Gerald. Personal letter to Allan Isbester. 21.08.1961 (Isbester Collection).
12 *Death of a Shetlander in Australia.* The Shetland Times Ltd, Lerwick. 03.01.1903.
13 Isbester, Capt. John, Letter J15, 07.12.1900. (Isbester Collection).
14 Isbester, Capt. John, Letter J15, op.cit.
15 In 2017 the piano remains a treasured Isbester family possession.
16 Music of Susie Isbester. (Isbester Collection).
17 Smith. Martin. Personal correspondence, 04.12.2013 (Isbester Collection).
18 Isbester, Capt. John, PC.CAI46, 03.11.1908. (Isbester Collection).
19 I was aged 18 at the time of this meeting, and was an apprentice aboard the SS *Clan Maclachlan.*

14 THE SECOND FAMILY VOYAGE

For this voyage, starting from Liverpool on 31 August 1902 and destined for Sydney, the entire family was present. John Isbester was aged 50, Susie 38, Kathleen 14, Arthur 13, Eric 6 and Allan 2. Susie probably knew that she was again pregnant, but nothing was to stand in the way of this adventure. More than 50 years later Kathleen corresponded with Margaret Simpkin, daughter of one of the apprentices. She wrote:

> We had such a happy eighteen months in the *Dalgonar*.[1] My father was very good to his boys [the apprentices] and took a great interest in their future. Father had a class in seamanship every Sat morning which all the apprentices attended. He always had the steward make a big cake for the boy who had learnt his set piece best. Most of the boys were ready for their first exam when their time was up. I remember your father as a rather short, thickset man – very powerful. He had a very happy expression and a very jolly laugh. He was a most capable officer, very dependable, my father thought a lot of him. In Sydney the ship lay off the harbour for a long time & when we went ashore we went in the ship's gig a long, narrow boat rowed by the apprentices. When we got alongside father said 'Way enough!' All the oars were lifted out of the water [and held vertically] then laid down & any boy who did not do that properly was told off. Your father had powerful arms. He always had his sleeves rolled up. One very bad night we lost a man overboard. Volunteers were called for to man the lifeboat. Your father was one of the first to volunteer. The boat was away over two hours but of course did not save the man. There is an old sailor's superstition that if you are taking home a dead man's effects that the ship is sure to have a man lost & that at midnight the two departed will fight over the chests with their effects – the apprentices dared me to go into the storeroom at midnight & touch the chests. I did – and found Sayle was sitting on one chest – but instead of yelling as the boys expected I gave poor Sayle a hard smack!! Sayle was always quiet and sleepy looking, and fat.
>
> We had a visit from Father Neptune – your father took part – I forget what he was. The men were all dressed up with long beards and hair. The barber had a huge razor & when the doctor had examined the chicken & said he was able to be treated, the patient was given a pill then lathered with soap, shaved then tipped into a bath of water. My brother went through it but I had footing – a bottle of rum for each watch. Eric was a keen sailor. He was only five but could go right up the main rigging. He knew every rope. He used to walk up and down the bridge with his oilskin and souwester on & twice blew the whistle and called all hands on deck.

> Fortunately the men liked him so this was no trouble. Allan, the next one, always wanted to be a girl so the men made a wig for him and called him Mary.[2]

John and Susie were both very distressed at the death of Thyra; they had both been with her for most of her infancy after the stranding of *Rossdhu*, and both wrote to friends on different occasions to say that they had so wanted a daughter. I believe that my father, a sensitive soul, was aware of this and, wanting love, decided to be the daughter for whom they longed. Kathleen continues:

> One of your father's duties was to give out the daily tot of lime juice. I can picture him standing by the bucket seeing that each man took his tot. The photo you have was taken after your father was made 3rd. While in Newcastle, Australia our 3rd was hurt and had to be left in hospital. My father had a man from a training ship as 3rd. He was just useless, did not know the ropes, etc. so in Frisco he was sacked and your father made 3rd. In the picture [Fig.14.1] the other boys were dressed as they were likely doing boat duty. They were a nice lot of boys & all got on well together. We, the Captain's family, had to keep to our end of the ship. The apprentices had their half deck & we were right aft. My father always said it was not right to go to the men's part as they must have freedom. Xmas Day all hands had a special

Figure 14.1 *The* Dalgonar*'s ship's company. San Francisco, August 1903 (1.Quayle, 2. 3. 4. 5. 6. 7.Joe Chandler, Steward, 8. Allan Isbester, 9 10. 11. 12. 13.Third Mate Simpkin, 14.First mate John Healey,15. Captain Isbester, 16.Mrs Isbester, 17.Norman Isbester, 18.Kathleen Isbester, 19.Second Mate. 20.Arthur Isbester, 22.Eric Isbester, 21–26 apprentices including Sayle and Hugh Norman McGill*

> dinner. The pig, usually called Dennis, was killed and all hands had pork and plum pudding. Then the men got up a concert and dance to which we were all asked. There was a tough old Irishman called Kennedy. When the Xmas rum came round a lot of the young men gave Kennedy their share, then got him to sing.

My father used to tell of the time that the sailors gave Eric some hard tack (biscuit) containing weevils, and when he had eaten it, showed him what he had eaten. When Eric went to his father in distress the response he received was 'You should be pleased. You're the only person on the ship who has had fresh meat in the last month.' Captain John knew that he couldn't rebuke the crew for sharing the food which he had issued to them. Another of my father's stories of Eric was that when on the bowsprit working with the crew, he earned their praise when he slipped but still clung on to the spanner he was holding.

Arriving in Sydney, the family would have been met with the distressing news that Captain Linklater had died. The families remained very close, as a letter from Susie to her friend, Mary Nicolson, in Lerwick shows. The letter is written from Tingwall in Glenfield, the Linklater home outside Sydney.[3]

> My Dearest Mary
>
> Very many thanks for the ties – it was far too good of you, dear – but you are always so good. We have all been in the bush almost a fortnight now divided between the Linklaters and Gairs, and the children have had a fine time riding and out all the time. Arthur looks like a regular bush man. On Tuesday the big two [Kathleen and Arthur, Fig.14.2] are going to a place four hours' journey from here called Nowra – they will stay there a week and I won't go home again till they come back – this is so good for the bairns and Jack takes a run up twice a week – but he is much worried at the ship – the first mate still in the hospital [Kathleen had written that Mr, Healey first mate, had had his right arm dislocated in a storm when about two days out of Liverpool[4]] & now the third got his scull [*sic*] fractured by a lump of rock salt falling on him – I am just afraid he won't live – It was his own carelessness and he had been warned about it. So Jack has no one to depend on at the ship at all … Your excellent [Christmas and New Year] show & all the festivities will be over now – I do hope you all still keep well – it seems hard to realise that you are all cold and us baking – I miss Capt Linklater but it's a mercy he died so peacefully. …

Figure 14.2 *Kathleen and Arthur ready for the bush*

This is an abominable climate here: all the grapes and fruit scorched off within a day's hot wind. & not 1000 miles away sheep dying in snow. It has been really cool and pleasant here two nights now but before that heat and mosquitos were dreadful. We are pretty well discharged now – but still no charter. We all send love & many thanks. Mrs Linklater wishes to be remembered to Mrs Nicolson & Mattie. Ever Your Very loving Susie.

Susie enclosed a cutting which read:

Accident on a ship

Whilst superintending the washing of the side of the ship *Dalgonar* at Daltons wharf, Millers Point yesterday afternoon the third officer named Ernest Shields (26) was struck by a lump of rock salt, which fell from a sling whilst being landed and knocked him into the water. Upon being rescued it was found that he had received injuries to his head and he was removed to the Sydney Hospital by the C.A and T.B. in an unconscious condition.

The documents contain no news of whether he survived.

A few weeks later *Dalgonar* had moved to Newcastle, NSW, to load coal for San Francisco. Characteristically Susie's letter to Mary Nicolson gives us an excellent picture of what is going on.

My Dearest Mary

Another letter to thank you for – we are always so pleased to hear from you – We are still lying waiting for our turn & may be three weeks yet & then for Frisco. I do wonder will Violet come to see us, This is a very quiet spot. No shifting about & no other ship very near – We have a few visitors, the Minister of the Bethel Mr Koulis & his family are very nice, he is getting a concert here I sent you the paper with the advt. [see below] The two Linklater girls are still with us. Maggie teaching the big children and Eric goes to school. I was glad to get them all to work – It's miserable hot muggy weather & baby [Allan] gave us such a fright the other night with a touch of croup. We often see John Morrison's son. Willie you see and the Linklaters are coming he is such a nice lad – We also had a visit from a Capt Young whose wife stays on Albany Street, she ought to be at sea with him & that's what I'd like to tell her [I detect a very clear hint that Captain Young had been behaving inappropriately, either womanising or drinking!] … We have been greatly excited over the trial of an old sailor of ours Nash He got drunk and was accused of indecent assault on an infant. We were sure it was a trumped up affair – the mother looked a virago – & such a fight as Jack had to get him off – a kind old man to our bairns and the man who noticed the broken mast and saved us all from kingdom come [no other reference to this structural failure has survived] and only drink the trouble; however he is out of this scrape but feeling it terribly. This is the busiest coal port I ever saw. They load without ceasing day and night. K & A even down a pit [i.e. a coal mine] the other night and enjoyed it – I can't think how they are ever to settle in Whiteness after this. All the three boys are looking ill just now, but this is a very trying month here – Kathleen looks well. I am disappointed not hearing from Maggie or the Dr again.

Our land bird[5] is still alive and Kathleen has a koselle parrot. She and Arthur send best love to you.

Ever Your loving Susie[6]

Figure 14.3 *Captain Isbester in Sydney with family and friends*

Many years later my father Allan Isbester wrote:

Father and mother both liked people and company and were excellent hosts – they drew people out and were adept at getting the right people to meet each other. They made lifelong friends in all the ports they visited – on the East coast of Australia and the West Coast of America. In Australia many settled Shetlanders [Fig.14.3] … In those days a ship stayed weeks and even months in port. My parents always got into touch with the Scottish church & the Seamen's Mission, and their ship always became the centre of social life for all the British ships in the port.[7]

An example is the concert given on the *Dalgonar* in Newcastle. The advertisement for the event read as follows.

Grand Musical Promenade and Concert

On board the Clipper Ship DALGONAR, Captain Isbester, The Basin, Carrington on WEDNESDAY March 4th in aid of the Newcastle Seamen's Mission.

The following artists contribute:- J Bevan, Geo.Jenner, S V and Reg Jansen, R Lamont, D Meldrum, Mrs D Evans, Misses Ada Gee, V Tresize, M Wells, N and Flo Boddy, Cowburn, Masters B Winterbine, and W Smailes, Japanese Trio, etc.

Tickets 1s

Hon pianist, Mr Geo Williams

J L Fegan Esq MLA, Chairman

Dyke Ferry Steamers to Ship 7.20, 7.40, 8 Return every 20 minutes[8]

Allan, despite his tender years, had convincing memories of the preparations for the concert.

I can remember the after main deck being decorated with Chinese lanterns between the cabin passage entrance and the apprentices' deck house, and mother's piano … being brought out onto the deck from the cabin. Job done by the officers and apprentices.[9]

On Saturday 4 April 1903 the Newcastle NSW *Morning Herald* carried the following news item.

Birth of a Son on Board a Ship. The shipping community was a little puzzled on Thursday as to the reason for the ship *Dalgonar* being gaily dressed with bunting. Enquiry elicited the fact that the ship's company had increased by one, without the intervention of the Shipping Master. To mark the advent of his youngest born son Captain Isbester hoisted the British Ensign, and on coming ashore was congratulated by many of his friends who claimed that the new arrival was a native of the city. This contention Captain Isbester refused to accede to claiming that, although his son was born on the waters of Port Hunter within the State his advent, taking place as it did, under the British flag aboard a British vessel, does not allow of his being considered a native of this State. The *Dalgonar* sails hence to-day for San Francisco and a competent nurse will accompany Mrs Isbester on the voyage.

Allan Isbester provides a footnote to the events surrounding the birth of Magnus Norman Isbester, always called Norman.

This had an amusing followup years later. In his early twenties Norman considered emigrating. He and mother found that he had no birth certificate. They applied to Somerset House who denied any record. Next they wrote to the Board of Trade outlining the circumstances of his birth on the *Dalgonar* & giving the date. They got a reply saying as there was no record of any woman being on board they must be wrong! Then mother remembered that father had had a tacit agreement with the owners not to mention any women in the log and only such males of the family as reached the age of 14 – thus only Arthur, the eldest, was mentioned (as assistant to the carpenter). Finally they applied to Australia House & found that Norman was technically an Australian.

Susie's next letter describes Norman's birth and the voyage to Frisco:

My Dearest Mary

I was so pleased to have your letter waiting for me, … We had an uneventful passage of 70 days I got such a nice nurse. Miss Denning she has brightened the time up for the children and I will miss her sadly when she goes – she will stay with me till she gets a position – but she is so very ladylike and taking I am afraid she will be soon suited and I would feel happier too could I see her settled before leaving. Frisco looks much the same – the climate lovely. We got in on Friday night, came to the hard on Sun. and on Mon. went in a body to the park and

> just enjoyed to the full a squat and roll on the lovely grass. Find many of our old friends still alive and all anxious to chum up – but as you may imagine I won't have much time for visiting and while nurse is here I want to take the children to see the sights – Norman is a very good child – and can be taken round without trouble. I was so disappointed that he was not a girl – he came in a great hurry and there was no one with me but the Minister's wife, & she nearly took a fit. I doubt if she has recovered yet. We have no idea yet of our movements. One of our ships has been here 15 months and there are 45 ships laid up in one leg here – but people say we won't do that, as a ship that carries what this one does can sail for less money than one that carries less but we'll see – The bairns are all well just now. Kathleen is stouter. Arthur's heart just the same and himself very peaked like Allan is off & on & I never feel very sure of him. Eric keeps thin but he can't falter – he is all the time in such a turmoil. Nurse and I are horrified at the price of things here, they ask 16/- for a babies coat that you could buy anywhere for 3/11 – & a dollar and a half (6/-) for a little white Muslin Mutch. A lady in tonight with a plain grey tweed on cost £8 – a common 1/- belt is 2/- & cotton gloves 2/- (half a dollar) & the people in the shops so snuffy. Altogether Sydney is a much more social place & the people much more hospitable. I just love to get Dr Hoops's letters, they are so newsy and amusing – Mr Neil – well, his affection is on the surface. We all join in love to Mr Nicolson, Tom and your own dear self. I could write more had I time, your very loving Susie[10]

Susie's next letter is from Port Costa, to which the ship must have moved to load grain. After mentioning that Olligarth had been rented to Dr and Mrs Hoops, and considering the possibility of renting a house near Lerwick to be convenient for the education of the children, she characteristically provides a very clear description of Port Costa.

> We are still in this ghastly place – it's like living in the north hill only more so. However we are always contriving to get company on board, though what I would like would be for the bairns to get away from the ship – we were better off in Frisco – for there we could go to the park every day and every day find a fresh spot. Such lovely grass and daisies – here it's a steep hill side unclimbable except by steps. At the foot the railway then miles of warehouses – then us and then the river and at the other side of the river more deserted-looking hills – to walk along the railway line with a blazing sun o'erhead and a baby in one's arms is no joke, and I have only tried it twice – The children however always contrive some amusement and just now are very well, which is the main point. Three weeks will likely see us near ready for sea. Arthur is getting to be quite a sportsman: one day he got two squirrels and yesterday it was a young eagle. I have got its claw to make a brooch – he and Kathleen have got bikes and so take little trips abroad on them. Kath has had one breakdown and got a hole in her elbow that is not like to heal.[11]

In the 1903 photo of the *Dalgonar*'s ship's company, my father is shown in the arms of Joe Chandler, the black steward (Figs 14.1 & 14.4). My father wrote;

Figure 14.4 Joe Chandler with Allan Isbester

I was a delicate baby – and the coloured steward took me under his wing. I was really fond of him and would go with him anywhere. We called him Stewardibus. Mother said if he was allowed to take me ashore he'd always come back sober – if not he'd as often as not come back drunk. Mother said that coming back to the ship with Father she'd often be hailed by me from the top windows of a pub in the dock area of San Francisco! (P.S. I've never drunk or smoked at all).

Stewardibus visited us in Ilford [in 1911 or later] and met me, as arranged, coming out of the Grammar School. We went for a tram ride – he had his modest drink while I waited outside – then trammed home to tea. I still loved him.[12]

I suspect that the name 'Stewardibus' was coined by Kathleen, who had been learning some Latin. My father used to credit her with the doggerel:

Boyibus kissibus sweet girliorum,
Girlibus likibus, wantee some morum.

The months spent at sea on *Dalgonar* were enlivened with entertainments, of which some relics remain. A note dated 2 January1904, and signed by Frank Bell, reads:

To Miss Isbester

The costume returned with many thanks, and in good condition, I sincerely hope. The festivities have come to a close. I am, yours sincerely,[13]

Intriguingly Frank Bell's signature is followed by a very discreet little x.
The undated programme for a concert reads:

Programme

Carpenter	Song	Across the Bridge
Mr Sayfy	Song	White Wings
Mr C Shearer	Song	Poor Little Joe
F Rhodes	Song	Way Down in Louisiana
Mr R Kennedy	Song	Jimmy Riley from Dublin Town
Mr A Ghent	Song	Daughter of Shame
Mr W McKay	Song	Within a Mile of Edinburgh Town

The Cook	Song	The Happy Irish Boy
The Sailmaker	Song	Poor Old Jeff
Mr Simpkin	Song	Off to Philadelphia
Mr McKinstry	Song	Wearing of the Green

Later selection at Company's pleasure

Carriages at 11.30[14]

Nobody really expected carriages at 11.30. Eric Isbester surely spoke for all the family when he wrote:

> I spent three years aboard and coursed twice round the world before I was nine years old. We had many happy days on board her. I have never been sorry for the experiences of life at sea in those seemingly now far off days.[15] [Fig.14.5]

***Figure 14.5** Norman Isbester at sea*

1 Davies, Kathleen. Letter KD1, 27.03.1956 (Isbester Collection).
2 Davies, Kathleen. Letter KD2, 02.03.1957 (Isbester Collection).
3 Isbester, Susie, Letter S1, 16.01.1903 (Isbester Collection).
4 Davies, Kathleen. Letter KD2, op.cit.
5 A cutting from an unidentified Sydney newspaper records 'A Land Bird at Sea – Captain J Isbester of the ship *Dalgonar* which arrived in port a few days ago, had a land visitor to the vessel while she was 400 miles south-west of Tasmania in the form of a small bird of the frugivorous order. The bird had evidently been blown from either the mainland or Tasmania, and had flown till it became exhausted and settled on the ship's wheel. It was easily captured by the first mate and recovered strength on a shipboard diet of oatmeal and soaked bread. It was brought to Sydney by Captain Isbester and is now flourishing in a cage. Birds are often caught on vessels close to land, but rarely is one of the non-migratory description captured at such a distance as 400 miles from the coast.'
6 Isbester, Susie, Letter S2, 26.02.1903 (Isbester Collection).
7 Isbester, Allan. Note CAI5. 1960s (Isbester Collection).
8 'Grand Musical Promenade and Concert' Advert from unknown Newcastle NSW newspaper. (Isbester Collection).
9 Isbester, Allan. Note CAI5. 1960s (Isbester Collection).
10 Isbester, Susie, Letter S3, 16.06.1903 (Isbester Collection).
11 Isbester, Susie, Letter S4, 08.07.1903 (Isbester Collection).
12 Isbester, Allan, Note CAI6. 1960s (Isbester Collection).
13 Bell, Frank, letter dated 04,01.1904 (Isbester Collection).
14 'Concert on Board '(Isbester Collection).
15 Isbester, Eric. Letter in *Sea Breezes*, May 1956.

15 TRAGEDY IN COQUIMBO

I have been told that on 23 August 1903, the night before *Dalgonar* sailed from San Francisco on what was to be her last visit to the port, John and Susie had spent the evening with old friends who, as a parting gift, gave them two fine decorated plates. The following day, as *Dalgonar* was slowly sailing away, John Isbester, looking back at the port with his telescope, could see smoke and flames in various places. The family tradition is that there was an earthquake in San Francisco that day and John and Susie learned later that although their friends had survived unharmed, their house and its contents had been destroyed. The two plates were all that remained! The great San Francisco earthquake did not occur until 18 April 1906, several years after *Dalgonar*'s departure, but 'For the period 1850–2004, there was about one potentially damaging event per year on average, though many of these did not cause loss of life or property damage',[1] so the story could be true.

Back in the UK following their arrival in Liverpool in January 1904 the family had to cope with the harsh realities of life in Whiteness, school for the three older children, and a solitary return to sea for John following what must have been a very welcome period of almost four months during which *Dalgonar* remained in Liverpool and John remained with her, or in Shetland.

As usual on *Dalgonar*, eight apprentices were carried for the next voyage to Sydney. Alexander Guthrie McKinstry, aged 19, born in Jubbalpore (now Jabalpur), India, had joined in 1901, as had Thomas Radcliffe Sayle, aged 19, from the Isle of Man and Frank Bell, 17, from Manchester. Those three had been on both the family voyages. Joining in 1902 for the second family voyage had been William Andrew Kelsall, now 19, from Manchester and Peter O'Neill, 18, from Dublin. The three newcomers in 1904 were William Jackson, aged 17, from Westmorland, Thomas Hewitt Robinson, 15, from Lancaster and William Ferris Rudd, 17, from Northumberland.

The voyage took the *Dalgonar* back to Sydney where, in a comparatively hectic six weeks they discharged, then loaded coal in Newcastle, NSW, for Coquimbo in Chile. Friends in Sydney sent a postcard to Susie thanking her for her letter, and saying that they had tea aboard *Dalgonar* but that the ship had been strangely quiet without all the family, Eric in particular.[2]

Amongst Captain Isbester's routine official log book entries about sailors deserting or being dismissed in Coquimbo is one which was distinctly non-routine (Fig.15.1).As usual with John Isbester's reports, its substance is admirably clear and to the point, and his writing is well formed and easy to read. His words include a few spelling mistakes which on this occasion I have not corrected.

> 18/11/04 About 12.20 PM
>
> About 11.15AM Mr Waldenstrom 4th Mate & App Peter Neill went for a pleasure sail with my consent in one of the Ship's boats. Neill informs me that at about 12.15AM in the act of waring the boat round to come back to the Ship the boat

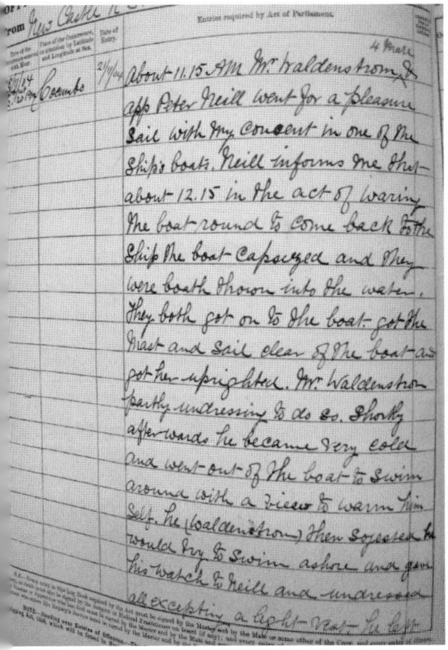
About 11.15 AM Mr Waldenstrom & App Peter Neill went for a pleasure Sail with my consent in one of the Ship's boats. Neill informs me that about 12.15 in the act of waring the boat round to come back to the Ship the boat capsized and they were boath thrown into the water. They both got on to the boat got the mast and sail clear of the boat and got her uprighted. Mr Waldenstrom partly undressing to do so. Shortly afterwards he became very cold and went out of the boat to swim around with a view to warm him Self. He (Waldenstrom) then sojested he would try to swim ashore and gave his watch to Neill and undressed all excepting a light vest he left

Figure 15.1 *Page 1 of Captain Isbester's entry in the official log book regarding the death of Waldenstrom*

capsized and they were both thrown into the water. They both got onto the boat, got the mast and sail clear of the boat and got her uprighted. [The boat was then upright, but remained full of water – waterlogged.] Mr Waldenstrom partly undressed to do so. Shortly afterwards he became very cold and went out of the boat with a view to swim around to warm himself. He [Waldenstrom] then sojested he would try to swim ashore and gave his watch to Neill and undressed all excepting a light vest. He left the boat about 50 yards and then came back saying that he could not manage it. He came back into the boat again apparently much exhausted and cold. and being still submerged in the water his condition did not improve having no clothes on. He afterwards made several attempts to get warm by swimming round the boat. At last he came over the bow of the boat and rested for some time, then crawled aft to Neill and shook hands saying it was all up with ~~him~~ me Neill held on to him but he shortly after droped appearently dead. That time would be about 2.30pm

Shortly after they left the ship I went ashore on business and came back about 1.30pm. The boat being not come back I and the officers searched the Bay with glasses seeing nothing till about 2.15PM, when we saw something on the water about 4 miles from the ship. I watched it a few minutes when I saw an ower [oar] raised on end and brought over to the other side of the boat. I then suspected it to be the boat capsized and manned our boat at once, pulled as fast as possible in the direction. I think we were about ¾ of an hour reaching them. Found Neill sitting on the stern of the boat holding Waldenstrom's head just above water. Waldenstrom was quite dead and cold. I took them into my boat and pulled back and took the body on board the Chilean ironclad *Prat* where the Dr opprated on him most energaticly for about an hour all to no effect. I then took the body back to the ship, dressed and laid him out in his cabin. Went ashore and called my owners. Mean time the helth officer from shore was on board and examined the body.

Getting no reply from home all arrangements was made and he was buried on Sunday morning. The Funeral was attended by Mr George L Ansted, the British Consel, all the British Ship Masters and apprentices in the port, and Mr Steel the ship agent, and a large number of representatives of the place.

The boat was about 4 miles or more from the ship and about 2 miles from the shore when I came to there assistance.

J Isbester (Master)

W McMorries (Mate)[3]

John Isbester and the rest of the ship's company must have wondered whether they had been given an entirely true account of what occurred in the boat in the three hours during which the 18-year-old O'Neill and the 21-year-old Waldenstrom were alone together. John Isbester showed good judgement, in my view, in avoiding any speculation in his report and limiting himself to what he knew and what he had been told. I think that he would have cursed himself for failing to tell his officers to 'keep an eye on the boat' while he was ashore. Waldenstrom, whose home address was recorded as 69 Gordon Mansions, London, had only joined the ship eight weeks previously, in Newcastle, NSW, signing on as fourth mate at a token rate of pay of one shilling a month. His previous ship was recorded as having also been *Dalgonar*. The ship did not normally carry a fourth mate and none was needed, so he was clearly being carried as a favour to someone, as John Isbester's attempt to inform the owners also suggests. Waldenstrom may have been a former apprentice whose sea service had been interrupted in Australia by accident, ill health, or an attempt to start a new life. The list of his possessions suggests that he had not been living in penury before he rejoined *Dalgonar*.

> Date of event: 18/11/04, Date of entry: 24/11/04, List of effects E M Waldenstrom
>
> One leather trunk containing, Two blue suits, One gunsey, One coloured vest,
>
> One Blue pants, One pair Brown shoes, One pair Black shoes, 2 Sleeping Suits,
>
> 4 Flennel Shirts, 2 White Suits, 2 Bath Towels, 4 White Shirts,
>
> 6 Colours, 6 White handkerchiefs, 1 Cap, 3 Singlets, 3 Drawers,
>
> 6 Pair Socks, 2 Pairs White Sheets, 1 Ned Quilt, 1 suit oilcloth,
>
> 1 Pair Rubber Sea Boots[4]

Coquimbo lies in sub-tropical waters about 30 degrees south of the equator, and these events took place early in the southern summer, but the coast of Chile is swept by the cold Humboldt Current. The critical factors in Waldenstrom's tragic death were probably his ill-advised removal of most of his clothing and the unnecessary loss of energy resulting from his vigorous swimming, but it is easy to be wise after events that would have cast a pall over the remainder of the voyage. The experience must have been traumatic for O'Neill, and it is good to see from the ship's official log book that he remained aboard for the following voyage. He must have had the understanding and support of his shipmates.

Dalgonar spent the better part of two months in Coquimbo followed by a month in Antofagasta, where an entry in the official log book records a story familiar to most shipmasters of those times.

> Patrick Monsey, AB, complained of having rheumatic pains all over. I sent him to the British Consul who gave him an order for the hospital. He (Patrick Monsey) did not go to the hospital but instead went and got drunk and was locked up. Two days later the Consul had him taken out of jail and sent to the ship's boat with a police officer and myself. He, Monsey, again deserted and I understand is again in jail to be put on board when the ship is ready for sea.[5]

In fact, Monsey was again released from jail, returned to the ship unannounced, removed his possessions and deserted.

From Antofagasta, *Dalgonar* rounded Cape Horn, arriving in Antwerp by way of Plymouth.

In Shetland life for the Isbester family was getting back to normal after the exciting times on *Dalgonar*, and Kathleen, aged 16, at school in Lerwick and staying there through the week, provided a reminder that life in Shetland could be tough. In a postcard addressed to her mother at Olligarth she says 'I don't think that I will [return to Whiteness] tomorrow night unless it's a night for riding as I can't leave before 5 and would not get home before 8 walking and it's so dark.'[6] The distance was about eight hilly miles through the countryside, walking on muddy tracks, so her lack of enthusiasm is understandable.

At this time the Isbester family and their friends were using postcards a lot to keep in touch with one another. The writing was often tiny, with every scrap of space used. John Isbester was apparently trying to assemble a comprehensive collection of Shetland views with family and friends being advised by Susie of the views he had not yet received. 'Father has no Fair Isle ones – he has Lerwick in all shapes and the whaling stations – but not Roe Bridge.'[7] Postcards were sometimes made to order using wedding photos or posed family photos.

From the time that my father, aged four, left the *Dalgonar* along with the rest of the family, he received occasional postcards from his father addressed to him personally. Some 20 of them survived in Allan Isbester's postcard album,[8] along with a much larger number written by his mother when she was visiting the ship in European ports and Allan was at home attending school and staying with family or neighbours. When of interest, they have been quoted in later chapters.

Dalgonar spent about two months in Antwerp, discharging nitrate and then, after drydocking, loading coke for Valparaiso. John Isbester remained aboard throughout so Susie joined him, and seems to have made the most of the opportunity. To Mary Nicolson she wrote extolling the virtues of the fine churches, art galleries and museums, and poking gentle fun at the Belgian soldiers:

> They are mostly short and look well fed but no smartness at all … the soldiers don't look a bit like drilled individuals – I have never seen one drunk – or in fact anybody drunk in Antwerp – but they drink for all that.

Allan and Norman were with her.

> The children are quite happy & Jack is so pleased to have them – except perhaps about twice a week, when Norman's temper is outrageous!!![9]

> While the cargo was going out a woman attended on [the stevedores] with a jar of beer and a tumbler – so much a glass. In the copious folds of her skirts she used to draw out

Figure 15.2 Allan and Norman with their three older siblings

the neck only of a bottle & give them little glasses of that – gin, I suppose it was – the woman who sold this on our ship looked such a nice body, just like our Mrs Scott.

We are laying at the entrance to a dock & to watch the endless procession of barges going out and in affords our food for thought – every barge a complete family in itself – & thousands of them. You could easily walk the length and breadth of the docks on them. I think they are used more for transit than trains. Always a wife and bairns. And the wife at the helm. Jack thinks they are proper help Mates!

This is the busiest port I ever saw. I can count from our poop six ocean steamers discharging wood – and three grain – and they are coming and going all the time. We are discharged – and Jack has turned out a satisfactory amount of nitrate. somewhere about 4000 tons. Now we are taking in (from a barge) 6.50 tons[10] slag ballast & then after being in drydock we will fill up with coke for Valparaiso – it is quite a nice voyage and should not be more than 9 Months. Jack seems all right now. He is thin – but he is always better when he is like that [Several references in the correspondence indicate that Captain Isbester had experienced a period of ill health] – if Olligarth does not suit me – I will cross from here to London and see Auntie for a week and then come by steamer to Aberdeen – we are such good sailors we are better on sea than on land. I trust Mr Nicolson is keeping well – Jack joins in best regards to him and Tom and with much love to yourself dear

Ever Your loving Susie

In a postcard from Olligarth Lizzie, a neighbour, reported to Susie in Antwerp:

Our cow is all right and the chickens is all living but three of my big ones. Your three is almost ready to lay only they are cocks. We are going to hoe the potatoes tomorrow. We are managing kinda midlin without you. I hope your enjoying yourselves. Lizzie.[11]

A few days later a postcard from Dolly, Susie's adopted younger sister, brought Susie in Antwerp up to date with events at Olligarth, where there were clearly still livestock to be tended and crops to be harvested.

Liz and I howed the taties [hoed the potatoes] last week. A. comes to heap them some day this week. The neeps are fine – will soon be for winding. Liz and I heaped Miss Harrisons taties on Monday. Our second cow has never arrived yet. Why didn't you ask Peter Anderson he was a more likely person than M C Brugg. She will never say if the ship is loading yet or not. All well, still no word from K. You said I was to write once a week so I have done so every Mon.[12]

On 19 August 1905 *Dalgonar* left Antwerp bound for Valparaiso with the cargo of coke. After five days at sea John Isbester made his first log entry. His spelling is uncorrected:

24/8/05 Jacob Rowe Cook of duty suffering from diarrhoea. Treatment. After giving him a light does of Caster Oil with 10 drops of Laudanum gave the Diarrhoea Mixture to no effect. His water and motion from bowels mixed with blood. Gave the Dovers Powder for one day to no effect.

Gave him the Witch Hazel Mixture to no effect. The motions and water almost pure blood.

31/8/05 He [Jacob Rowe] died at 4.AM and was buried at 4PM Aug 31st. 05 Latitude 43° 37 North Long 17° West

J Isbester (Master)

W M Morries

Jos A Beesley (Steward).[13]

It seems likely that Jacob Rowe, who was aged 58, knew that he was a sick man when he signed on the ship. With no job he would have no pay, so it was in his interests to conceal his illness, become a crew member and hope to be cured aboard ship. The captain of each British ship was provided with a basic medical chest and a manual, *The Ship Captain's Medical Guide*. In cases like Rowe's, when the damage was internal, the master often had two impossible challenges; to diagnose the problem and to provide a cure. If he had not previously met a similar case his chances of an accurate diagnosis were slim, and in any event the likelihood of a cure for an internal injury was vanishingly small. In port or close to port a sick man could be put ashore and help was normally given willingly, as with the doctor on the Chilean warship who had attempted to revive Waldenstrom. But away from land and before the days of radio communication, a sick man had to take his chance. Rowe could have been suffering from a whole range of conditions, from ischaemic colitis, through infective causes such as salmonella and e. coli, or from ulcerative colitis to duodenal ulcer.

The cause of death suggested in the official log book is Dysentery[14] which could be correct.

The one person to benefit from the death of Jacob Rowe was a 20-year-old ordinary seaman, F. Woollams of Fremantle, who was promoted to acting cook with pay increased from £2 a month to £2.10s a month. He must have made a reasonable job of it, because five months later he was given a further increase to £3 per month for a job which he kept until the ship reached Iquique in mid-April, where he paid off with the useful sum of £20 9s.

After discharging the coke in Valparaiso during a three-month stay *Dalgonar* spent a month in Iquique then 40 days in Antofagasta, all on the coast of Chile, before setting sail for Rotterdam, which was reached in October 1906 at the end of what proved to be a 14-month voyage.

Susie was soon aboard to stay with John, and snippets of news can be gathered from her postcards to the children. Allan is told that his father has become very stout. Kathleen, also at home in Olligarth and now aged 18, seems to have been taking on quite a lot of responsibility. She is told to ensure that Johnnie points the byre and to store the potatoes in the stable.

In Rotterdam there were

four fine sailing ships lying beside *Dalgonar*. Mr Grundy [apparently the Gracie Beasley agent] is here now. As sad and sadder than ever – still no charter. We don't

> want to take Frisco – the expenses there now are so great and the men go – and no others to be got. This is a lovely bright morning. We are asked to the *Acamas* to tea. The Capt and his wife both come from Maryport, Mrs Flynn's place, and they do talk broad. Still no word what we are to do and only 1000 tons [of ballast] in so it will likely be a hurry and rush up at the end. … After this address care of August Bolten Hamburg. The Acamas …tows to London tomorrow. I will miss Mrs Nelson. Sun afternoon. We are still here [in Rotterdam] & the weather is such that there is not much sign of going. Last night was a gale and rain. Oilskin and seaboot weather, today is some better but glass very low. I hope we will get a chance at the back of this gale. I stayed in bed today till dinner time. That is no comfort except at the fire. Love to all. Yrs Mother.[15]

To the ship in Hamburg, Kathleen wrote to say that she had arranged for her brothers to provide her with a list of the Christmas presents they wanted, and she planned to buy them on the next visit to Lerwick.[16]

Susie in Hamburg wrote to her son:

> I am wearying for you my Allan – but can't leave poor father all alone – a little new apprentice has come tonight and he is really not much bigger than Eric, – but such a plucky little fellow – he is sleeping in the halfdeck all alone – this New Year's Eve – I do hope you are well my darling.[17]

Joining a first ship in a foreign country in the depths of winter would be a daunting experience for any 14-year-old.

When *Dalgonar* sailed from Hamburg back round Cape Horn towards Astoria in Oregon, Susie went not to Shetland but to Ilford, near the London docks, to look for a new home. She and John had made the decision to leave Shetland!

When writing to Mary Nicolson a few years earlier, John Isbester mentioned that Susie was interested in living in London, but continued 'Surely the last place on Gods earth for anyone to go to live except people of means or in business.'[18] He probably continued to think that, but two practical reasons forced him to accept that a home in London made good sense. As long as his home was in Shetland he had to face three days of travel in each direction if he took leave from London or Liverpool. That was a big, big bite out of two or three weeks' leave at the end of a one-year or 18-month voyage, and though Susie could travel to be with him on the ship it was more difficult, as well as undesirable and expensive, for the children to travel too. The second practical problem was the schooling for the children. Arthur seems to have needed some special schooling and was already at a school in the Ilford area, and Kathleen wanted to go to a catering college. There was no thought of abandoning Olligarth, the cherished family home in Whiteness, but a rented home in London was needed. Several Shetland friends and relatives, including shipmasters, were living in or near Ilford, which in 1907 was a pleasant, semi-rural, outer suburb convenient to the Royal Docks and with parks and open countryside close by.

In January Susie was staying with her widowed aunt, Elizabeth Gifford, at 29 Cecil Road, Ilford, in a house named 'Busta' to echo the former Gifford Shetland home. L.L. in Whiteness wrote to assure Susie that 'We are doing all right and the bairns is well only we shall be glad when you are back. The roads is open now only awful muddy & torn up. … Eric wants to meet you at Lerwick if you hire a hack.'[19] It sounds as though Eric was wanting the rare treat of a ride. Susie had clearly been informing friends of her imminent move to London. Amongst the replies was one from M.W., writing from Whalsay (one of the islands composing Shetland).

> My dear Mrs I. thanks so much for PPC. Glad you are well but sorry you are leaving Whiteness. Whatever will they all do without you? I would so like to see you. I hope you will not leave before the end of April when I might see you as then I will be in town to meet my sister coming from afar. Glad so many are sighing for me. Tell them to cheer up a good time coming. Love.[20]

M.W. sounds to me very much like a minister, perhaps one who used to lodge at Olligarth when circumstances brought him to Whiteness.

An idea of the sort of home that John and Susie hoped to find in London can be gained from Susie's postcard to Kathleen. By this time Susie was back in Olligarth, and Kathleen was staying with Elizabeth Gifford and house-hunting in Ilford. Susie wrote:

Figure 15.3 *At 24 Bengal Road, Susie with Allan and Norman both wearing the kilt*

> I think the end house would be nice. We would only have neighbours on one side. I have an idea the garden is exposed. What like is the back garden and what is the rent?[21]

By mid-July the move to Ilford had been completed, and the new address had been circulated. No 24 Bengal Road, a terrace house, was to be the Isbester family home for some years to come (Fig.15.3). The name 'Olligarth' was given to it, but seldom used. My father, Allan, and his brother Eric moved from the Whiteness school to schools in Ilford. Although Allan was only in the Whiteness school for two years, he remained lifelong friends with his classmate, Davie Sinclair, later commodore of Currie Line.

A few days before reaching Portland, Oregon, John Isbester had an experience which intrigued members of the scientific community. It has been reported as follows.

> The British ship *Dalgonar*, from Hamburg to Portland, Oregon, Captain Isbester master, was in Longitude 136 west and Latitude 46 north on June 25th 1907. This is about 250 miles off the northern California coast.

> The weather was clear and sultry, and when the Captain took the noon observation for declination [*sic* – actually for latitude] with the sextant he noticed a very large spot on the disc of the Sun. The spot was of immense size and the Captain was much surprised at its general appearance, for it was unlike the commoner Sun spots which he had seen almost daily for many years. It had a singular motion and the Captain in trying to describe it said It looked like an inverted balloon. It moved with easily noticeable speed and passed off the Sun's disk late in the afternoon.[22]

The writer continues:

> This is the testimony as I secured it, and from it I concluded that the Captain had witnessed the transit of an intra Mercurial planet.

An intra Mercurial planet is a planet with an orbit closer to the sun than Mercury, and the report lists 11 previous reported sightings between 1720 and 1898. Captain Isbester seems to have been the very last person to sight Vulcan, the intra Mercurial planet, as no sightings have been reported since 1907!

Susie's friend Violet, writing from Portland, Oregon, with a postcard incorporating a fresh photo of a suntanned John Isbester gave Susie the good news that he had reached port:

> Here is the man you lost. I found him, and put him on paper to keep him from getting away again. How are you all? I hope well. You should have come to Portland, nobody gets sick here. Violet[23]

An unnamed Portland friend of John Isbester sent Allan a card showing a warehouse knee-deep in 'a Puget Sound salmon catch' with the message: 'When your dad gets home you will be able to sample these fellows, he is buying a lot of them in cans.'[24]

Several postcards refer to Susie having been unwell at the time of the move to Ilford, but no details are known. Susie received a further report from Violet when *Dalgonar* left Portland for Dublin:

> Jack got started off yesterday. He came up and had supper with us the night before he left. We all hated to see him go. I think he has had a nice time in Portland. I only wish you had been here too. He is looking so well. As ever, Violet[25]

Dalgonar spent six weeks in Dublin discharging, then seven weeks in Liverpool loading for Sydney, during which period John Isbester would have had the opportunity to experience their London home in springtime, a pleasant time of year.

---

1 https://en.wikipedia.org/wiki/List_of_earthquakes_in_California.
2 S.A.W. PC9. 21.11.1904, (Isbester Collection).
3 Dalgonar OLB ended 28.06.1905, pp.18–21. National Maritime Museum.

4 Dalgonar OLB ibid, p.22.
5 Dalgonar OLB ibid, pp. 24–26.
6 Isbester, Kathleen. PC13. 31.10.1904. (Isbester Collection).
7 Isbester, Susie. PC38 Nov. 1906 (Isbester Collection).
8 Allan Isbesters PC Album (Isbester Collection)
9 Isbester, Susie. Letter S9, 26.07.1905. (Isbester Collection).
10 6.50 tons of ballast seems an improbably small amount, but that is what Susie's letter clearly says.
11 Lizzie. PC15. 07.07.1905. (Isbester Collection).
12 Irvine, Dolly. PC7. 19.07.1905. (Isbester Collection).
13 *Dalgonar* OLB Ended 13.10.1906, p.14. Liverpool Record Office.
14 *Dalgonar* OLB, ibid, pp.10–11.
15 Isbester, Susie. PC32, PC33, PC35, PC37, PC38, PC41. 20.10–19.11.1906 (Isbester Collection).
16 Isbester, Kathleen. PC43. 12.12.1906. (Isbester Collection).
17 Isbester, Susie. PC.CAI6, 31.12.1907. (Isbester Collection)
18 Isbester, Capt. John. Letter J15. 07.12.1900. (Isbester Collection)
19 L.L. PC57. 11.01.1907. (Isbester Collection).
20 M.W. PC47. 08.03.1907 (Isbester Collection).
21 Isbester, Susie. PC4. 13.03.1907. (Isbester Collection).
22 Weston, L.H. 'The Intra-Mercurial Planet Vulcan', *Parachemy*, Winter 1973.
23 Violet. PC8. 19.07.1907 (Isbester Collection).
24 Anon. PC.CAI64. 19.08.1908. (Isbester Collection)
25 Violet. PC5. 07.10.1907 (Isbester Collection).

16 FROM LIVERPOOL TOWARDS SYDNEY

It was 30 May 1908 when *Dalgonar* sailed for Sydney on a voyage which has been unusually well documented. That voyage, the ship carried two passengers to Sydney, one of whom was Arnold Franz McJannet, a 32-year-old solicitor from Irvine in Scotland. He was making the voyage for health reasons, and he kept a diary or log book for his parents, who were paying for his trip. At the end of the passage he had the record typed and presented Captain Isbester with a bound copy of the text[1] which lacks only copies of his photos. When Joseph Conrad read the document, he wrote 'I think this log or diary of the voyage to Australia in a sailing ship is quite interesting. The writer takes the reader with him.'[2] There would have been little in the diary to surprise Joseph Conrad, but when the document is read more than 100 years later it provides fascinating insights into the day-to-day experience of life aboard *Dalgonar* – the weather, the ship's movement, comfort and discomfort, the food, marine life, ships seen, rats, shipmates, entertainments and boredom. The diary is too substantial, and at times too mundane, to include in its entirety, but extensive extracts are included in this chapter and the next, and more is to be found in the appendices.

The diary commences:

> On Board the Steel Clipper *Dalgonar*, 100 A.1. 2565 Tons Register. Australasian Line.
>
> Captain. – John Isbester.
>
> 1st Mate. – George Georgeson.
>
> 2nd Mate, – J.S. Williams.
>
> 3rd Mate. – Laurence Sinclair.
>
> Twenty two of a Crew, seven Apprentices, and two Passengers P.G. Littler, Meadowcroft, Carrs Crescent West, Formby and myself.
>
> We left Brunswick Dock on this day, the 30th day of May in the year Nineteen hundred and eight, and in the Seventh year of the Reign of His Majesty King Edward the Seventh.

McJannet records that a photographer from the Carbonara Co. of 4 & 6 Wilde Street, London Road, Liverpool, was aboard the tug *T A Joliffe* to take pictures of *Dalgonar* (Figs 16.1–5). The tug towed them through the Irish Sea at a rate of about 6–7 knots and passed the Tuskar Rock lighthouse at the south-east tip of Ireland after about one day. Sails were set in light airs when clear of the Irish coast, and in misty conditions a sailor was posted forward to sound the foghorn. Late that evening:

[Above] ***Figure 16.1*** *Leaving Brunswick Dock, Liverpool*

[Left] ***Figure 16.2*** *Under tow*

[Below] ***Figure 16.3*** *Becalmed*

[Upper] ***Figure 16.4*** *Alone*

[Lower] ***Figure 16.5*** *Under full sail (National Maritime Museum, Greenwich, London)*

> We came across the Fishing Yawl *Irma* from Brixham, and two men made off from her in a small rowing boat. They hailed us, came alongside on our starboard, and made fast. The Captain bought some fresh Fish, which we had for Breakfast this morning, and in exchange they received a Bottle of Brandy, a pound and a half of Tobacco and a pailful of Bread. Bread, I should explain in the Ship's parlance, means hard biscuit. The two weather-beaten young salts told us that the fishing was bad, and that they were some days out. They wished us a good voyage and praised the Ship

The following morning McJannet

> had a cold sea water bath in which the Steward had kindly emptied a pailful or two of warm sea water. It was very pleasant and invigorating, and gave me a good appetite for Breakfast.

It was a miserable morning, with thick fog and drizzling rain. The foghorn was constantly sounded. *Dalgonar* was still beating off the south coast of Ireland. In the afternoon:

> The crew engaged in washing the decks [Fig.16.6], and this Ship has now a more presentable appearance. The only sails we observed all day were three Fishing Yawls on the horizon. We are still beating westward in the Irish Channel. Wind is light and sea calm. The Captain heaved the lead in the forenoon and afternoon, and made seventy and fifty fathoms respectively I was aware for the first time that the apprentices have a Cat and her Kitten with them. These young Sailors all come from good families, and look thoroughly happy and contented.

Figure 16.6 *Washing the decks, port side, abreast the main hatch*

2nd June, A dull morning and little wind. Black, a Sailor, was promoted to Bosun. He had sailed with the Captain before and it means an increase of £1 per month in pay to him. He receives, therefore, £4 instead of £3, an A.B.s pay. This means a substantial addition in a long voyage of a year or so. We hailed a Steam Trawler *Fane,* from Fleetwood, which approached on our Port Bow at 11-30a.m. The Captain shouted through his trumpet 'Fane Ahoy! Report me all well', and an answering cry of 'Yes' came back. She crossed our quarter to make out where we were from, and then headed for Ireland. We think we should be reported to-morrow and that our friends will then know how we are. I had a talk with the Carpenter, and he is going to fit me up a shelf in my Cabin to put my Books tidily on. His workshop is in the starboard bow of the Ship right at the bow, and he has not much room to work in. He is only now getting the place put to rights, after he cleared out a lot of rubbish which was heaped breast high.

Evening:- We have had little change all day – light and variable winds and sometimes a dead calm. We are heading N.W. just now still off the South Coast of Ireland. At 7 p.m., we saw the Irish Coast through the glasses, and about an hour afterwards the Captain put about. A Duck Egg for Tea was much appreciated …

3rd June. We saw Galley Head Light – five successive flashes and then a pause – last night, so that the Captain's prediction as to where we were was correct. We passed through a lot of fishermen and one of them waved circularly a light to ask us to pass to leeward of him, so as not to go over his nets. A dull morning and a heavy roll on, the sails being square set and nothing to steady her. We are steering South West, and though not making much progress – 2 or 3 knots – are fairly on our way. Water for drinking and washing purposes is valuable on board ship, the sailors being allowed four quarts per diem each. Naturally they take advantage of any rain fall to preserve the water by placing buckets where they are likely to accumulate a quantity of water … We observed several shoals of porpoises and a large sun fish. The latter looked just like a big blob of oil, but as it came nearer one saw a large fin sticking out of the water, a white skin and a shape like an enormous sole.

4th June, Lat.49.19 N. Long 11.13 W. We have an enormous number of meals – Breakfast – Porridge, Meat and potatoes, Tea. Dinner at 12-30, Soup, Meat, Potatoes and a Vegetable, Pudding. At 3 pm Tea. At half past five an egg, usually two, and thereafter Meat and Potatoes, and at 8-30 a Cup of coffee and Biscuits and Cheese. A good breeze all day, and we are making eight knots.

We passed in the morning a three-masted barque making for the English Channel and when approaching her we hoisted the Ensign and [the *Dalgonar*'s identifying signal letters] MLDG. She hoisted an answering pennant to shew that she understood. We then pulled down our five flags and put up three flags representing three letters of the alphabet URZ. These letters signify according to the International Code of Signals for the use of all nations, prepared under the authority of the Board of Trade, 'Report me all well'. The barque then hoisted the tricolour, which shewed that She was a Frenchman and that she understood. She would log the fact and where and when she saw us, and on reaching Port

> would report it and thus you get news of us through the Shipping News in the Newspapers. We then bade her farewell by hoisting our ensign and dipping it three times, which she endorsed by doing the same with the tricolour. The International code is arranged alphabetically and almost any request, query, or answer can be made by signalling with flags.
>
> 6th June, We are now opposite to the Bay of Biscay, but miles from land so as to escape the norward inward current to the bay and the southward outward current. We are still making some eight, and sometimes nine knots … with the easterly wind that is driving us on to the trade winds. Latitude 43.41 N., longitude 15.56 W
>
> 7th June. A dull day, with still an easterly wind sending us on at the rate of about seven knots. We have made 159 miles in the cycle of 24 hours. The speed decreased towards evening, shortening to four knots. Latitude 41.24 N., longitude 17.46 W.

After reflecting on the fact that as the equator is approached the days get shorter, and after describing the system of bells to mark time aboard ship throughout the day, McJannet turns to the wildlife, describing the stormy petrels which have now replaced the gulls to accompany the ship. Then:

> 8th June, We sighted an Allan Liner at Breakfast time, and, in the afternoon, a Brigantine, both making North Westward. The wind, which has been most favourable from the time we left the Channel, has to-day died down to a calm, and in the evening we are resting gently on the broad bosom of the North Atlantic. … It is beautifully calm, and there is no motion except from the swell of the ocean. The carpenter has made us a Draught Board, and … we will sometimes sit down in the evening to a quiet game.
>
> 10th June, …We are now about 35 degrees North, and South of the Azores; to be exact – in latitude 35.30 N., and longitude 21.22 W. It is very much warmer with a blazing sun overhead. A breeze sprung up this morning, and in the forenoon we were making about four knots.

A passenger's life on *Dalgonar* was good:

> 11th June, Lat. 33.26 N., Long. 21.48 W. I find my average day just now made up in the following manner. At six o'clock in the morning I am awakened by the sailors swabbing the Poop Deck, and shortly afterwards a plunge into the cold sea water, which does not now require any added warmth, gives me, combined with a sharp walk on Deck, an insatiate appetite for Breakfast. After that meal we haul out our Deck Chairs, the awning over mine being now quite indispensable, and, with a book, pass an hour or so. We are hail fellow well met with all on board, and there is always something of interest to distract our attention. We feel ravenous by Dinner time. … Thereafter the afternoon is quietly whiled away with an interval for afternoon tea until Tea. … In the evening when the sun is sinking, the coolest and most pleasant part of the day, the Officers have more leisure for conversation.

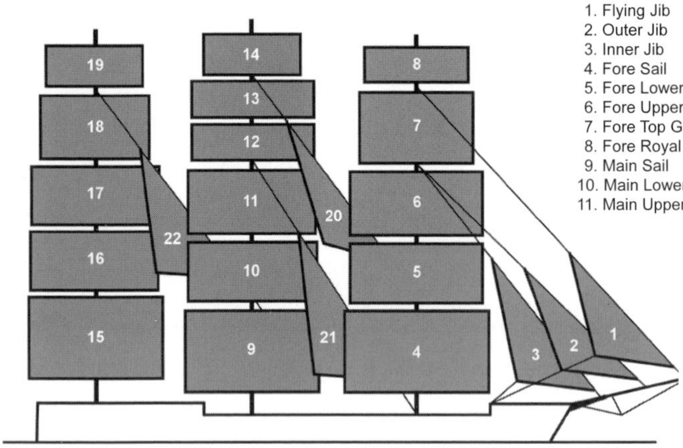

Figure 16.7 *Dalgonar's sails as labelled by Arnold Franz McJannet*

We have many a pleasant game of Draughts, and conversation from grave to gay, from lively to severe. To rest at ten, and I sink back to easy slumbers.

We are having Lime Juice at dinner, which is also served out to the crew at noon. The heavy mainsails have been taken in and replaced by thinner and lighter summer ones more suitable for the light airs. [In his logbook McJannet provided a list of all the sails carried by *Dalgonar*: see Fig.16.7]. We have put out a fishing line with a large hook. To the hook is attached some white linen, and about half a yard of steel twisted into a rope. A fathom or two of thick line attached to a stick tied on to the stanchions aft. The stick is whittled down to a point to bear the drag of the line and hook, but when a large fish bites, the stick breaks and thus shews that we have him on. Of course the line is also attached to the railing. So far we have not been successful but we live in hope.

Our greatest speed is said not to exceed eleven knots, so that we cannot travel faster that a little, a very little, over twelve miles an hour. The *Dalgonar* was not built for speed, but for carrying capacity. She is aptly described at a floating Warehouse. I find the distance in nautical miles from Liverpool to Sydney by the Cape is 12,798 but I expect we shall traverse a much longer distance. … Each day's sailing, … is, roughly, an average of 190 miles in the twenty four hours.

They are a cosmopolitan lot, the crew. Some of their names for instance are:- A. Malit, Wm Sodergoist, David Jenkins, Mathow Schmit, a Dutchman who cannot steer, Wm. Fargher, G. Jansson, Knut Uddgreu, Martin Murphy, of course an Irishman and a regular dare-devil. He has rings through his ears, and tried the Navy for a year. Asked why he did not stick to the service his reply was epigrammatic: Booze! P. Schwarz, J. Schroeder, seems a German, A. Wragg. The Apprentices' names are:- Charles Hore, known as Charley who is in his last year of apprenticeship, George Grimshaw Rose, a nice curly-headed little fellow, 17 years of age, and always smiling, Fred Richardson, John Blakeway Topton, Arthur Griffiths Jones, a Welsh boy – his name gives him away – Walter Owen, a boy of 20 who has been a failure in several other occupations and is

> sent to sea as a last resource, and John Woodcock Marsh. They are all Lancashire lads, chiefly from Liverpool and Manchester, with the exception of Charley, who is from Queenstown in the Emerald Isle. It is impossible to mistake Charley's nationality, because if his appearance does not betray him, his brogue certainly does so.
>
> A light Wind in the forenoon dying down to a calm at midday, and thereafter a dead calm all day. A very warm afternoon – 77° in the shade – necessitating lighter clothing and dispensing of all underclothing. Work ceases at 4 o'clock on a Saturday, and, thereafter, the crew have Boat Drill and the Apprentices muster on the Poop to undergo an [oral] examination by the Captain on the work they have to study for their Examination for Second Mate. [The apprentice doing best] receiving a Cake as reward.

A joke played on the mate with a dummy egg reminds us that the hens aboard provided fresh eggs which had their date of delivery written on them to ensure they were eaten in date order.

> The sun disappeared below the horizon at 7 p.m., tonight, which is 10 minutes to 9 Greenwich time [ship's time was being adjusted to take account of the longitude], We have now practically no twilight, and I am writing – 7-20 p.m., – in oil light. Our mileage for the 24 hours at noon to-day was only 52 miles.
>
> 15th June was Jones' Birthday, and he receives a large Cake as a memento of the date. The fact is perhaps not worth chronicling, but, at any rate, it is of great importance to Jones.

Passing into the tropics on 18 June, McJannet welcomes the first sight of a shoal of flying fish, foresees much hotter weather and records seeing the Southern Cross for the first time. On 18 June they were 'abreast of the Cape Verde Islands, but, as we are roughly 60 miles off them, we cannot sight them'. McJannet hails the sight of shoals of common porpoises playing around the ship, a welcome sign, he suggests, of wind to push the ship onwards.

> Our fishing line has not yet hooked anything. We now have a game of Quoits, which have been made for us, varied, in the evening when darkness sets in about seven, with a game of Draughts. I forgot to mention on Sunday that we had some selections on the Captain's Gramaphone [*sic*] as a treat on that day.

Tantalisingly, we are not told what the music was!

> We have now completely settled down to sea-life routine, and are treated with uniform kindness by all on board. The Captain in particular being one of the most considerate, kindest and most genial of men.

On 19 June within 15° N of the equator, the steamer *Urmston Grange* was sighted making for Madeira, followed shortly after by a large Italian steamer heading in the same direction.

> Both Ships [appeared to be] taking their line from St Paul Rocks, [a short distance] north of the Equator, or from Fernando Noronha, which is south of the Equator off the east coast of South America and north of Pernambuco.

On 20 June the wind was light and the heat terrific.

> Work ceases practically at four in the afternoon to-day … The bosun is a good flute player and he has organised a foc-sel [fo'c'sle] band consisting of the Carpenter, who has managed to fit up a very passable drum out of a Salt Pork tub and wet canvass, and others of the crew as Bones, Triangle and Kettle Drum. The Kettle Drum being an old biscuit tin played with right good will by the old Swede. The band marched round the Deck, headed by a Drum Major waving a pole and followed by the remainder of the crew and Apprentices. Littler and I took the opportunity to pay our footing on board and we asked the Captain to serve them out a tot o' grog. We each received three cheers, and the Band and followers drank our health in one good bumper each. Grog is not a very ancient drink, having been first introduced by Admiral Vernon in 1745, at which date he put an end to the use by the English Navy of Ale, and substituted for it rum diluted with water.

On Sunday 21 June, McJannet:

> Overheard the Half Deck which is the nautical term given irrespectively either to the Apprentices collectively or to the house containing their Bunks, concocting a joke to be played upon Marsh, one of their number, who is a nice boy, but being newly from his Mother's apron strings and having no brothers or sisters, is what might be called a little soft. They represented to Marsh that the Captain made a practice of asking the newest Apprentice-Seaman to dine with him in the Cabin on a Sunday, and that they had been informed by the 3rd Mate that the old man, as the Captain is euphemistically called, in conversation with him (the 3rd Mate) had expressed the wish to have Marsh's presence at Dinner time. Marsh was, at first rather sceptical as to the distinction to be conferred upon him, for, of course, it is considered an honour to receive such an invitation, but I entered into the joke (for another purpose as the sequel will show) and corroborated, with a solemn face, what the Apprentices were telling him, by stating that the Captain had, at Breakfast, mentioned that he must have some of the boys in, and that he would begin with Marsh. This additional testimony dispelled any wavering doubts that the young man had, and he began to brush up his Uniform, took out a collar and black tie, and made himself presentable. In the meantime I informed the old man of the prospective joke, which much amused him. We arranged with the Steward that a place at table should be laid for the boy, and that he be received just as if the Captain's invitation had really been given. At one bell Marsh duly appeared looking spruce and tidy in his new Uniform with brass buttons, but rather flushed in the face owing to an unaccustomed tight collar and the strangeness of his position. On his entering the cabin bearing his blushing honours thick upon him his

Messmates bursting in their glee signalised the completion of their practical joke as they thought by three hearty huzzas. Great was, however, their consternation and chagrin to find that their supposed victim did not reappear. In a tumultuous realisation of the failure of the plan they softly, one by one, crept onto the Poop, and, looking through the open sky-light, beheld Marsh calmly enjoying a good dinner in our Company.

In the intense tropical heat – calms with temperature 90° F (32°C) in deep shade – appetites were poor and McJannet was wearing 'a pair of canvass shoes, flannel unmentionables, a shirt, having the sleeves rolled up to the elbows, and my wide hat, which I could not do without'.

On 24 June, a tropical shower supplemented the water supply.

Immediately all hands, among whom I include my two, were busy collecting rain water. I have been energetically washing, and now look with pride upon towels, shirts &c. hanging on the line to dry, which they do very quickly.

The first four weeks of the voyage must have been sailed in pretty kind weather. McJannet reports that on 25 June:

We are making Eastwards to-day with a southerly breeze. The sea is very lumpy, and the motion is uncomfortable. The Steward put on the table for the first time the wooden guards or racks [known as 'fiddles'] to prevent the dishes waltzing on their own account. However, the breeze has tempered the tropical heat. The rats are becoming more audacious, and two big fellows have [been disposed of].

26th June, Salt fish for Breakfast to let us know it is Friday again. At 8 bells before that meal all hands were on deck to wear ship and we are now steering S.W. It is a beautiful day, not too hot in the shade, and the sea calm.

29th June, The sailors sang with glee The Dead Horse. I overheard some of the hands saying that they would bury the dead horse today. On enquiry as to the meaning of this obscure and mystical expression I found it to mean that the first month's pay being now due, and, it having as a rule been advanced and spent on shore before leaving Port, Jack is now henceforth earning money for himself. The Captain on a hand joining the Ship will grant him, if requested, an advance note of a month's pay payable three days after the ship has left. This note will be cashed by any Seamans' Boarding-House Keeper, who, you may be sure, exacts a very substantial discount for doing so, and Jack then has some ready money to get happy with. The crew came to-night aft and sang their song, being rewarded by a tot o' grog from the Captain.

McJannet was later told the traditional way to Work Out the Dead Horse – see Appendix 2.

1st July, Latitude 3.48½ N. Longitude 17.26 W. We are still tacking trying to get South. Littler and I are like Lilies of the Field – we toil not neither do we spin – but to-day, being the first of a new month, we have set our hands to pulling a rope when the occasion arises. With a Yeo! He! Ho! Once again! Hi! Hup she comes! [McJannet seems to have been an accurate reporter. It is safe to assume that this really is the sequence of shouts and grunts that accompanied the hauling aboard *Dalgonar*.]

3rd July, There is considerable motion to-day and footing is precarious. We are driving on, and hope to cross the line to-morrow. We are fairly in the S.E. trade and will probably sail on this tack – port tack – for a month.

4th July, This is a red letter day in our Calendar as we crossed the line at midnight. Our position to-day at noon being 1°.10 S. Long 21°.16 W. The course is S.26°W. and the distance travelled in 24 hours 142 miles.

Explaining that Captain Isbester disliked the more brutal tradition for line crossing ceremonies, McJannet goes on to describe the good-natured and entertaining humane and civilised process he observed aboard *Dalgonar*:

Neptune and his Court – crew members in outlandish dress – assembled on the decorated fore hatch and were welcomed by the Captain. The passengers were allowed to pay their dues with a couple of bottles of grog. The Captain was appointed Examiner in Chief and five apprentices were dragged forward. They were blindfolded then one was told he was to be fed a spoonful of sugar. Then he was fed … a spoonful of sugar! This process continued with cheese, bread, water and tea. The candidates were then weighed, measured and examined for physical defects of which plenty were found. until the Examiner declared himself satisfied. [For a fuller description see Appendix 3]

5th July, Lat. 4.12 S. Long. 22.1 W. A fine day, but we were shipping a sea or two. We are so accustomed to the motion that we do not feel the slightest inconvenience. There is already a perceptible coldness in the South East Wind, which is sending the good Ship along at eight knots. [Fig.16.8]

7th July, Lat. 9.31½ S. Long. 25.35 W. Course S.34 W. 195 miles. It is too warm to have anything except a sleeping suit covering one at night. The torrid heat through the day is, I am glad to say, greatly tempered by the S.E. wind. We have been on the Port Tack for some days, and there is little or no alteration in the sails. Life on board is monotonous at times – especially when waiting on a meal. All our fresh meat was finished, of course, long ago, and we now subsist on tinned foods. We have a nice Cake to our afternoon Tea, and we wind up the evening with Coffee or Tea and Walnuts. The food is plain, but well cooked and wholesome.

8th July, Lat.12.26½ S. Long. 26.39 W. I do not think that I have mentioned the curious phenomena I saw the other day, one was the extraordinary luminous appearance of the sea at night. This phosphorescent light assumed the form of brilliant stars, or round masses of greenish hue, some small and some 18 inches or so in diameter. They floated by the Ship in such masses as to light up the sea for yards around, and formed also behind her a large and fiery train.

The other was while I was in the bow. I saw we were approaching a large patch of water, which exhibited a brown and dirty appearance. Now, the dark and deep blue ocean presents always the same colour, and I, at first, thought that we were on the edge of a shoal. The brownness of the water arises from the spawn of fishes, which is deposited in such numbers as sometimes to form an area of several miles extent The one I saw was not so large however.

10th July, Latitude 18.04 S. Longitude 27.36 W. Distance 185 miles. We have reached the southern limit of the S.E. trades, and are now sailing in a 4 or 5 knot breeze. The Captain, Mate and Third Mate are all Shetlanders, and they represent in themselves three stages in the age of the Islands. The Mate is an old Shellback of 65, the Captain about 50 [in fact 56], and the Third Mate a young man of 19. The Second Mate, a red-haired youth of 21, is from Birkenhead, and has just obtained his Ticket, as it is called. In other words he has recently passed the Board of Trade Examination for a Second Officer.

Figure 16.8 *The view from the poop, looking forward, the sails drawing nicely*

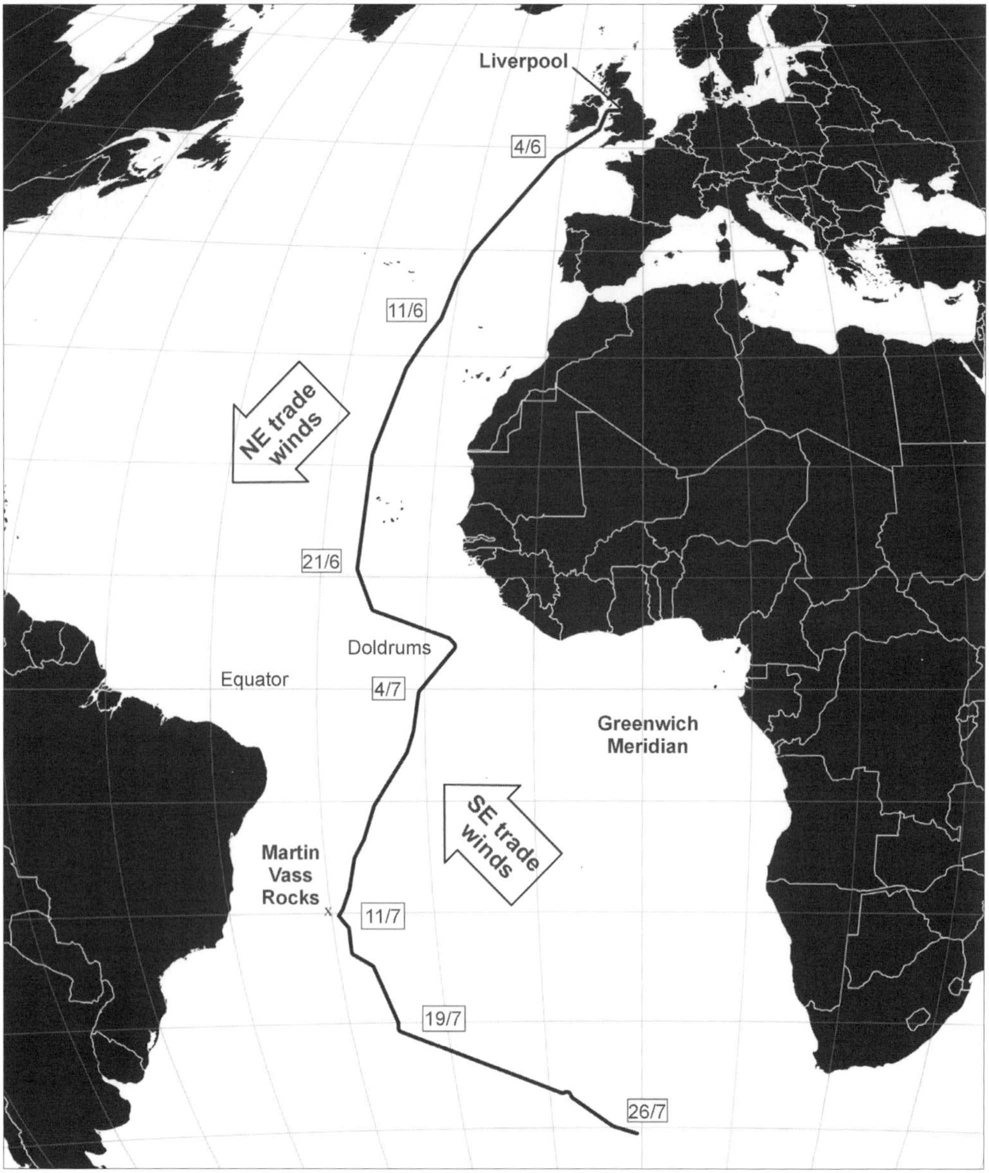

Figure 16.9 Track from Liverpool to Martin Vass Rocks and the Greenwich Meridian

11th July, We are in latitude 19.47½ S. and longitude 28.29. W. and have made very little progress since yesterday. We are in a calm, having passed out of the zone of the S.E. trade. We are close to Martin Vass Rocks. [Fig.16.9] There being no wind it is much warmer but very pleasant. My tobacco has, unfortunately, become very much mildewed, and notwithstanding every effort I made to make it smokable 3 lbs had to be flung overboard. I have, consequently, now to fall back upon the Ship's Tobacco, which is not bad. One very objectionable habit of the sailors is that of

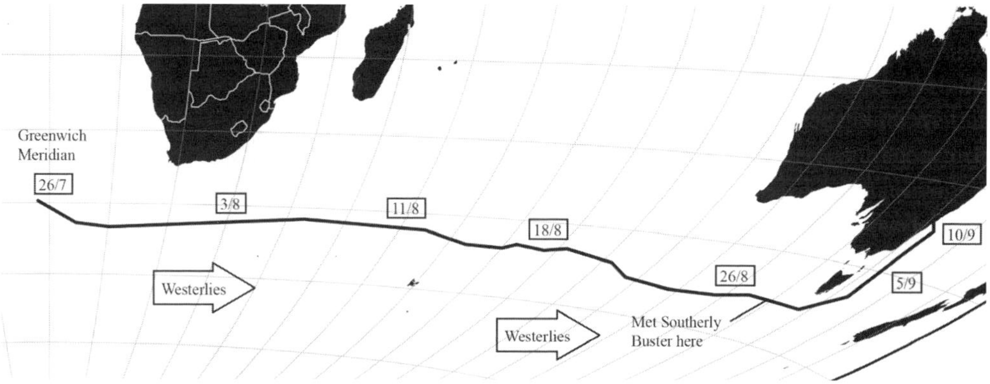

Figure 16.10 *Running the easting down: track from the Greenwich Meridian to Sydney NSW*

> chewing tobacco, and they do not care where they spit. I suppose not being allowed to smoke while on duty they have recourse to this form of enjoying Tobacco. There is no twilight here, and when the sun sinks darkness overhangs like a pall, but these few evenings, after a brilliant sunset, we have had lovely moonlight nights. It is almost light enough to read.

From Martin Vass rocks *Dalgonar* entered the second phase of the voyage, running the easting down (Fig.16.10) described in Chapter 17.

---

1 McJannet, Arnold Franz. *The Log of the Dalgonar*. 1908. (Isbester Collection).
2 Conrad, Joseph. Undated note written after 1913. (Isbester Collection).

17 RUNNING THE EASTING DOWN

During the first part of the voyage from Liverpool, while in the Atlantic, the ship's company had experienced the pleasures of summer sailing. The weather was warm, or often hot, the food was good and the experiences for McJannet were new and interesting. The second part of the voyage, when the vessel turned east, still offered new experiences but there were hardships too, with cold weather, rough seas and a shortage of fresh provisions: in the Southern Ocean it was the depths of winter.

> 16th July, … A heavy swell which rolls us like this and – count seven quickly – like this. … Lat. 25.9½ S. Long. 25.00 W. A heavy squall struck the Ship in the early morning and split up the Main Royal and also the Fore Royal sails. We are sailing with all the Royals down over a very heavy sea. Things that are not tied down securely are flung all over the Cabin. We take our tea out of mugs for security. A full rigged three masted Ship was seen on the horizon beating Northwards. She proved to be French.
>
> Sunday, 19th July, latitude 31.45 S. longitude 20.20½ W. Distance 190 miles. Quite a chapter of events. The cat has had kittens and neglected to nurse them. They died soon after birth. Two Molly Hawks, large Sea-birds, are flying around. I saw a whale. We have made a kite. The Canary has not yet laid an egg. Ham and eggs for Breakfast and a fowl for Dinner.
>
> 20th July. Latitude 33.3 S. Longitude 17.50 W. 150 miles. A most uncomfortable night owing to heavy rollers from the S.W. I have had my Bunk narrowed and narrowed again, so that now when I lie on my back an elbow touches each side. This is necessary as the Ship rolls very heavily, indeed I understand that she makes an angle of 45°. I was fortunate in catching a Cape Pigeon by the wing with some cotton thread. One practically fishes for sea fowl, if a line and hook and piece of salt pork can be called fishing. Sometimes cotton thread is used for a line in the hope that a bird may be caught also by the wing in flying past. A Molly Hawk was also caught and one of the sailors has skinned them and fitted them up for a Taxidermist. We had another Cape Pigeon on Board, and, after I had snapshotted it, we let it go. It is curious that they cannot fly from the Deck, and that they turn sea-sick after a minute or so. The Molly Hawk was a vicious one, and severely scarified Richardson's hands when he held it. Another nearly proved a victim, but as I was hoisting him over the rail the line slipped from the hook and he got off with a troublesome fish hook in his gullet. It died down to a calm this afternoon, after a squally night, and this made the fishing easier. An albatross is our aim.

21st July. Lat. 33.38 S. Long. 17.4½ W. Distance 53 miles. Owing to calms little sailing is being done. The *Dalgonar* rolls heavily, and at Dinner we had difficulty in consuming soup. A lot of Cape Pigeons, Boobys, which are a species of Gannet said to be of a tame and stupid disposition, and to lay their eggs on bare rocks, Albatrosses, three tremendous big ones, and other sea-fowl are constantly flying around.

23rd July. I awoke to find a gale blowing; and all sails, except the Lower and Upper Top Sails and Fore Sail, reefed [He means stowed]. Shortly after Breakfast the Mizzen Upper Top Sail was also taken in. It is a stiff gale, but a moderate sea. We are confined to the Cabin as the cold wind is intense. One satisfaction is that the Ship is steadier, and the motion, when [she] takes a header or a roll, is preferable to the monotonous roll from side to side that she has lately been making. The wind is from the South West and we are driving on Eastwards with a point of two of Southing. We sailed past, during the night, the three Isles, the largest of which is called Tristan da Cunha, being about 40 miles off. They have intercourse with few Ships, but they get news at least once a year as a British Man-

Figure 17.1 Water on deck – looking forward from near the entrance to the saloon

of-War calls yearly with the mails, &c. ... The gale increased in strength in the afternoon, and a very heavy sea was rolling. This is a Wet Ship, as she lies like a log in the water, letting any sea go over her. [Fig.17.1] Matters are not so pleasant now for shore hands. We are confined to the Cabin and the Chart room. It is a great and precarious climb to get up the companion Ladder. I am not exaggerating in saying that the Decks are flush with water, and that waves come over the Poop Deck, 22 feet high. We are now sailing under very little sail – Fore Sail and Fore Lower top Sail, two Main top Sails and Mizzen Lower top Sail. Playing at Draughts is difficult as, notwithstanding all we do, the Draught Men are Knocked about. I have some difficulty in writing and have to wait on a lull before putting pen to paper.

24th July. After an uncomfortable night, morning saw the gale moderating and after Breakfast it died away, but left a high sea. It is now cold on the water, and the stove has been fixed up in the Cabin and set alight. I am now wearing lacing boots, having worn a pair of white shoes up till now. The Deck is made of Pitch Pine Wood with an underlayer of steel. The wood is, however, easily marked, and sailors are careful to wear boots that have no obtruding nails. I have had the nails of the heels of my Boots filed down by the Carpenter. Another hint – get the feet of your Deck Chair covered with Canvas, as otherwise they are bound, with your weight and the motion of the Ship, to make an impression on the Deck. The Captain was able to take the altitude of the sun, and found us to be in latitude 37°18 S. and longitude 7°48 W. having sailed 148 miles from noon to noon.

McJannet describes the routine for taking observations of the sun, noting that there is a delay or about four seconds between the time that the first mate takes the observation on deck and the time he roars 'Time' for the captain by the chronometer in the cabin. McJannet speculates that this delay could cause the calculated position to be 'faulty by a few miles or so', but his fears are groundless – the error would be less than one mile.

25th July. A wet sheet and a flowing sea, and a wind that follows fast is what we found, and we are confined to the Cabin. Rain, flowing sea and wind aft. The Ship takes a sea now and again, and then the main deck is from 3 to 4 feet deep in water until it escapes through the lee scupper holes. In latitude 39.31½ S. longitude 4.48 W. 194 miles.

26th July. Again a nasty roll, and a 3 or 4 knot breeze. We have discontinued a sea water bath in the mornings, as it is now too cold. The Cabin is well heated with the Coal Stove. In latitude 40.40½ S. longitude 1.33½ W, distance 164 miles. There is still a heavy roll occasioned by a heavy sea coming up on the Starboard Quarter. As additional security to the wooden boards on the table we use small bags of sand and canvas with which to safeguard the crockery ware from flying off. My Porridge Plate is, for instance, hemmed in fore and aft and on the Port side by sand bags, the Starboard being safeguarded by the wooden board across the table, Mugs replace cups and saucers, and as for Soup it must be partaken of as quickly as possible from a plate held in the hand. Everything requires to be firmly secured. The Cruet Stand to the table, Boots to my Trunk, and Drawers in my Chest of

Drawers by a wooden latch. You will notice that we are in the rolling forties [i.e. the 40 degree South latitudes] with a vengeance.

27th July. We crossed the Meridian of Greenwich during the night, and our position at noon was – latitude 42.38 S. longitude 2.07 E. the distance travelled being 188 miles. We have now come back to the same time as at home, but we have five hours less daylight. The lamp is lighted at half past four in the afternoon, and it is dark up to half past seven in the morning. A fine bracing day, with sunshine intermittently. The heavy roll is still with us. We reckon that we are now about half way to our destination, but the second half will, in all probability, be quicker covered.

28th July. In latitude 43.56 S. and longitude 6.31 E. At noon we [had] sailed the greatest distance – namely 208 miles – in the 24 hours we have yet done. Running the Easting Down as we are now doing, our daily average of mileage should increase, as we should have the wind pretty well aft, the prevailing wind being westerly.

29th July. Cribbed, Cabined and confined by 9 × 6 × 8 [probably L×B×H in feet], the size of my Room, I spent a sleepless night owing to the wind having died down and causing persistent heavy rolling. Some snow fell during the night hours, and it was much colder than hitherto. The wind freshened in the morning but was unfortunately accompanied with rain, and Littler and I are encompassed in the cabin as it is uncomfortable on deck. We propose to go no farther South than 45° which is far enough south in the Winter here – that is from May to September – owing to the length of the nights (dangerous on account of icebergs) and the extreme cold. The object of going so far south of the Cape of Good Hope is to get stronger and more constant winds, which are found nearer the Poles, and the degrees of longitude are lessened. The highest degree of South latitude it may be prudent to take depends mainly on the season of the year, the ice, the winds, the state of the Ship, and the well being of the passengers and crew. If the winds are not good and strong you require to bear south to look for them. The Southern Summer – August to April – is the best time to make a quick passage as you do not require to go so far South to look for these winds as you will in winter The shortest passages, therefore, will probably be made in the Southern Spring and early Summer, when daylight, the winds, the state of the weather, and all, except ice, are most favourable for reaching high Southern latitudes. [When McJannet discusses navigational matters, I think it reasonable to assume that he is quoting John Isbester or a navigational publication found aboard. Certainly the sensible, informed views he expresses sound like those of an experienced and responsible navigator.]
A [great] circle [track] between two points on the globe is the shortest distance; and we are making what is called a composite track, that is – we have completed a [great] circle [track] from Martin Vass Rock to about here – the shortest distance – and we will now run due East until we get South of Tasmania, when we will, of course, head North. Latitude 44.17 S. Longitude 11.13 E.

31st July. We were roused earlier out of bed by an easterly, and consequently of all things to be abhorred, a head wind. Instead, therefore, of sailing towards

Figure 17.2 Dressed for the weather

the East and towards our Port, we are heading in a South Easterly direction. It is a bitterly cold wind and some snow fell. This is our ninth week out, and the thought that we will never reach land is obtrusive; perseverance and patience will, however, win the race in the end.

2nd August. A Lime Juice Drink is still served out to the crew at twelve noon, but to-day being again cold, owing to the easterly wind, only Jones, the youngest and the smallest water-dog on board, turned out to receive his portion. The Upper Top Sail Yard [Which one? Fore, Main or Mizzen?] came down suddenly with a crash, grazing a man's arm in its fall. As the weight of it is about three tons and the fall sixteen feet [much more than 16 feet – more like 60 feet] it is a mercy that King, the Sailor in question, was not more seriously hurt or instantaneously killed. It appears that there was a flaw in one of the iron clips fastening the yard to the mast, and when it at last gave way the whole yard was precipitated on to the deck. We have had quite a chapter of accidents, and the Steward, in his capacity of Surgeon, has been busy rubbing on embrocation to sprains, boils, swellings &c. The wind gradually died down towards evening, and I am glad that we are now on our course. We feel the monotony and confinement, as with fog and damp and cold we cannot get into the air, but our feeling of ennui should be dissipated by the wild west wind. [Fig.17.2]

3rd August. This is Bank Holiday with you, and I hope you had all a pleasant change to Troon or some trip or excursion. The day makes no difference on Board – the same routine, tempered by the weather, and the same horizon. We are tossing and turning about and making little progress with a wind now aft, but it is variable.

Littler and I have our Deck Chairs set each on one side of the Cabin Stove, and there we sit in the evening after Tea, or through the day if it is a bad one, like Darby and Joan. I have grown very much stouter both in face and in body. The clothes I wore when I came on board are so tight now that, with my heavy underclothing, the waistcoat will not button, and my trousers cannot possibly meet across the abdomen. The Jacket straggles across the chest with difficulty. In fact if I go on increasing in bulk at this rate I will soon have what is called a corporation, and I will require to purchase new suits to be respectable on shore. My increasing stoutness is an unfailing source of wit at table. I am in excellent health, only one's spirits are apt to get damped with the increasing monotony. The crew have been busy all day repairing the damage done by the fall of the yard. A sunshiny day, and we're enabled to find our position to be latitude 43.12 S. and longitude 30.00¼ E.

5th August. Latitude 42.45 S longitude 34.08 E. A day similar to yesterday, only squally and a sea comes onboard now and again.

6th August. A westerly gale was raging when we awoke. We were told that it sprung up suddenly at 4.a.m., and carried away the Foresail. It abated somewhat in the afternoon, but a heavy sea made everybody uncomfortable. We were sailing with only the lower top sail on each mast. In the evening a calm set in, but a heavy sea on each quarter and one astern made sleep to me impossible. Through the night a breeze sprung up, and on 7th August we have an 8 knot breeze, and some sunshine. It is not so cold now and it is longer daylight, our latitude being 42.45 S. Longitude 41.16 E.

8th August. Such a pleasant day we have not experienced since we saw Martin Vass Rocks almost a month ago. Bright sunshine all day with a bracing fair wind aft. We were doing 8 knots and a bit over, but in the evening we have again that bugbear a dead calm. In latitude 42.17 S longitude 45.46 E.

11th August. It is difficult writing with the Ship labouring heavily, but as our latitude is to-day 43.13 S and our longitude 61.14 E we hope for warmer and better weather, which we were told to expect from about longitude 60 E, and penmanship will become easier.

Our manner of life is as regular as that of any monastery. We generally rise now a few minutes before eight, having been awakened by the Steward, and as soon as we have breakfasted our pipes are glowing by the cabin fire till nine or ten. We then take a turn on deck – see what sails she is carrying, how she is steering and how the wind lies. At twelve we dine, and, thereafter, I retire to my books until afternoon tea at three. Then perhaps another turn at gentle exercise – twenty five steps one way and then back again. Tea at half past five, and to books and a game of Draughts, and we have earned a night's repose at ten.

14th August. Latitude 43.7 S. Longitude 74.13 E. Distance 154 miles. The Captain and Officers, with one exception, continue in their thoughtfulness and kindness to their two passengers.

After grizzling about the crusty attitude of the mate and the inadequacies of the steward, McJannet continues:

I cannot say, however, too much in praise of Captain Isbester, and I am most fortunate indeed in having such a cheery, honest, kind-hearted and homely skipper, and anything I may have previously written about him – and I can only write in his praise – is now, through a better acquaintance, heartily endorsed.

I must also say a word about the Cook, the black sheep of a good family in the North of Scotland. He has had a rough and hard time of it during the bad and dirty weather we have had. Seas continually washing through his Galley, and he complains he is never dry from early morning – half past four – till his work is done at nine at night. He is a small, knock-kneed undersized wizen faced man, and was with the Captain twenty years ago as Cook.

16th August. That bald Sexton Time has given us our twelfth Sunday on board, and it has been signalised by a larger sea than usual coming over and washing right along the passage to the Cabin, penetrating and filling the Second Mate's Room, the Steward's Pantry, and with a last convulsive effort trying to put out our stove. In latitude 43° 49 S. Longitude 82° 48 E. Dist. 235 miles.

Quantities of water on deck and washing into the accommodation were facts of life on the sailing ships of this period. The regulations eventually achieved by Samuel Plimsoll a few years earlier allowed *Dalgonar* a freeboard of at least 6 feet, which means that in calm water when the ship was upright the ocean would be at least 6 feet below the deck. However, as readers will have realised, the seas were rarely calm and a ship under sail is seldom upright. Provided that the hatch covers were well secured – a vital consideration – the ship was not in danger of sinking, but with water on deck seamen and apprentices could go for weeks continuously in wet clothes, and if unwary could be knocked over and even swept overboard by heavy seas.

19th August. 43° 21 S. Lat, 96° 19 E. Long. Course E ½N. Distance 192 miles. The labouring of the *Dalgonar* was very heavy all day, so much so that it was impossible to stand on the Poop Deck without holding on to something. The Sailors forming the crew are hardly worthy of the name Sailor. The name as applied to them is a misnomer; if by a sailor is meant a man rejoicing in the strong winds, able, good hearted and open handed, and taking hardships as they come without a grumble. [It is likely that McJannet is quoting the views of John Isbester here.] The men here, with hardly any exception, live for food and grog and … a slight injury to limb or finger disables them from work for a few days. If they would be longer than that, and the Captain thinks the sick hand a malingerer, he has a short and ready way with him. Being sick he is naturally placed on a low, very low, diet, and, of course, he is not able to smoke. He is further told that he is very ill, and a Bible is placed beside him for his edification – the first time probably that he has seen a Bible since his Boyhood – and when he wishes to go forward an Officer goes with him, taking his arm, in case the poor fellow should faint on the way. He is thus debarred from smoking, from light literature and from all conversation, besides being slowly starved. The Captain says it is surprising how quickly they recover through his gentle and considerate treatment. He has never failed yet, no matter how bad the case was. Fancy that!

22nd August. Latitude 45.6½ S. Longitude 110.34¾ E, Course S. 78 E. Distance in 24 hours sailing 167 miles. A day similar to that of yesterday, only much colder, the Thermometer registering 41° Fahrenheit. We are to-day 85 days out from Liverpool, and I must candidly confess that I will not be sorry to see land again. We have today ended a week's competition at Draughts between the trio of us in the Cabin, the Captain, Littler and myself, and, after a hard fought fight, the Captain came out first. I was a fairly good second, and Littler, usually a slow but cautious player, a bad third.

23rd August. We are some 600 miles South of Australia. Marsh, the Peter Simple Apprentice, yesterday complained to the Steward that he had had a sleepless night, and was feeling very unwell. The Steward reported this to the Captain, and Marsh was ordered to appear before him. I overheard the dialogue between Marsh and the Captain, being in my cabin at the time just before Breakfast. Captain, in a deep gruff voice for the occasion 'Well! boy what's the matter?' Marsh, with a very doleful look in anticipation of immediate sympathy, 'Please Sir, I have pains all over me.' Captain, in a rising crescendo of astonishment, 'What!' Marsh 'Pains all ov---e---e---r S---i---i--r.' Captain, 'H-m-m GET ON DECK!!!' Poor Marsh, disconsolate, departs for the Poop Deck, from which he is shortly afterwards brought down to the Captain and given a strong doze of Black Draught, being ordered to take his Breakfast, and, thereafter, report himself on the Poop. Marsh duly appeared, having donned his overcoat, and a face dismal in the extreme. He was commanded to walk up and down the Poop Deck, and given a Bamboo Cane to support his seeming trembling limbs and faltering footsteps; the Captain occasionally walking with him to accelerate his speed. He then ran through the Musket Exercise to remove the stiffness in his joints. He was, to put it shortly, kept on the move till 8 bells (12 noon) when it was his watch below. Needless to say his recovery was as complete as it was rapid. The Captain saw from the first that the boy was shamming and that he had the foresight to complain when it happened to be his watch on deck. From information that I can rely on I was told that Marsh's watch below (from 12 noon until 4 p.m.) was much interrupted, the Black Draught proving exceedingly virulent.

24th August. I awoke this morning after a most refreshing sleep, the Ship being steady during the night and the heavy sea having moderated. Bright sunshine in the early morning, but some rain afterwards. We have had really bad and dirty weather running the Easting Down, and it is, in the opinion of the Mate and the Bosun, the worst passage in these latitudes that they have individually experienced. The Decks have been awash since the 16th day of July with scarcely any intermission with the heavy seas. All on board have felt the discomfort, and especially the crew has suffered severely – scarcely ever having a dry stitch of clothing on them. Oil-skins are certainly of some use, but they offer little protection to a cold sea washing down the neck. The men must just take a sea when it comes in the best way possible, as they cannot leave hold of a rope that they are at the moment pulling on. The Decks too are so slippery with the salt brine that walking in heavy sea boots is precarious, and falls are numerous. One hand – Long Murphy as he is called in contradistinction to Little Murphy, two Irishmen of the same name but not of the same kindred – is laid up by a severe blow he sustained by a larger sea than usual coming onboard. I forgot to jot down the other day that I saw the Aurora Australis, a similar phenomenon in the Southern Hemisphere to the Aurora Borealis in the Northern. It was a long streamer of light shining above a cloud.

We sailed 249 miles from noon to noon, and our position is in latitude 45.49½ S. longitude 120.41½ E.

25th August. The food, being the same week by week, is beginning to pall on one, and it is noticed that our sea appetites have not such a sharp edge to them as heretofore. Of course a supply for one here would serve a small family easily on shore. The bald-headed Cook, as the Steward calls him, is getting careless, I suppose through being heartily sick of the difficulties that beset his office. He makes splendid bread, however, as good as any of our home bakers could bake. Mike, the Kitten, has grown into a big Tom Cat, and he has already proved himself a victor over several misguided rats who assayed a tussle with him. Betsy Jine, his mother, is of a very quiet and retiring disposition, passing her life peaceably by the Cabin Stove. The Canary gives a feeble chirrup now and again, and takes his food like a sailor.

27th August. We are 90 days out from Liverpool to-day. It is a long time to be without information of the world's doings. In latitude 45° 15 S. longitude 135° 37 E. and we are making better progress than we have done.

28th August. Our position at noon was 45.22 S. lat., 140.35 E. long., and our rate of progress during the week was 10 miles per hour. It is considered that this is remarkably good sailing. We have had the Patent Log fixed up, and it records about an average of 110 knots [actually nautical miles, not knots, the latter being a measure of speed] in the 12 hours. There is a fairly extensive Medicine Chest on board, and the Steward is able to cope with the minor ailments that afflict the men. The Steward is an all round man, and he includes the profession of Doctor and Surgeon among his numerous avocations

29th August. I was writing the foregoing lines last night having just finished a game of Draughts with the Captain, and when he and Littler were intently engaged in a similar game, eight bells having just been struck ending the last Dog Watch, I suddenly heard a loud roaring sound of wind, and paused, pen in hand, expectantly. The Captain, at the same moment, looked up from the Draught Board. The next instant he made one bound out of the Cabin, ran up on deck, and shouted 'Hard down! Hard down! Hard down!' The noise had been increasing in violence, and we – Littler and I in the Cabin – sat spellbound, not knowing what was going to happen. Tremendous rain pattered on the Deck and Sky-Light above us and with the hissing of the wind, and enormous seas we could also hear coming onboard we were quite frightened. Next we heard confused shouts in the pitch darkness, and then we could distinguish the captain's voice yelling 'All hands on deck!' Littler, who says he had not heard the sudden gusts of wind, on hearing this seized his coat and cap and was making for the Deck. He was very much excited, and indeed the events warranted it. I remained seated where I am now writing, and though I was much alarmed I managed to calm him, pointing out that he would be of no earthly use on deck, but that, on the other hand, he would be in the way. I said we were helpless, and that we were best where we were, and where the Captain would know to get us should anything happen. He eventually calmed down, agreeing with my proposition. We had been struck by what is locally known as a Southerly buster. In the Australia Directory, compiled chiefly from various surveys made by order of the Admiralty, seamen are warned to be prepared against these Southerly busters, as the first gust is generally of a violent character and apt to occasion damage, unless due precautions have been taken. We had been experiencing a strong westerly wind which, you will have noticed, continued for several days driving us on to Tasmania at 10 knots per hour [*sic*]. At the time stated the wind suddenly jumped to the South South East, and the Southerly buster, in all its fury, was upon us. As a rule, the Directory goes on to say, these changes can be foreseen by clouds rising to the Southward; sometimes, however, very little warning is given, and the change takes place with a cloudless sky. The Captain had remarked that the Barometer was falling, and on hearing the first sudden gust he knew what had happened. His first object was to get the ship before the wind and he ordered the ship Hard Down to prevent any damage.

(Captain Isbester, in common with all British seamen, was in 1908 still using helm orders carried over from much earlier times – orders which reflected the position of the (by then often imaginary) tiller rather than the rudder, and which had not been amended when the wheel replaced the tiller! McJannet's log records that the order he actually gave was 'Hard up!', which nowadays would suggest a turn into the wind rather than away from it. European nations had from the 1870s begun to correct this anomaly, but it was only in 1933 that British shipping made the change, a change which must have been at least as momentous as when the Swedes changed from driving on the left to driving on the right.[1]) McJannet continues:

We ran before the storm until nearly all sail was taken in, and in about a couple of hours it had much subsided and we were on our course under three lower top sails. It had driven us North Eastwards towards land. The Captain then came down to reassure us. He was simply drenched from head to foot having, as explained, run on Deck without Cap or Oilskin. We learnt that the Mate, who had just gone below, on hearing the shout for all hands, essayed on Deck. He had just got one leg over the washboard, which is put in, during rough weather, at the entrance to the passage to here [ie to the saloon or cabin], when the sea caught him and washed him down to the Starboard side, and then, on the Ship rolling, to Port, where he stuck in the Bitts, as they are called, and had to be hauled out forcibly. He was not hurt but, of course, as my Father would say, he got wet. A half tumbler of grog soothed the Old Mate's ruffled feelings when he came below to change. But it did not alter his exacerbated temper. The Bitts, you must know, are the posts, so called, to which the Ship's moorings, or ropes are made fast. The sudden change in the wind was entirely unforeseen, and though temporary excitement was rampant, no damage to the ship was done. The sea which carried away the Mate also came in along the passage, so that the sea must have been about four feet or so in depth, as the step and wash-board are 3½ feet high. This necessitated bailing out.

Such a pleasant day as we have to-day may be said to properly belong to those described in the earlier pages of this Journal. We have a head wind, however, and there is little progress North Eastwards to get round Tasmania, or Van Diemens Land. This being a quiet day for work, and the weather genial, of course the men forard must wind it up with a fight between two of them. A good hard tussle with plenty of stiff blows. Malcolm, a nice, good natured New Zealander, who I like, and who is the pick of the bunch forard, and Foster, a Minister's son, were the contestants. The cloth was badly defeated. In latitude 45° 8 S. and longitude 147° 33¾ E at noon.

The crew are supplied with Tobacco from the Captain's Stores, receiving a lb every three weeks. They are charged for it at cost price which is cheap as it is duty free 3 shillings per lb. Last Saturday night the whole crowd came aft and requested Tobacco, when they had been supplied with their regular quantity of a lb. each only a fortnight ago. The Captain peremptorily refused them any. They, of course, have no cash to pay, and the quantity and price of the Tobacco each Hand receives is marked against him, and deducted from his pay at the end of the voyage on return to a home port when the crew is paid off. Their request for my lady Nicotine a week too soon is an indication of their intention to desert at Sydney because they have an inkling that we will arrive there by the end of the week, and the more they get out of the old man the better for themselves.

We are in latitude 43.39 S, longitude 149.58 E. and abreast of Hobart to the East, but a long way off land. Another good day, but still a head wind. We take an occasional sea, and Ross, an Apprentice who boasted that he had never been caught by a sea coming over, was nabbed by an extra large one as he was walking along the Deck, and to the amusement and gratification of his companions, thoroughly drenched from tip to toe. His boasts were damped.

4th September. Latitude 39° 49 S. Longitude 151° 44¼ E. Still being baffled about with a head wind. Steering N.E. We wore Ship in the evening to N.W. and the Captain and I hauled the weather main tgallan brace taut, and thus I earned my Supper.

6th September. Latitude 38° 10½ S. Longitude 152° 3½ E. A hundred days out from land. Pleasant weather with occasional squalls. We had our usual Sunday Dinner. Item. A fowl was dragged through some luke-warm water – Chicken Soup. Item. Two of the Roosters were slaughtered yesterday. Boiled Fowl. Potatoes, Carrots (tinned). Item. Some hard brown whitish substance called Pudding. Item. Lime juice.

Figure 17.3 *Entering port after a stormy voyage*

7th September. Similar weather. We can now dispense with the stove, and, at intervals, can enjoy the sunshine sitting in our deckchairs on deck. The crew are engaged giving the Ship a wash down trying to make her presentable going into Port.

[At the end of a stormy voyage a ship would look very dilapidated, with paint stripped from the steel hull and rust stains widespread, [Fig.17.3] but the wooden decks could be made immaculate, the brass could be burnished and any trace of rubbish removed.] At noon in latitude 37°39 South, Longitude 152°4½ East. After Dinner a Strong Wind sprang up from the South West to the rejoicing of all, for it is what all have been hoping for and some praying for – A fair Wind! It increased in strength as the day went on, and we're at times easily making 11 knots.

8th September. We sighted Land about 1.00 am, and we made it to be the two heads of Jarvis Bay. I do not suppose that we can possibly make the offing of Port Jackson to-day, but we should surely anchor to-morrow. I am glad that we are now in sight of our destination. Our supply of Potatoes is exhausted, and we have to fall back upon the tinned variety, our Ash [hash] consisting of tinned meat with absolutely no flavour – the meat being tasteless, fibrous matter – and as for the tinned Potatoes – well you might as well be eating soap. There is no difference in taste, and the appearance is much the same. We feel the want of some tinned fruits which would lend some variety to our meals. It is said that some are aboard, but they have never been found. The tinned vegetables are also not up to much. We have three classes: Peas, Carrots and Turnips. The Peas are not bad, but please do not mention either the Carrots or Turnips. However, we hope soon to be at an end of these little hardships when we hope to enjoy first a good fresh hot water bath, and secondly a good fresh meat square meal with fresh adjuncts.

The boys in the Half-Deck, who were rejoicing exceedingly at the fair wind, are now greatly disheartened. It may be not amiss to give you an idea of their mode of living and how they learn their profession.

They enter into an Indenture with the Owners, paying at the same time a premium of Fifty pounds. They are indentured for four years. They sleep, eat, spend their leisure, and do their studies in a small iron house amidships which is always in semi-darkness, even on a bright day. What with their bunks and chests lining three walls of the house, and a board for a table lining the fourth side, there is not room to swing a cat inside. In dirty weather it is constantly awash both inside and out. It is bearable in fine weather, but the fetid air that meets one on looking inside in bad weather is horrible. Now, they learn the use and the name of each rope &c. &c. and everything needful and useful in their business, but, at the same time, a great part of their time is occupied in cleaning brass work, scrubbing, cleaning the hen coop, carrying coals, water, our Dinner &c. from the Cook's Galley, and keeping the time [by striking the ship's bell]. They are divided into watches just like the men, and have to turn out at all times and in all sorts of weather just like them. The food that they get is no better than the crew's, with this exception that they may occasionally obtain some of the leavings of the Cabin Table. Remember they are young gentlemen of good family! On this Ship, and I am told it is the exception, they receive good treatment in so much that they are never kicked or cuffed, and that the Captain takes some degree of interest in them. He has a School every Saturday afternoon in fine weather, and the [leader] of the class obtains, as a reward of merit, a cake baked by the Steward. On the whole they are a happy lot, and like to appear and to be called Hard Cases; a generic term for endurance, devil-may-careism, and good nature. Part of their premium is repaid to them yearly.

The Owner has a very good bargain, do you not think so? He obtains payment of a considerable sum – we have seven Apprentices so the premiums amount to £350 – and at the same time obtains labour, giving, in exchange, miserable accommodation and food for boys in their situation in life. The profession of the sea is after all a monotonous and poorly paid one, and, after what I have experienced and witnessed, I would give the same advice to an aspirant for the sea as Punch gave to young men about to get married. DON'T!

We had the company of a monster Whale where we lay in latitude 34° 02 S., longitude 152° 10¼ E. A four masted barque is on our Starboard bow just visible, and a tramp steamer sailed past us just visible through the glass. These were the only signs of life on this idle ocean.

10th September. We were only thirteen miles south of Port Jackson on turning in last night, and on awaking this morning we found ourselves, to our great surprise, some forty to fifty miles North of that Port. We had a 5 knot breeze but thought we were making no headway owing to a strong current. As we got inland the current must have been absent, and the wind drove us North. After Breakfast we saw North Head Lighthouse when we were bearing South having wore ship. About one a.m., smoke was seen on the horizon and soon a tug came into view of our glasses. She proved to be the Gamecock of Newcastle, and said she had been looking for us to the Southward for some days. She handed a Sydney Newspaper on Board. How would my Father like to be without a Newspaper for one hundred and four days? From it we see that Lord Dudley is the new Governor General of Australia, and that he landed in Sydney yesterday. Everybody now wears a large smile, and, if appearances are not deceptive, they are thoroughly glad that our long, and at times uncomfortable, journey is nearing its end. (Later) We entered Port Jackson … about seven in the evening, and anchored in one of the Bays for the night.

---

1 Harland, John. *Seamanship in the Age of Sail,* Bloomsbury Publishing plc, London, 2015, pp.176–177.

18 LIFE AND DEATH

While in Sydney, Captain Isbester had a day in court.[1]

> Thomas Black, 54 and Patrick King, 26, were charged at the water police court with having, while engaged as seamen on the British registered vessel *Dalgonar*, on or about August 20th last, between London and Sydney, embezzled certain cargo of the vessel namely, 1720 yards of shirting, value £35 16s 3d, the property of John Isbester, master of the *Dalgonar*.
>
> Captain Isbester stated that the vessel left Liverpool on May 20th [*sic*] last. Among the cargo there were several bales of shirting totalling in all 2200 yards and 10 bundles of twine. On September 16th Black deserted the ship and witness took charge of his chest in which he found a ball and a half of twine and two pieces of shirting. Two pillowslips were found in King's chest. In all 1720 yards of shirting and £2 8s worth of twine were missing.
>
> Hubert Porter, an able seaman on the *Dalgonar*, said that while on the high seas he saw King take off a hatch and go down into No.1 hold with a candle. About 20 minutes afterwards he returned with a bundle.
>
> Charles Hore, an apprentice on the *Dalgonar*, said that on the way out he bought a hammock from Black for a shilling and some coffee. The hammock was made of twine similar to that produced.
>
> The men had nothing to say except to deny the charges.
>
> For embezzling the shirting the accused were each sentenced to 10 weeks with hard labor and for embezzling the twine Black received ten weeks imprisonment.
>
> On a further charge of deserting from the *Dalgonar*, to which he pleaded guilty, Black was sentenced to 12 weeks gaol.

Stealing cargo was most likely to be a problem when general cargo – assorted manufactured goods – were carried, as was the case on this voyage. No.1 hold was most distant from the poop and therefore least likely to be overseen, but Black cannot have been well liked aboard if fellow seamen were prepared to give evidence against him. One wonders whether, in fact, Black and King were the only culprits. The severity of the sentences was, presumably, the norm for those times.

Exceptionally from Newcastle, NSW, we have the postcards that John Isbester sent to two of his sons on the same day. To the eight-year-old Allan he sent a view of the Paramatta river and wrote 'Dear Allan. I got your letter all right. I am sorry to hear that you have not been well but hope you are better long ago. We are still not commenced to load. X Father.'[2] Five-year-old

Norman received a view of Balmoral Beach and North Head, Sydney, and the message 'Dear Norman, You were surely kicking the big bare [*sic*] out of your bed but got your leg strained. I hope it is all right again. X Father.'[3] Characteristically, each child received an individual message on a distinctive postcard.

Dalgonar followed the familiar route across the Pacific with coal from Newcastle for Coquimbo, then loaded a full cargo of wheat in Talcahuano, Chile, for Queenstown for orders. At Queenstown the orders were for Hull where she arrived late in September 1909, some 16 months after her departure from Liverpool with McJannet aboard. A stay of more than two months in Hull (Fig.18.1) was doubtless welcome, as was the relatively short travel time between Hull and Ilford. Susie stayed aboard the ship for some time and sent an affectionate postcard to son Allan when he and his siblings had to return to Ilford, probably for school after the half term holidays. She wrote:

> Oh but it was lonely without you all last night. I could do nothing but cry, the ship felt so empty. I do hope you had a nice journey. Didn't we all have a lovely time when you were here – love to all. Mother[4]

Allan was not singled out for special attention; there would have been an individual postcard bearing a halfpenny stamp for each of the children.

After a return to Ilford she wrote:

> Father was so glad to have me back – & had been so lonely that on Monday he nearly wired for me to come. So you must not grudge me to father for I assure you he is just the best father any little boy could have.[5]

Figure 18.1 *Alexandra Dock, Hull, from Susie's postcard*

Figure 18.2 *The family about 1911. From left: Allan, Arthur, Kathleen, Captain John, Susie, Norman and Eric*

It may be that Allan was finding his father's absence difficult. John Isbester sent him a sensitive postcard, reading:

> Dear Allan, I think I am lonely without you but you have sense to know that it cannot be helped. You must attend school and I must attend to the ship. No word of us going to sea yet so we may meet again.[6]

The card was signed 'With love from Mother and Father' but was clearly written by his father. Happily, the family (Fig.18.2) was to be all together in South Shields for Christmas and the New Year.

From Hull, *Dalgonar* moved to the Tyne to load coal for Seattle. In South Shields she moored at the Jarrow Slake buoys staying on the Tyne for a period that happily included Christmas and the New Year and sailing for Cape Horn and Seattle on 6 January 1910. John Isbester was able to send Susie some money before the ship sailed, writing:

> My dear Susie,
>
> Got your wire this morning, glad you had a fairly good journey. I hope you are none the worse of it. Everything points to getting away tomorrow. Enclosed find cheque for £12.00 … Love to all Your own Jack

Later in the day he took up his pen again:

> My Dear Susie
>
> This just a line to confirm that we are all ready for sea in the morning pilot and Tugs ordered. I wrote you a line or scrible today. Sent you a cheque for £12 and

£3 postal orders. The stevedore gave me £3 – I have got my slippers and have got 12/- in my pocket yet. I will need to give Charley a shilling or two and the pier head etc. Your wire came tonight while I was ashore after the slippers. I am glad everything is all right with Arthur. I think he is very lucky. Kath seems to think he is downhearted. The cook has been to work today and things are shaping better. Only two or three of the sailors came as they found out that the ship doesn't go before tomorrow. I am done with the Owner's letter and it is now 10.30PM, so will go to bed. I haven't filled the hot water bottle. The weather is very fine and Mild. This will be posted from the pier head, Charley of course. So tata and Love to all your Jack

8AM Just going to run up and post this myself and wire you in another hour we will be getting in motion byby Love to all, your Jack

It is good to see that the Old Man, doubtless encouraged by Susie, had equipped himself with slippers and a hot water bottle! Arthur had emigrated to New Zealand, and there is an undercurrent of uneasiness in family references to him. The £3 from the stevedore would probably have been a normal payment to ensure co-operation and smooth working relations. This practice was widespread at the end of the 19th century, and probably still exists today in some corners of the maritime world. Fifteen years earlier Sir Francis Jenne, President of the Admiralty Court, had ruled in a case in which the master had, over the course of the voyage, been given payments of £10, £10 and £5 by stevedores and the managing owners were claiming the money was theirs:

> I regard the gratuities as presents simply given by the Merchant to the Captain for doing his duty both to the Merchant and to his Owners, and for doing it extra well[7]

Figure 18.3 *Lewis Davies, first mate*

Serving as first mate this voyage was Lewis Davies, aged 30, from Llechryd, in Ceredigion, west Wales. (Fig.18.3) Like Captain Isbester he had started his seagoing career on deck, serving both in sailing and steam ships as an able seaman, having probably worked initially as a fisherman. His first job as an officer was as second mate of the barque *Harlech Castle* in 1904, and following two years in this rank he was appointed first mate of the three-masted iron barque *Carnarvon Castle* in October 1906, having gained his mate's certificate of competency. The similarities to Captain Isbester's career do not end there, as this newspaper report reveals:

> The steamer [*sic*] Carnarvon Castle, bound from Liverpool to Melbourne full of general cargo, was in Latitude 42[S] Longitude 104

> E., when a fire was discovered in the midships hold. Anderson, the cook, who first discovered the fire, states that the captain ordered the covering to be taken off the main hatch. The cargo was jettisoned and the deck between the main hatch and the galley was torn up in two places. Water was then poured in by means of buckets and pumps. The fire seemed to come from the lower tween deck. [The cargo is elsewhere[8] described as spirits and other inflammable goods.] All hands fought the flames until ten o'clock that night, but the fire gained so rapidly that the whole of the tweendeck between the bows and the mainmast was one mass of flames, and the heat was so terrible that all hands were driven to the afterdeck, all, more or less being seriously burned. The captain then told them it was hopeless to attempt to save the ship, and ordered the lifeboats to be got ready for sea.[9]

Another report[10] states 'Two boats were launched, the captain and sixteen men going in the lifeboat and the chief officer Lewis Davis (*sic*) and ten men in the other boat.'

The person quoted in the remainder of this report is not identified but he was in the lifeboat of first mate Lewis Davies. He was a competent observer who kept track of the weather and the lapse of days. This may have been Lewis Davies himself (though the words do not sound like those of the person in charge of the navigation), or it may have been Anderson the cook or another experienced hand. The report continues:

> When the crew of the *Carnarvon Castle* left the burning vessel, in each boat were placed jars of water totalling 25 gallons for ours and 30 gallons for the captain's. The boats stood by the ship all night. The vessel was wrapped in flames from stem to stern, from the deck to the trucks. About midnight the mainmast fell against the mizzen and caused the mizzen topgallant mast to fall overboard. By daylight the ship was smouldering and clouds of steam were rising from the red-hot sides. It was impossible to board her again, and the captain gave orders to shape a course East by North by half North, and make the best speed for [Cape] Leeuwin, which was about 1,100 miles[11] off. Each boat was 22 feet long with five foot beam and lugger rigged. Our boat made considerably more headway than the captain's for the first six days, and we had to put back several times to keep company; The weather was moderate at first, but there was a stiff blow from the north east on the seventh day out. A strong breeze then sprang up from the northward, and in the morning we could see nothing of the captain's boat. We were put on rations of two pots of meat and meal among eleven men, and two condensed milk tins of water a man a day. After separating from the captain we encountered a strong south east gale, and were hove to for 40 hours. With great difficulty the boat was kept from swamping. The wind continued for the next two days from the same quarter but it did not blow so hard, so we were able to make a fairly good run. On the night of the eleventh day the South East wind strengthened to a gale, and all the bread was spoiled by the seas. We had to heave to. Starvation was then facing us and the water was running short, each man having half a milk tin a day. We had now only meat to eat and the biscuits sodden with salt water. Then the men began to drink salt water. ... I used to drink eight or ten mouthfuls of salt water every twentyfour

> hours and, owing to taking only small quantities was none the worse. The weather was then moderate until three days before we reached Fremantle, when there was a stiff South Westerly wind. Just before we got this breeze we were becalmed for a day, a shark swimming around the boat for three hours. We sighted the smoke of two steamers, but those on board did not see us. At four o'clock on Sunday morning we rounded Rottnest Island and started to run across to Fremantle. We were entirely exhausted and as we climbed on the wharf we fell down. We suffered terrible privations through hunger, thirst and loss of sleep, and being continually wet through, none of us closed our eyes for the last three days and nights. In the gale on the eleventh day several times we thought we would be lost and almost gave up hope.

When landed in Fremantle they were housed in the Sailors' Rest 'where every care was bestowed on them'.[12] The captain's boat reached Cape Naturaliste, 100 miles from Fremantle, later the same day. Three of his crew died during the final days of their ordeal. Writing many years later John Davies, son of Lewis, recorded that his father had been presented by the Mayor of Fremantle with an inscribed watch for his services 'in navigating for 25 days in an 18ft open boat of ship *Carnarvon Castle*, abandoned on fire Lat 43S, Long 97E'.[13]

Astonishingly, on 9 March, only 14 days after he had staggered ashore in Fremantle, Lewis Davies joined the three-masted full-rigged ship *Iredale* in Wallaroo, South Australia, as first mate![14] He made two voyages on the *Iredale*, spending a total of almost two years aboard her before obtaining his master's certificate in the autumn of 1909. He signed Articles aboard *Dalgonar* a day or two before she sailed for Seattle, but from the letter to Mrs Isbester[15] in which he mentions that he has been corresponding with her daughter Kathleen, we can deduce that he had been aboard the ship for some days or weeks in South Shields and that romance had flourished over the festive period. The main theme of his letter, written from Quarter Master Harbour in Washington, was a sombre one. Lewis Davies had to write a pleasant letter to his potential future mother-in-law while discussing events involving the captain, her husband. He made a reasonable hand of this difficult job.

> Dear Mrs Isbester
>
> Your favour of the 3rd Inst, duly to hand safe. Thanks very much for same and pleased to learn you to be well.
>
> The stone which was sent from the North Sea was picked up by the hauser and not with the anchor. It was the Captain who suggested that this stone should be sent, and I complied with the order. Expecting to hear about it on arrival here, but no word neither from you nor Kathleen, I thought sure I had offended you. I often hear from her and I am always pleased to hear of her welfare and also the boys.
>
> Yes it was rather a trying time getting clear of the North Sea, more especially beating all the way out into clear waters. What anxiety you must have endured until the good ship was spoken. Your anxiety then would have been a trifle eased, but again the trip was so long, causing you renewed anxiety. On the whole the trip proved rather comfortable, if only we could have avoided the accident to the

Figure 18.4 Dalgonar, *looking aft from a position about one-third of the way up the foremast. The white apprentices' halfdeck (i.e. cabin) is in the foreground. Beyond is the poop, with lifeboats to port and starboard and the smaller gig.*

unfortunate boy Collins; the other death was a natural one and did not spread a gloom over the ship's company. I'll endeavour to relate you the life of Collins for the brief time he was on board, during same he always seemed to be perfectly happy after recovering his seasickness, and always a favourite on board especially with the Captain. Often he used to tell him yarns and the boy tell him, always very interested in the proffession [*sic*], even the Captain was instructing him in the Rule of the Road, stars and shipwork. a very intelligent willing and obedient, well brought up and always civil. No sooner had he recovered from his seasickness he asked if he could go aloft, but this was forbidden until well in the tropics. One day I told him he could come along with me and seemed delighted. This day being Sunday I was at liberty to spend a few hours with him also instructing him in the art of climbing etc. [Fig.18.4] Telling him to be always carefull one hand for himself and the other for the ship After this we could not stop him climbing. Often I cautioned him also the men did so. You can see I can growl too when there is occasion. The boy was very careless aloft, his whole ambition was in climbing, anxious to know everything. On Sundays he used to take his Bible into the Main top [Figs 18.5 & 18.6] to read. Probably he thought that he would not be disturbed [there]. All I regret is that the accident had never happened, and as regard the treatment he received both before the occurrence and after. No father could have done more for his own son than what Captain Isbester done for him, he seemed very interested in the boy. On the morning of the death I was below from 4 to 8 AM. On entering the saloon where the boy laid, I saw the Captain bending over him and crying bitterly as though he was his own child. I can assure you it touched me much. He was buried the same day with all due respect to the body. Captain read the burial service but he was so deeply touched we knew he could not see the part as he was blinded with tears and chocked with grief. I can quite sympathise with his dear Parents especially the Mother when they learnt the terrible news. The boy was perfectly happy and always in good sound health, enjoying his first experience to sea to the full. It was nobody's fault that the boy was aloft on this particular night. The both first voyagers were told not to go aloft and especially on rough and dark nights. This boy insisted on following wherever the other boys went as you can see for yourself, what good would they be to the men. The other boy had not been aloft yet and was not up on this night, and is a quite different boy throughout. I know the parents will blame me for this to a certain extent, but how am I to stop them when they insist on climbing? Am I then to go to every man (after giving the order to furl the sails) and ask them who goes there? Then I am in for a good deal of trouble and worse still have the old Man to growl and say that I am not fit to be an officer.

When sending a crowd of men aloft at night, with no lighting on deck, it would indeed be difficult to detect an unauthorised apprentice amongst the others. Lewis Davies continues:

Dear Mrs Isbester, a little bit of news about the afterguard. I do not think we could expect to be with a better Old Man and not at all worried with growls, although

Figure 18.5 *Looking forward from a position on the mizzen mast to the main top and the main yard. The boat on skids on the port side is the pinnace and the deckhouse beneath the pinnace is the crew forecastle and donkey boiler house with warping ends protruding from each side.*

Figure 18.6 *Looking aft from the foremast with, at the foot of the photo, part of the open main hatch*

sometimes I get, but I suppose I deserve it. The three mates are quite good chums. I believe if it wasn't for the different hues in the colour of our hair we could pass as brothers, but often you see brothers quarrelling and fighting, it hasnt come to that yet. The glad news has come at last, we are chartered to load wheat here, where for I do not know. hope it will be for home, nice time to round Cape Stiff [Cape Horn. Writing on 19 August, with the cargo yet to be loaded and the length of the Pacific to be traversed, Lewis Davies was anticipating a December or January, ie summer, rounding of Cape Horn.] The hold is nice and clean just finished today. I can assure you that the ship looks quite different now as when she was at Shields. lovely warm weather we have had throughout our stay and a good chance to keep her clean. I gather from Kathleen's letters that she doesn't intend going back to Swiss Land and has been very fortunate in securing the best post in England and so near to you. Captain was delighted to hear so and he expressed his joy by reading the letter to us, and then having us to hunt out the place of the good post on the atlas. It was I who found it first. Now I draw this to a close hoping it will find you all enjoying sound health. Please convey my kind regards to Arthur and boys also to Kathleen. I remain your very sincerely,

L Davies

> P.s. If anybody could have avoided that terrible accident then it is useless to think there to be a Supreme Being. God's will be done on sea as well as on land. All our days are numbered and soon we will have to answer for our wrong doings. only a few live to a ripe old age. others are cut in the bud. I hope you have no objection to my corresponding to Kathleen. Please pardon me for any mistakes and etc. I am a very poor letter writter. For more close particulars of the trip you may ask Kathleen. Both Mr Owen and Sinclair sends their kind regards to you all.

The excessively deferential tone of the letter rings a little strangely in our ears, but probably reflects the reality of 19th-century life when a shipmaster was Master under God, with the almost unchallenged power to hire, to punish and to fire.

The letter's margin contains unaddressed and unsigned comments, probably written by Susie Isbester:

> Sunday night. Isn't this awful weather. I am sending you all this letters to amuse you. Just Burn when read. You will see by this letter that Jack did not send the boy aloft, you see it was the mate who had given him leave to go. Poor Jack, he was Heartbroken over it.

Clearly the death of the apprentice Collins weighed heavily on Captain Isbester. He valued the apprentices greatly and took his responsibility for them seriously. When he took to the boats on the loss of the *Centaur*, he took all the apprentices in his boat instead of sharing them between the two boats as might have seemed normal. A friend writing to Susie[16] referred to this voyage as the captain's 'unfortunate voyage', and this is doubtless how he saw it. He had told McJannet that he had sailed the wide oceans 'without loss of life or accident' from 1900 to 1908.[17] This was not strictly true – his daughter Kathleen had mentioned a boat being launched in a failed attempt to rescue a man overboard[18] and there was the tragic case of fourth mate Waldenstrom who had died while sailing one of the ship's boats – but this was surely the standard to which he aspired. In his early years of seafaring hardly a voyage had passed without loss of life, and John Isbester had clearly decided that lives were precious and as master his responsibility was to protect them.

On leaving school in Shetland, Kathleen had trained in London as a domestic science teacher and taught first in Switzerland but, as Lewis mentions, she 'then obtained an organising post in Chiswick, Middlesex, where her combined domestic science centre was the first of its kind, and became a show centre for visitors from all over the United Kingdom'.[19] In 1910 she was aged 22.

In the summer of 1910, Eric and Allan Isbester were sent to Shetland for the school holiday, and Susie booked them to travel by the steamer from London to Leith and then on to Aberdeen and Lerwick, a journey that would have taken some four or five days. Their mother teased them afterwards that their trip had been very expensive because of all the meals that they had eaten. She claimed that she had thought they would be seasick and would save on the cost of meals. This was the holiday when Eric and Allan stayed for a very happy month at Quoyness, the beautifully situated croft in North Whiteness where their hostess was Maggie Gair, the former Maggie Smith to whom John Isbester had once been betrothed. While at Quoyness Allan received a postcard from his father in Seattle, hoping they were having a good holiday.[20] The postcard featured *Dalgonar* at anchor, her hull storm-scarred but masts and rigging looking immaculately placed

[Right] ***Figure 18.7*** *The storm-scarred* Dalgonar *in Seattle*

[Below] ***Figure 18.8*** Dalgonar *at anchor, in process of unshipping topgallant masts to pass under the Martrou transporter bridge at Rochefort*

(Fig.18.7). Before Christmas 1910 Susie wrote from Ilford to her friend Mary Nicolson and brought her up to date with family news. Kathleen was working very hard at her post at Chiswick and gaining the warm approval of the Board.

> Arthur [now aged 21] writes very cheerfully [from New Zealand] – but I think he is having a struggle. He took an 100 acre farm outside Wellington & hopes to make it pay grazing cattle. Arthur Gifford [Captain Arthur Gifford, Susie's uncle in Wellington] seems hopeful of him succeeding – but the boy is living alone and doing everything for himself. I believe he never gets a decent meal but when he goes to Gifford's and the Gifford children's chief joy seems to be to spend the day beside Arthur – I am afraid he has taken on too much – but he says never venture never win – he still keeps true to his Nellie.[21]

Eric, Susie continued, would go into engineering at the end of the school year (as he did, aged 15) and Allan, now in Standard 6, and Norman were both doing very well at school.

Dalgonar left Portland, Oregon, early in October 1910 and reached Rochefort on the Atlantic coast of France in mid-March 1911 after calling at Queenstown for orders. At Rochefort the topgallant masts had to be housed, a task requiring the safe manoeuvring of heavy spars up to 200 feet (61 metres) above the deck, activity calling for cool heads and plenty of skilled seamanship. In a postcard to Kathleen Susie claims that the picture (Fig.18.8) shows *Dalgonar* with 'our masts housed so as to pass under the bridge',[22] but it actually appears to show the upper yards for the fore and main masts unshipped in preparation for housing the topgallant masts. In the postcard she adds 'Do let me hear the worst from NZ', doubtless with her worries about Arthur in mind.

After six weeks in Rochefort discharging *Dalgonar* was towed to Liverpool to load once again for Sydney. The tow would have been because she was needed in Liverpool promptly and/or because the winds were absent or adverse. Alternatively, it could have been because the topgallant masts were still housed and the temporary Run crew, signed on for the passage from Rochefort to Liverpool, were not trusted to rerig the masts efficiently.

Lewis Davies left *Dalgonar* in Liverpool and a fortnight later was sailing as third mate on the *City of Baroda*, a steam ship. He held a master's certificate, but on going from sail to steam he had to start at the bottom again. He remained seriously committed to Kathleen, whom he married 11 months later, and he had clearly recognised that the future lay in steam, not sail. As a man contemplating marriage he had to consider his prospects. Fifty years later Kathleen wrote 'My husband never liked steam but loved sail. The officers used to say that if they passed a sailing ship they had to hold my husband down or he would jump overboard and join her.'[23]

John Isbester, meanwhile, embarked once again for Sydney where, as Susie wrote,[24] 'Jack is well and having a good time with all his Sydney girls who seem to think age no disadvantage'. Clearly the Isbester and Linklater families and other Sydney friends remained very close. From Sydney, *Dalgonar* sailed the familiar route to Newcastle thence to Coquimbo and Taltal and finally to Queenstown and Dunkerque.

Meanwhile back in England, son Eric had reached the age of 15 and started an engineering apprenticeship. He may have wanted to follow his father's footsteps but his eyesight was not good enough. In a letter to her friend, Mary Nicolson,[25] Susie wrote

> Eric started work yesterday & is being so good & helpful & pleasant, if only it lasts, I never heard him go out this morning & he had fed himself & made his bed. I got home at ½ past 9 [in the evening] with a terrible headache to find that Eric had bathed and fed the little boys and washed up all dishes and had the porridge water boiling. While it boiled he and I folded the washing & while it cooled he turned the mangle for me – & then fetched up coal [from the cellar] and broke sticks & fed the guinea pig so it was just 11 when he got to bed – I like him to be there by 10 – but he thinks it will be all right in the morning – he rises at 5 & gets a 6 o'c train then he is home by 6 – he will have to take an evening class just for plain English but is quite willing to do so – won't he be proud on Fri when he gets his first 6/-.

Apart from feeding the guinea pig, these were all tasks common to most families in those times. As always, Susie joined the *Dalgonar* when she reached the discharging port, in this case

Dunkerque, in September 1912. From postcards[26] it is clear that the children were also there for part of the time, and when *Dalgonar* moved to London to load for Melbourne there were further opportunities to visit.

---

1 *Evening News*, Sydney, NSW. 08.10.1908.
2 Isbester, Captain John. PC.CAI58. 10.11.1908. (Isbester Collection).
3 Isbester, Captain John. PC.CAI65. 10.11.1908. (Isbester Collection).
4 Isbester, Susie. PC54. 20.10.1909. (Isbester Collection).
5 Isbester, Susie. PC.CAI13. XX.XX.1909. (Isbester Collection).
6 Isbester, Captain John. PC.CAI29, 10.11.1909. (Isbester Collection).
7 Jenne, Sir Francis. *Masters' Gratuities and Slopchests*. MMSA Reporter. Vol.XXI. 1894, p.1124.
8 'Burned at Sea'. *North Wales Express*. 05.04.1907.
9 'Burning of the S.S. *Carnarvon Castle*' *Colonist*. Volume XLIX, Issue 11870 26 February 1907 p.3.
10 'Burned at Sea'. Op.cit.
11 There are inconsistencies between the reported positions of abandonment and the distances sailed in different reports but they do not detract from this remarkable account of survival in extreme conditions.
12 'Burned at Sea'. Op.cit.
13 Davies, Lewis. *Welsh Mariners' Index*. *http*://welshmariners.org.uk/search.php.
14 Davies, Lewis, Seaman's Discharge Book. Property of grandson Philip Davies.
15 Davies, Lewis. Letter LD1. 19.08.1910. (Isbester Collection.)
16 Aggie in Lerwick. PC25. 10.08.1910 (Isbester Collection).
17 McJannet, Arnold Franz. *The Log of the Dalgonar*. 07.09.1908. (Isbester Collection).
18 Davies, Kathleen. Letter KD2 02.03.1957 (Isbester Collection).
19 'She had a colourful life'. *The Shetland Times Ltd, Lerwick. 13.12.1963.*
20 Isbester, Captain John. PC.CAI27, 08.08.1910. (Isbester Collection).
21 Isbester, Susie. Letter S5. 12.12.1910. (Isbester Collection).
22 Isbester, Susie. PC46, 20.03.1911. (Isbester Collection).
23 Davies, Kathleen. Letter KD5, 19.07.1960. (Isbester Collection.
24 Isbester, Susie. Letter S10. 03.12.1911. (Isbester Collection).
25 Isbester, Susie. Letter S6. 09.01.1912. (Isbester Collection).
26 Isbester, Susie. PC51. 21.09.1912. (Isbester Collection).

19 THE FINAL VOYAGE TO MELBOURNE

In London during a six-week period in October and November, *Dalgonar* loaded a full cargo of cement in barrels for Melbourne.[1] This should have been a happy time for Captain and Mrs Isbester (Fig.19.1) and perhaps initially it was: their home was only 5 or 10 miles from the docks, and John would be able to spend plenty of time there. When he required to be aboard ship Susie could be with him. It was during this period that John Isbester was given the devastating news that the owners intended to sell *Dalgonar*, his cherished command for the last 12 years, at the end of the forthcoming voyage.

Figure 19.1 *Captain and Mrs Isbester*

So what, as he starts his final voyage, do we know about Captain Isbester?

Growing up in 19th-century Shetland, as John Isbester did, was different from an upbringing anywhere else in Britain. In the 1960s the oral historian Paul Thompson, interviewing people born between 1870 and 1906, found:[2]

> The most generally progressive parents in Edwardian Britain were to be found in a particularly primitive region. Among the families of the Shetland crofters, children were treated less unequally than anywhere else in Britain. Here too the authority of parents was accepted, but it was imposed with reasoning rather than punishment. It was the only part of the country in which physical punishment was not socially approved. On the crofts, on which parents often lived with grandparents, children were not forced to eat food they did not want, their conversation was welcomed, and when they had finished they could leave without asking. They also shared in the common social life of the community, including even dances. There were very few public houses, but instead men and women called frequently on each other, customarily walking into the house without a knock on the door. When there was company Shetland children stayed up late ... with their parents round the fire, perhaps making kishies [baskets] as they talked.

Even at a distance of two generations I can recognise gentle and civilised child rearing as an Isbester family characteristic, and so too, it seems, did the family friend[3] who brought this research to my attention.

John Isbester's single minded determination as a young man to succeed in his chosen profession was not unique but it was exceptional and admirable. We have noted the commitment with which, in his early years at sea, he seems methodically to have sought to visit all the great seaports of the world and it was exceptional that even as an OS or AB he completed every voyage, never deserting or being left behind as did so many of his shipmates.

He was devoted to his wife Susie and had, over the years I suspect, relied on her tactful guidance for many of the social and religious aspects of his life. Aboard ship his word was law and in society ashore he could express a trenchant view and tell an entertaining story but away from ships, sailors and Shetland his views on what to wear, who to meet and what to think had, in the early years of their marriage, been usefully influenced by Susie. He was no longer the man she first knew who had not remade his bunk for a month, or who could not remember which weekend he was supposed to change his underclothes! He needed no prompting to love their children and his letters contain numerous expressions of his interest in and care for each of them.

For twenty eight years as a shipmaster he satisfied his employers with his navigation, seamanship and ship management skills, frequently on ships where competent support and assistance were in very short supply. The explanations of his navigation given by McJannet in Chapter 17 are authoritative, convincing and in accordance with best practice. His powers of observation and enduring curiosity, or his sense of mischief, are illustrated by his observations of what might have been Vulcan, the intra-mercurial planet.

Captain Isbester was respected by his nautical teacher Captain Robert Cogle who wrote that he had passed all his professional examinations at the first attempt and that it had been a privilege to know him[4] and by Captain Dunn-Taylor who was privileged to serve as second of the *Dalgonar* 1905–1906 … [Captain Isbester was] a strict disciplinarian, beneath a rugged manner he was the most sympathetic of men and I have much cause to thank him both for what he taught me and for the way I was treated by him. Captain Thompson, from Shetland, wrote that Great Sailor who commanded the ship *Dalgonar* for so many years and set such an excellent example to us boys who hoped one day to follow him.[5] In a later letter he wrote from what I have heard of Capt Isbester [from Shetland men who had sailed with him] he was a man who knew what he wanted and used his best efforts to secure it which he did.[6] For the Society of Cape Horners the *Dalgonar* … was … fortunate with the three masters who commanded her during her twentyone year career, as all of them were universally respected and liked by the crew and possessed the qualities of making a happy ship.[7] For the solicitor Arnold Franz McJannet, passenger to Australia, I am most fortunate indeed in having such a cheery, honest, kind-hearted and homely skipper … a rough and ready sailor of course, but as bright and true as his clear blue eyes and, I think, as honest as a man can be in this world.[8]

John Isbester's consideration for his apprentices, regularly teaching them navigation and seamanship with a cake for a reward when they did well, teasing them when opportunity presented itself and keeping them with him when forced by fire to abandon ship are all the actions of a decent man in an age when brutality was not uncommon. His determination that Line Crossing ceremonies should be the occasion for fun and entertainment, not bullying reflect well on him too and his readiness to encourage sports days and concerts must have been welcomed by ships' companies looking for distractions during almost endless voyages. His insistence on the crews of his boats tossing oars like crews from the Royal Navy are testament to the importance he attached to a smart display.

John Isbester smoked a pipe and occasionally a cigar, and he drank whisky, rum and wine on occasion, though there is no suggestion anywhere that this was ever a problem. He never wrote letters while at sea except when a pilot was aboard and had the con, and it is quite likely that he never drank at sea either, except for a token tot on special occasions. References to any physical activity in his letters are very rare, and it seems that he conformed to the 19th- and 20th-century convention that shipmasters expected others to do any walking, climbing, hauling and rowing that was required. He suffered from asthma, and if like mine it was seasonal asthma induced by pollen, then going to sea was the best thing for it as there is no pollen away from land. He admitted to Susie that he was not regularly wearing his false teeth,[9] a practice much more common in his day than now, and in a letter written on his final voyage[10] he mentioned being given tabloids (tablets) for his head, which could mean headaches or something worse. As he offers no explanation the condition was presumably one of which Susie already knew. For 'all his girls in Sydney age was no disadvantage' according to Susie, but he was 60 years old and the years had taken their toll. He did not want to retire, but he was feeling the effects of his age.

In the latter part of 1912 when *Dalgonar* was loading in London, Captain Thomson of Sandsound in Shetland, then a young third mate, wrote to Captain Isbester, asking for the third mate's job aboard *Dalgonar*. As he explained many years later in a lively letter, typically Shetland in its relish for the whos, wheres and whats:

> I started my career at sea at the age of fourteen with my father who was skipper of the *Zephyr* owned by Nicholson & Co. Scalloway. This was 1905, and the following winter I baited lines and mended nets for Davie Williamson the youngest of John Williamsons sons at the Slate, Whiteness, taken in just as one of them. There was sons: Robert, Peter, James, John, Henry and David. They owned the smack *Village Bell* which they had lengthened by 20 feet by K T Jamison at Sandwick, and James who I think had served under Captain Isbester, also Andrew Anderson of Haggerstay. So I was well versed in the technique of life on a deep water ship. The following season I sailed as cook and bushrope boy with Laurence Williamson in the *Betsy Sim*. The following winter I served in Nicholson's sail loft as an apprentice to sail making, under those fine seamen Magnus Erasmuson and Findley Johnston from *Affort* both deep water sailing ship men. March 1907 came and the smack *Mersey* was being refitted for the coasting trade and I was taken on by skipper Walter Goudie and Eddie Leask as mate. Both were well up in years and had been skippers of smacks and schooners fishing at Iceland and Faeroe and Rockall. The *Mersey* had been a Liverpool pilot boat bought by Captain Peter Tait a deep water man at the period when the cod fishing was at its peak; as you know at that period Shetland had a number of smacks making three or four trips per season landing their catches in Shetland as green fish. The fish was cleaned and sun dried on the beaches and shipped to Spain, Portugal, Italy and Brazil as prime bacalao. The

> *Mersey* was one of those smacks, heavily rigged, for the small crew of master, mate and two ordinary seamen. It was splendid training, and after two seasons at the herring fishing, a winter at the sail making I expect that inwardly I was beginning to think I was no end of a good sailor.[11]

However, Captain Isbester wrote back explaining that 'the Senior Apprentice gets the job', as in due course he did. Captain Thomson spent no more time in sail but obtained an extra master's certificate and served in command for 15 years with Eagle Oil before becoming their marine superintendent.

An immediate consequence of the decision to sell *Dalgonar* was that no new apprentices were employed, and the voyage started with only three apprentices, all nearing the end of their four years of sea service. All three had been aboard *Dalgonar* for the voyage to Seattle and for the subsequent Sydney voyage, totalling some three years of sea time. Alfred Lloyd May, aged 18, was the senior, and seems, like the 15-year old Wilfred Henry Banks, to have served on another ship for six months before joining *Dalgonar.* Their indentures both commence in Liverpool at a time when *Dalgonar* was on the west coast of South America. Such a switch was always a possibility if a ship was lost or a master retired. Joseph Sidney Ocnard, aged 16, who began his apprenticeship aboard *Dalgonar* in South Shields was the junior.

An unusual amount of detail of Captain Isbester's final voyage survives because Susie kept all his letters from that voyage. John Isbester sent Susie a card[12] from The Downs (off the Kentish coast) where, on leaving Gravesend, *Dalgonar* had anchored when faced with strong westerly winds which prevented them from sailing down Channel. Completing a brief note[13] written while under tow and off the Isle of Wight John Isbester explains that the glass is in the garret i.e. the barometer is high and that they are experiencing calm, misty conditions with light adverse winds, so that any change must be an improvement. The steward and the boys (the apprentices) asked to be remembered to Mrs Isbester.

Arriving in Melbourne in March 1913, John Isbester received letters from his family telling him of their Christmas holidays and of the adventures of their dog Fergi. Allan at Ilford County High School for Boys was doing well, and his father wrote him this affectionate letter.

> My dear son Allan
>
> I am so glad to hear that you are getting on so well at school. I hope you keep well and go on improving.
>
> So you had your Xmas and New Year beside Kath. That would be like home all right but it appears poor Fergi did not think so when he made off to the railway station. And when he could not get a train to suit him he started along the lines, however I am thankful that he was found again. And that he did not collapse altogether when he saw you all land in Cardiff. I'm sure I think it's a wonder he believed his own eyes.
>
> Well I expect to hear from your own self sometime shortly, but don't put any French in or I won't be able to read it. X
>
> Your Loving Father[14]

South-easterly gales had prevented them berthing on arrival in Melbourne, but while at anchor they had been able to send and receive mail. Writing to Susie two days before her 49th birthday[15] John congratulated her (though not quite in these words) that they would have more freedom for lovemaking when she reached the menopause. Turning to shipboard news, John reported that the steward was doing well and bossing the inadequate cook who, like a lot of the crew, was likely to desert 'as soon as the ship gets alongside'. Responding to something that Susie had written to him John remarked 'Yes the Whiteness girls are surely a bit hot tailed, the thing is their simplicity getting taken advantage of when they leave home.' We have to assume that he was thinking of the situation just before the First World War, and not of his wife or his mother in earlier years when they were both Whiteness girls! After deploring the absence of news of Arthur, John Isbester reports that they currently have four cats aboard, the old cat Maggy and three of her kittens, two toms with the sailors and one she which stays with Maggy and the afterguard and were 'prancing about the cabin just now at a great rate'. Next he turns to the inadequacies of the mate and crew:

> Yesterday we sent down the foretop gal yard, parrell broke of course. The mate and his watch was the whole day over it, which should have been done in an hour or hour and a half. I just wish Smith [from the owners who had employed the mate?] knew how little the old mate can do with men. The men are the most useless I was ever at sea with. If we had had any sudden change of hard weather the ship would simply have run away with us. … The poor old mate is very crestfallen – he can do nothing with his men and the second never tries to do anything. I expect to pay him off shortly.

Remembering Susie's thoughtful surprise during their passage to Melbourne, John reported:

> Oh at breakfast Xmas morning the mate presented your parcels quite unknown to me. We opened them before starting to eat and called the two boys [the two boys here referred to are, I think, apprentices May and Banks – apprentice Ocnard was already acting as third mate] and carpenter to get theirs, the steward too. It was a very nice surprise, they were all pleased. I had the two apprentices to dinner with us. They appreciated it – we had 3 hens so were not so badly off. The men had grog and there was Xmas pudding etc. and in the evening I had a good strong rum toddy for them. They all mustered aft and cheered and thanked me for the good Xmas etc. Then we had crossing the equator, New Year's Day & Night of course. And then my birthday [9 February] so the Capt did not get much of the rum to himself.

Susie's gifts were a thoughtful, imaginative and unexpected gesture. Over the years she did a great deal to support John and to make doing a voyage with him a happy and memorable experience for him and for his shipmates. John continues:

> The mate and 2 mate don't eat eggs so I have not done badly. The hens laid a good few. We have 1 doz yet and the steward attends them well. One of our pigs died

shortly after leaving before we got out of the bad weather. The steward has to attend to the pig too, the cook is too lazy for that.

Dalgonar 'remained in Melbourne for five weeks discharging cargo and taking ballast, while Susie at home in Ilford had plenty to occupy her'.[16]

---

1 *Dalgonar*. Formal Investigation Report No.7640. 01.04.1913.
2 Thompson, Paul. *The Edwardians.* Weidenfeld & Nicolson, London. 1975. p.63.
3 Baillie, Donald. Personal correspondence. September 1995. (Isbester Collection).
4 Cogle, Capt. Robert S, Letter to *The Shetland Times Ltd*, Lerwick, undated early 1914. (Isbester Collection).
5 Dunn-Taylor, Capt. R.W. Unidentified newspaper, 1914. (Isbester Collection).
6 Thomson, Captain J. P., OBE ExC. Letter JPT1 12.10.1968. (Isbester Collection).
7 Thomson, Captain J. P., OBE ExC. Letter JPT3 15.12.1968. (Isbester Collection).
8 Woollard, Commander C.L.A., R.N. *The Last of the Cape Horners.* Arthur H Stockwell, Ltd, llfracombe. 1967. p.246.
9 McJannet, A.F. *The Log of the Dalgonar*.14.07.1908. (Isbester Collection).
10 Isbester, Captain John. Letter J26, 06.04.13 (Isbester Collection).
11 Isbester, Captain John. Letter J37, 11.08.13 (Isbester Collection).
12 Thomson, Captain J. P., OBE ExC. Letter JPT2 12.11.1968. (Isbester Collection).
13 Isbester, Captain John. Letter J18, 21.11.1912. (Isbester Collection).
14 Isbester, Captain John. Letter J19, 22.11.1912. (Isbester Collection).
15 Isbester, Captain John. Letter J20, 09.03.1913. (Isbester Collection).
16 Isbester, Captain John. Letter J21, 09.03.1913. (Isbester Collection).
17 Isbester, Susie. Letter S15, 07,04,1913. (Isbester Collection).

20 MELBOURNE

John Isbester wrote five letters to Susie whilst in Melbourne, one of which he claimed was probably the longest he had ever written, though he writes modestly that half a page would probably have served just as well. We have plenty of evidence of his preoccupations – the inadequate mates, the troublesome crew and the foolish owners of the ship. There were the gleams of pleasure, too, when things went well: 'Ocnard, the third, shapes well and the men work with him.' Joseph Sidney Ocnard, aged 17, was being given the chance to prove his worth in a very tough school.

The Ship's Articles[1] show that Ocnard actually signed on as bosun on 12 May 1913 when the ship was in Newcastle, NSW, his promotion from apprentice being backdated to 28 April, so prior to that date the promotion was an informal trial. Second mate McAllister was dismissed in Melbourne, since when Ocnard had effectively been working as second rather than third mate though a second mate was employed for a couple of weeks for the run from Melbourne to Newcastle in April. Interestingly Captain Isbester preferred Ocnard as second mate/bosun to the 19-year-old senior apprentice Alfred Lloyd May who was later promoted to third mate at sea during the subsequent passage from Newcastle to Callao. The third apprentice, William Henry Banks, having completed his required seatime, left the ship in Newcastle to return to England and sit for his second mate's certificate. From that point on Captain Isbester had no apprentices instead of the six to eight to which he was accustomed. He must have missed them as stimulating and entertaining members of the ship's company and as a very reliable and useful part of the workforce.

After *Dalgonar* had moved from the anchorage to a berth in Melbourne John Isbester had more to tell.[2] He was having lots of trouble with the sailors who were 'drinking, rowing and laying up'. He had told them

> that if they would straighten up and go to work in a proper manner I would give them 5/- today [Saturday 15 March] and the afternoon off and 5/- on Monday St Patrick's Day. After that if they did not behave I would have to deal with them. Oh they all agreed that would be all right, they would of course be all right. I have my doubts. They are only waiting for a chance to get away.

The money that John Isbester offered his sailors would not have been a gift: it would have been an advance on the wages which they had earned on the passage from London to Melbourne, money that they would forfeit if they deserted. Next, John Isbester had a bit of a grizzle about Gracie Beasley's lack of foresight and faith in his passage-making skills:

> We just commenced discharging [on Tuesday] and I had a cable from the owners on the same day. When will the ship be all discharged and ready for another cargo? I replied 18 or 20 days. We are evidently not fixed yet. Now the freights are going down. I don't expect we could get 30/- and if they had fixed two months ago they might have had 40/-. Are they not smart and far seeing? They might have taken a little risk on us making a fair passage, our passages have all been very equal, still between 97 & 109 this last of course was 104.

Other ships, their captains, and voyages made and planned were always of interest.

> One of the Invers ships, of Aberdeen, is at the quay astern of us. The Capt has just been on board a few minutes. I did not know him. They were 127 days to Adelaide. They are here with part cargo and chartered to load wheat for Caligo West Coast and there they will have to ballast for some other place. So it will be sometime before he gets to his wife. He is a man about 40 I should think, ginger or inclined to be red.
>
> The old mate has just been in for a stamp. He makes such a palaver before he can say what he wants he makes me tired. I am going to pay the second mate off in a day or two. He has of course never been ashore but is not good with the men at all. … So far only one man has cleared out but there's no comfort with them in port.

Monday Night, St Patrick's Day.

> I have 4 or 5 Irish Men so of course gave them a holiday and 5/- so I expect they are all helpless by this time, 9PM. Well I got your third letter today with Allan's and Eric's enclosed. I am glad to hear from them. I have wrote them. I am glad to hear that they are both better. I am sorry to hear about Mrs Garrick being so ill over having the baby. Something must have been wrong that they had to take it away before the time.

John Isbester's diagnosis is not out of the *Ship Captain's Medical Guide*:

> The Capt has surely been poking her and capsized things.

After responding to more news from Susie, John mentions visits to friends in Melbourne and continues

> We are about one third discharged and no word of a charter yet. Now I don't expect we will get 30/- even. I feel sorry for the Owners. I hear that some of our men is likely to clear out tonight. Good riddence [*sic*] to them – they are the most useless lot I was ever at sea with. And of course all the best will go, wages here is £6 Per Month and our men only having £3.10, you can't wonder. At any rate I

> believe there is men to be got. I have not had a line at all from the owners yet, but they sent me £1,000 and if we load here it will take about another £1,000 to clear us out of here.

John Isbester passes on news of the Linklaters and other friends in Sydney and Melbourne, and then turns again to shipboard matters.

> The old mate is ashore tonight of course the sailors having a holiday – they had nothing to do. He is getting a new spring for his gramophone. You know I am going to pay the Second off tomorrow. Tonight he is just a fool with drink and positively useless drunk or sober.

The excellent stewed apples that the steward was serving him each evening, claimed Captain John improbably, were turning his thoughts to amorous matters. Writing with the freedom that comes with almost 30 years of marriage, he had been thinking of taking Susie from behind 'with your corsets on'!

> The steward asks me to remember him to you and the boys. It's a pity Allan did not mention him. Allan writes a good letter now. This will surely be about the longest letter you ever had from me but I think half a sheet might have done just as well. The Carpenter came this morning to speak to me about getting discharged!! I chased him off. He said he could do so well here, 15/- a day. [That would be close to £20 a month as against the £5.10s he was being paid aboard ship.]

His letter ended in typically affectionate terms:

> Love to all. and to my own Dear Susie Pusie Your own Loving Jack.

Further letters from Captain Isbester[3, 4, 5, 6] tell of an active social life, with visits to and from various friends from the Shetland and wider communities in Melbourne. He was a guest of Jack Leask, married to Annie Williamson from Hoove, a former Whiteness neighbour, and having high tea along with Jemie Williamson, a carpenter, and Annie's brother. Also introduced was John's cousin, Robbie Anderson, an infant at Haggersta during John's own childhood there and now working on Australian coastal ships. They were meeting for the first time in 22 years. John was not much taken with him:

> He is a great big slovenly man. He is out here sailing for a spell. Wages is good on the coast and I think he has an idea of bringing the family out later. No word of a Charter. The Owners have made a Mull of it again. I Cabled them on Thursday that we would be ready on the 28th inst. but have got no reply yet.

The mate's name was Mull. Captain Isbester had a poor opinion of him and seems to have adopted 'make a Mull' to mean 'make a mess'.

> Two more of our men cleared last night as I expected. That makes about 10 deserters now. I think that will be about all now. The steward is keeping as good as gold. Our [remaining] men are all pretty well and settled now and this being another holiday I have given them another 2/6. [Two shillings and sixpence = one-eighth of £1.]
>
> Tuesday Morning 25th. Yesterday Robbie and Williamson came for me about 11 o'clock and we went up to Leasks, and after taking Dinner there we all took the train to Fern Tree Gully about an hour's run from Melbourne. We strolled around there for about 3 hours and had a lunch or tea. Got back to Leasks about 7.30. and sat there and yarned and had supper, and I got onboard about 11PM, sober, and the steward had my stewed apples and milk on the table ready so I had that too.
>
> I was up about 6.30 this morning, raining heavy, so I am afraid the discharge will be delayed today. I am not sorry as I have no word from the owners yet. …
>
> Robbie Anderson is a great lot worse than Andrew – that havering silly way of speaking about women and most slovenly in his dress.

On Sunday 30 March 1913, life for John Isbester became much more hectic:

> I have never been over the rail [ie ashore] today not even to the kirk. Yesterday I got a cable: 'Take in Ballast at once and wait orders.' So I expect it will be Newcastle and the west coast. The Owners have made a Mull of it. They might have had the ship fixed at a good rate two months ago. We have still about 450 Tons [of cargo to discharge] aboard and won't get any ballast for another two days, so we will just about catch her before she turns over. I can understand she is not fixed and they may fix yet for grain. so I am going to wire them tomorrow whether I am to take ballast to wait or ballast to sail. The fools.

Captain Isbester, considering the implications of his orders and knowing that the ship, under the weight of masts and spars, would capsize if all the cargo was discharged from its position low in the ship before ballast was loaded, recognised that the orders to take ballast had come just in time. However they were not clear. If *Dalgonar* was to wait in Melbourne for a cargo of grain, she needed only about 600 tons of stiffening ballast to keep her safe in port. If, however, she was to put to sea for the passage to Newcastle she would require about 1,000 tons of sailing ballast to keep her safe in the more unsettled conditions found at sea. Captain Isbester mentions later[7] that there were new people in the Company office. Clearly they did not impress him:

> Last night I had Mr and Mrs Sinclair and Mr and Mrs Andreds to tea and till 9.30 and had a very pleasant evening with them and Jack Robinson. Capt Robinsons son came about 7PM and left at 9PM. His boat was sailing at 10PM. I was glad when Robbie did not turn up, he is so raw and untidy. Today I got up in good time intending to do a lot of writing after breakfast but when I was going to start Robbie came and had Dinner and tea with us and left at 9. The poor soul, I could not be but pleasant with him but was awfully tired of him – he is such a haver of

> old yarns, so terrible slow. I think he is just about as bad as Robbie Tulloch was. He eats turn about with his knife and fork.

Robbie Anderson was clearly a trial, but because he was family, he was to be treated with consideration. The letter continued:

> Last week the ring came out of the head of my gold watch when I was putting it on in the morning, and it dropped on the mat in front of the bed and bent the case so that it stopped going. I will keep it till I come home and send it to Christies.
>
> I saw one of Bella Leask's girls at Leasks the other night. She is not as good looking as Mary Banks.

Mary Banks was presumably the comely mother of apprentice Banks. She probably visited the ship in London at the start of the voyage to arrange for her son to be sent home as soon as he completed his apprenticeship and met John and Susie at that time.

John's letter ends with the discreet salutation 'X top and bottom you know', which seems to hint at where the kisses would be applied were he and Susie together.

John's next letter, written on Monday 31 March, is brief and asserts

> Yes by all Means let Allan give up the scouts and I don't care how soon Norman does too. Oh. I have forgot all about Normans birthday in another two days. I am sorry but tell him that he will just have to have it over again when I get home. Your Own Jack.

He reopens it to add:

> All Fools Day. I have just got cable today that the ship is chartered to load coal at Newcastle. Of course I don't know as yet where for.

John and Susie would have been hoping for a cargo of grain from Sydney to Europe, getting him home within six months, but an intermediate passage to the west coast of North or South America would add three or four months to the voyage. Using their intimate language John wrote that lovemaking must wait for a long time. Then, returning to business,

> The cargo will be out in about 3 days then ballast, bending sails and getting crew etc. My hands full as usual. Tomorrow is Norman's birth. I hope he is well and has a good time. Love to all. Your own Loving X Jack. Oh I have bought a lamp for my room that hangs over the table. It's an awful comfort. I can't think how I have not done so before.

Writing from Melbourne on 6 April, John reported that they had taken 200 tons of ballast and finally completed discharge the previous day. Using pilot and tugs, they had moved from the dock to a berth in the Yarra river to load the balance of the ballast – 800 tons – which might take another week.

Turning to his active social life, John reported that, on returning aboard after ordering pilot and tugs he found old Mr Sinclair on board. In the captain's absence the officers had invited him to have dinner with them. He had 'just come to spend an hour with me so he stopped till we got our new berth here, then left asking me to pay them another visit which I may do'. Immediately afterwards Jack Leask, husband of Annie Williamson, boarded to invite John home to tea, where he met Bella Leask and her married daughter with husband and baby plus Bella's two young daughters. John reports:

> Bella minds a whole lot about me when we were at school that I had forgotten. She is the third time married her present works farm work in the country and is only home about every month. She is 54 and just so old and ugly. Three shore men husbands has surely been too much for her, however I could not help asking her and the married daughter and husband to the ship with Leask and Annie for tea tonight.

Recurring themes in John Isbester's letters are his happy mingling with Shetlanders wherever he finds them, and his readiness to be polite even to those who he finds unattractive.

> Robbie came on board with me last night and I have only got clear of him now 10AM. I think he is slower than Robbie Tulloch was, but I can't help being nice with him … The little steward is keeping just as good as gold, very pleasant with everybody that comes on board and really does the Table very well. Everybody notices how nice he is.

John Isbester's attitude to the mate seems to have mellowed a little: 'The old mate does his level best, but doesn't say much.' Matters may have eased a little with the desertions of most of the troublesome sailors. 'The third mate is shaping well for a second.' Ocnard's promotion from apprentice to third mate had not been made official but Captain Isbester was already anticipating his promotion to second mate – a much more substantial promotion. When second mate (or bosun, the post to which he was eventually promoted – perhaps more appropriate for a young man who as yet had no qualification) he would under the captain's watchful eye be in charge of the navigation watch for 12 hours a day at sea, with authority to supervise the sailors in their steering, keeping a lookout, setting and handing sails, and maintenance and cleaning work about the decks. 'I met the Second Mate that was discharged. [He said that] one day he would be glad to come onboard as anything, but I told him that I had no use for him.' Captain Isbester clearly valued ability and reliability over qualifications.

> We are 19 in all on board now so I will ship 7 or 8 before leaving for Newcastle, and hope to get a slant [of wind]. There comes all our old friends again. I had a letter from May Henderson's husband. I know you will just be mad on me still going without teeth.

John turns to family matters, asking whether Kathleen was expecting yet and saying that Arthur's failure to write to his mother was shameful, but she should give him time. Was it worth writing to Arthur's wife? John wondered. Relations between her and the family seem to have been chilly.

> This will not go before Tuesday so I will add a line later. I am just wild at the owners not fixing the ship to load here. They might have had 30/- after we arrived here but I hear they wanted 31/3 [thirty-one shillings and threepence] so it may be better for me that we have a long voyage since they are going to sell her when we come home or give me the sack.

This is the only time in the correspondence that the possibility of being given the sack is mentioned, and I assume that this would occur only as a consequence of *Dalgonar* being sold. 'So I had better do all I can this voyage. We are likely to land home in winter again.' John seems to be almost welcoming a longer voyage, on the basis that more days mean more dollars …

> Tuesday 8th we are ballasting but want about 600 yet. It's doubtful whether we get away this week. Last night a Mr Spence came on board, second mate of a boat, saw A Gifford [Susie's relative, Captain Arthur Gifford, in Wellington] about 3 months ago. Arthur asked him to see me. He was here till 10PM.

If he had any news of Arthur Isbester it was nothing that John wanted to pass on to Susie. 'Cousin Bob [aka Robbie] goes away today.' Doubtless a circumstance for which John was grateful. He continues with a reference to a wedding with which Susie had been assisting, possibly one of the sort of which Susie had experience – a wedding taking place when the father was away at sea.

> I hope you get over the wedding all right and don't kill yourself for other people. It's a mercy that you and Mrs. got on all right at the whist drive. She likely has nothing else to do either and would be clear of ship talk.

In fact Susie described the circumstances of the wedding in a lively letter[8] to Miss Jamieson, one of her circle of Shetland friends, currently staying in Leeds:

> I am sorry I can't say come here – but for the next month I am full – having a Captain's wife and two little boys from Modisty, Walls [in the west of Shetland] staying with me till they find a house for themselves. The Captain, George Laurenceson [Fig.20.1] sailed from Liverpool on Sat. & he thought so highly of me that he confided his loved ones to my care – we have had Laurencesons very much to the front with us lately as this lady's brother – Willie Laurenceson (who was Kathleen's best man) also thinking highly of me – entrusted me with his wedding – & I had his bride an Orkney girl with me for three weeks – & on Easter Mon got them safely married – a nice little wedding we had – all the Shetland friends at it – Giffords, Walkers, Henrys, etc – and Kathleen came through for the

event, & she & the bride furnished the nest. Kathleen is still here & will be till the 16th then Cardiff receives her – & perhaps Miss Henry is going with her – & in a month from now she expects her Man [her husband Lewis Davies, back from sea of course] – after that happy event she would be charmed to receive you – if you are still in this land – but maybe your stay won't extend that length of time. We had Miss Henry here tonight. Very bright, & she and Mrs L indulged in Shetland talk. Mrs H was not with her and we all feel freer to indulge in Shetland lore when she is absent, for she does not admire the bed rock and our sentimentalities regarding it are met with sniffs.

I saw the Scarffs the other night – your friend James Russell – has left the sea and gone out to Canada – to try and make his mark there. Capt Scarff has been off duty a few weeks with fluid on the knee – Mrs Scarff is well & has her student son at home – & finds that he is in demand now at dances etc. Sons always bring you friends of a kind. Even my big fat Eric has his admirers who court his mother – but Eric, poor man, finds his work and his sleep as much as he has time for. Allan also is very busy – & is looking forward to 18 days absolute idleness at Whit. Norman's brain work has not begun to trouble him – he is a scout first & a scholar afterwards – he went to camp four days at Easter & came home with four days filth on him & the Lord only knows what in him – & it took me the rest of his

Figure 20.1 *Captain George Laurenson, his wife Barbara and their children, from left: Douglas, Laurie, George, Mary, Jimmie and Babs (Photo from about 1922)*

holiday to get him fit for school again – the Mother of sons lies not on a bed of roses – Kathleen's visit has been a great heartener & I don't know what I will do without her – she is the one member of my family that causes me no anxiety & surely because of that it has been ordained that I am not to have her – why didn't you bring our friend Mrs Nicolson away with you? – it seems impossible to uproot her from Lerwick – I am tired of urging her to come – & I am sure she needs a change – Kath and I went up to Town & saw Mrs Walker-Pole – and very pleasant it was to see her once again. This weekend we have had Arthur Sandison & his wife – married life seems to suit them – for I never saw either of them look better – Mrs Gifford and all the family are well – the Old Lady is the most sprightly one amongst us – & puts all our grunts & groans to shame. My Old Man is in Melbourne and goes from there to Newcastle N.S.W. to load for Callao – Peru – so dear knows when I will bask in the sunshine of his presence again – but I must not grumble his presence is sunshine & I had a long bask this fall – I am longing for his letters which have not come yet and of what more shall I write – not of the doings of these wild women called suffragettes – for that you can read in the daily press – Nor of Lloyd Georges doings for over them I would fain draw a veil – nor of the weather – for the state of it is patent to all – so there seems no more to say – Aren't you going to aristocratic Purley? or is Leeds the only favoured spot. I thank you for your concluding petition for me – my handiwork – for which you so devoutly pray – consists of openwork babies socks for sales of work, & if the powers above would prevent me from dropping stitches I would be very thankful – I think I'd better stop this drivel – & I am sure you think the same – if you feel like visiting me three weeks hence – I shall be delighted & will endeavour to give you a perfect rest cure – Kathleen sends her love – so do the boys send theirs – & hoping you will soon be yourself again.

I remain your loving friend

Susie Isbester

Meanwhile, back in Melbourne, *Dalgonar* sailed for Newcastle, NSW, in the middle of April.

---

1 *Dalgonar* Articles of Agreement commencing 13 November 1912, Copy (Isbester collection).
2 Isbester, Captain John. Letter J22, 16.03.1913. (Isbester Collection).
3 Isbester, Captain John. Letter J23, 20.03.1913. (Isbester Collection).
4 Isbester, Captain John. Letter J24, 25.03.1913. (Isbester Collection).
5 Isbester, Captain John. Letter J25, 30.03.1913. (Isbester Collection).
6 Isbester, Captain John. Letter J26, 06.04.1913. (Isbester Collection).
7 Isbester, Captain John. Letter J36. 10.08.1913. (Isbester Collection).
8 Isbester, Susie. Letter S15. 07.04.1913. (Isbester Collection).

21 NEWCASTLE, NSW

John Isbester's letters to Susie give us insights into his work, his social life, his interests and his preoccupations. They give us some clues as to the sort of man he had become after 28 years of command and married life. They are, I think, worth quoting extensively. For the convenience of readers I have tidied his spelling and punctuation which were often chaotic, though he could, when necessary for a report, log book entry or letter to a son, write carefully. It is as though when writing informally he chose to write in the vernacular, while formal communications required a different approach. Writing to Susie from Newcastle on 29 April 1913[1] John Isbester had a tough winter passage from Melbourne to report.

> My Own Dear Susie,
>
> It's now two o'clock in the morning. I have just finished a long letter to the Owners so will commence this to you. We got here at 9AM yesterday [after a] 13 day passage. Head winds and calms and gales in the [Bass] Straits. We were battering about the rock for six days. However we are here all right to find that we are chartered to load coals for Callao, Peru, and that is not a loading port, so goodness knows when we get back. I have never had a line from the Owners since we left home or even Captain Kitchen, so I have surely offended them all.

It is not uncommon for those in lonely, responsible jobs to think that they must have done something wrong when their employers do not communicate. The employers are often busy men who see no need to communicate when from their point of view all is going well and there is nothing special to say, so Captain Isbester was probably worrying unnecessarily.

> I think it's just likely we will go in ballast to the Sound or Columbia River for grain home or wood back to Australia. So we will just wait and see.

John had received news of an acquaintance becoming a widower.

> I was really sorry to hear about Mrs Ramsey and just expect he will go to the dogs now except he marries soon. He will be able to get a wife yet – when Capt Williamson of Liverpool is getting married as soon as the 12 months is up. I did not write in sympathy.

It sounds as though John Isbester thought that Captain Williamson was seeking consolation rather too quickly!

In his next letter[2] John described having travelled on Saturday to the Linklaters in Sydney, only about 70 miles away, returning on Monday afternoon.

> I only saw Maggie, Jennie and Mr L. They are well. Jennie just got the engagement ring on that day. The young man is a brother of Charlie's wife, an engineer. I saw him and I think he's all right. I saw Capt Williamson, Herry & May and the Marms. They are all well.
>
> [I have received] a letter from the Owners today with the charterparty. Nothing in their letter, only a comment about getting the Ship put in good order etc. Freight 26/- so we ought to do something [i.e. make a profit] this voyage. They have sent me in now £1,500 and of course think that will be ample, but I don't.
>
> We are just now under the crane to take in stiffening, and will likely go back to discharge the balance of our ballast tonight.

Ballast and stiffening both being forms of extra weight loaded to prevent the ship from listing or capsizing under the weight of her spars, it might be wondered why one of those forms could not perform both roles. I suspect that the significant factor was whereabouts in the ship the weights were placed. The main hatch was located in the middle of the ship, and the ballast for the sea voyage from Melbourne to Newcastle would have been stowed in the middle of the ship. (Fig.21.1) But before it would be safe to unload the ballast to make space for the coal cargo, it would be necessary to load some stiffening ballast. That would have to be loaded in the empty spaces towards the ends of the hold, accessed through the smaller forward and after hatches. Once the sea ballast had been discharged from the centre of the hold and the space had been cleaned, the first of the coal cargo could be loaded through the main hatch, and then the stiffening could be unloaded through the forward and after hatches before they were used to load more coal.

> There is no more peace till we get to sea again. On Saturday after I left, the mate and others caught [the steward] going ashore with a tin of tapioca and brought it back. They are not supposed to have told me but I have got it and say that I can't let it pass with a comment – he is very attentive today.

Captain Isbester's next letter[3] begins:

> This is Sunday again and it's an awful day of wind and rain the whole day. We are at the wharf on the Newcastle side, loading. [Susie knew the port well, so there was no need to spend time describing it.] We have in nearly half our cargo and have to shift over to the cranes next week to finish. 4 or 5 more days ought to do us.
>
> Yesterday was a soldiers' parade. Capt Thompson and I went to see it and met the Hendersons, and of course had to go there to tea. I got back about 10.30, found the steward lying on the deck dead Drunk, carried him into his room and put him to bed like a baby. This morning roused him up about 7. He got up but had lost all the keys. However I got a key to open the pantry so I got a little coffee and in a few minutes after that the steward was missing. 4PM he is not back and no keys to be found. …

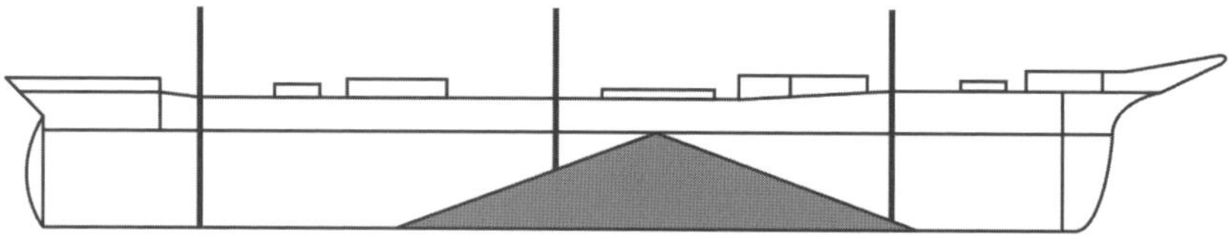

1. Ship arrives with 1000 tons of ballast

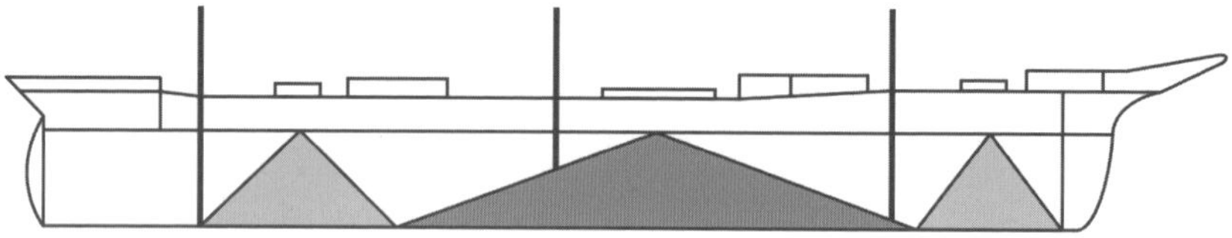

2. Loads 600 tons of stiffening

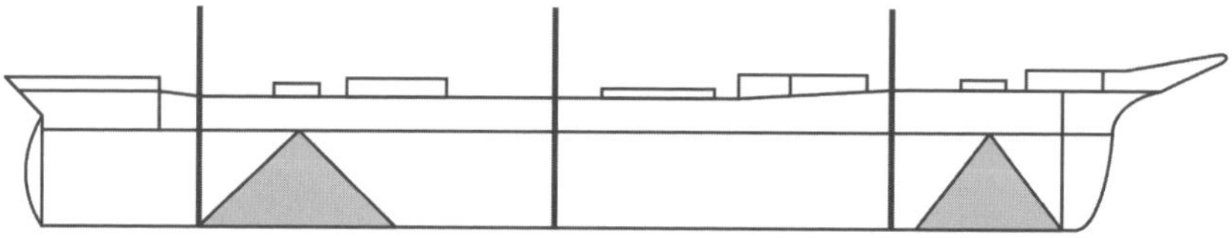

3. Discharges ballast

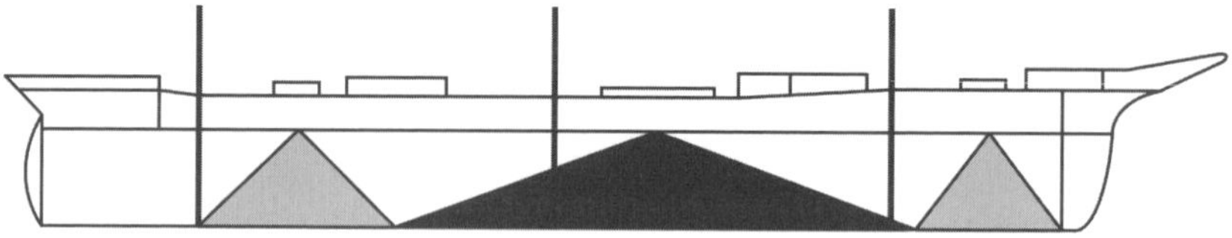

4. Loads part cargo of coal

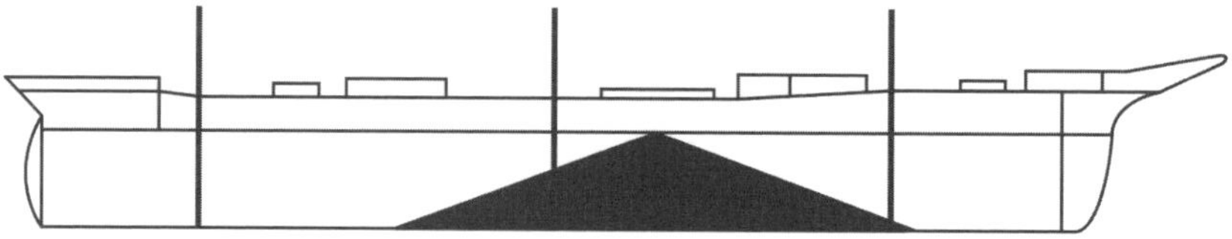

5. Discharges stiffening

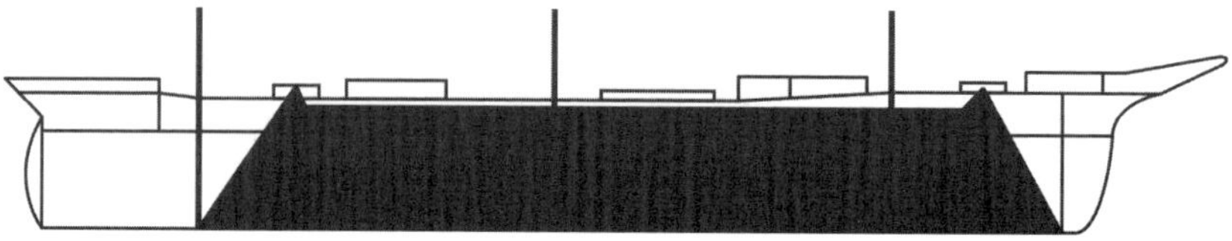

6. Completed loading full cargo of coal

Figure 21.1 *Ballast, stiffening and cargo sequence*

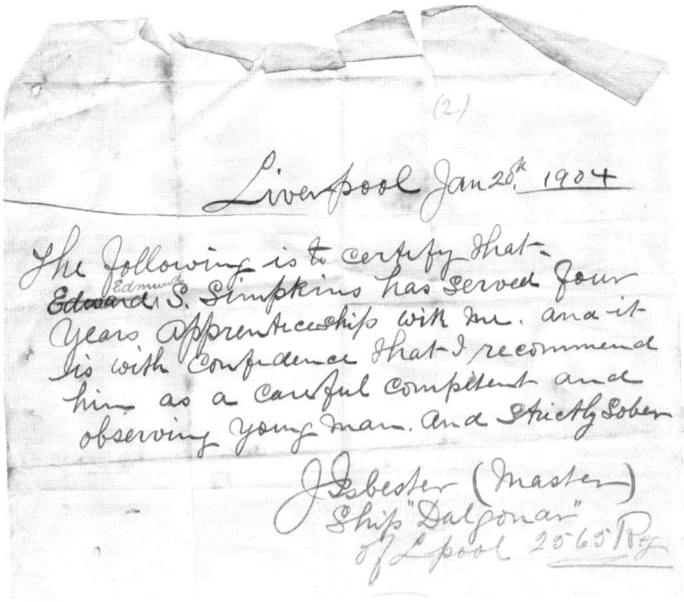
(2)

Liverpool Jan 26th 1904

The following is to certify that
~~Edward~~ Edmund S. Simpkins has served four
Years apprenticeships with me. and it
is with Confidence that I recommend
him as a careful competent and
observing young man. and Strictly Sober

J Isbester (Master)
Ship "Dalgonar"
of L'pool 2065 Reg

***Figure 21.2** Typical apprentice's reference issued on completion of service*

On Friday last I had a cable from the Owners Release App. Banks at Newcastle and give him what money he needs. So yesterday he is off to Sydney with £6 in his pocket, thinking to get a chance in a steamboat home. He is 14 days short of his time but is in a hurry to get home to try for his certificate this year. Whether he gets it or not I have sent him away in good shape with a Reference. [Fig.21.2]

A similar reference, issued by Captain Isbester to apprentice Simkins in 1904, read as follows:

The following is to certify that ~~Edward~~ Edmund S Simkins has served four years apprenticeship with me, and it is with confidence that I recommend him as a careful competent and observing young man, and strictly sober.

Captain Isbester had also written to Mr Banks about his boy – 'all smooth of course' – which seems to mean that his report was favourable. He continues:

Now May is promoted to Third Mate and of course Ocnard Second. (Acting).

Capt Thompson was to come here this afternoon and we were to go to church, but he will never come with this weather. Last week the railway was flooded for about 5 days, water 10 feet [3 metres] deep over the lines – no coals could be got down. They only started running yesterday. Now today it has been a deluge so I expect the lines will be flooded again.

I am just wild about the steward. We of course are taking in stores and he particularly would need to be here. We don't know how he got the money to get drunk yesterday. This [letter] will not go before Tuesday so I may add a line again. Tata to all, your Jack.

> Wednesday. The mail leaves today so I must finish off. Well we are under the cranes and I expect to finish off in another 1½ hours. I am just feeling sick. I got the steward on Monday and he promised to go on all right, but as soon as he gave me morning coffee yesterday he cleared ashore again. I have a warrant out for him but as yet have no word. Of course if I get him again I will keep him in gaol till we go. We have been hauling ship all night so feel out of shape. Had no bed made or boots cleaned for two days.

The steward's fall from grace was made all the worse because Captain Isbester and his visitors had previously been so complimentary about his work. The fact that he was behaving like an alcoholic would have been a bitter disappointment. Would he have lapsed had Captain Isbester not left the ship and gone to Sydney for two days?

> I got your No.4 yesterday. Did you notice in the home papers that Capt Nicholson (*Sad Jester*) [perhaps a ship] died on 27th Feb?
>
> Two more of our men deserted two nights ago. So we only have 5 left. Now I must stop as I have to write the owners and get ashore to ship them and hunt for the steward. Your own loving Hubby.

In his final letter from Newcastle[4] Captain Isbester had a disturbing account to give of the difficulties that a sick captain could experience.

> This is Sunday night, 9.30. We are now at the buoys loaded and to sail tomorrow afternoon. This forenoon I devoted to getting all the Owners' papers ready. Now I have nothing to do but write my leaving letter.
>
> Capt Thompson of the [ship] *British Isles* is a home Man [I think that this means a man from Shetland]. His ship was loaded a day before us, but since Thursday he has been in bed very sick, not able to get his shore business done. So after dinner today I went to see him and found him in bed almost not able to speak, and his dirty underclothes on and his bed in a most untidy state, and he had never tasted food since Friday. I asked his steward about him. He said he asked him in the morning if he wanted anything. He said No, so of course he was not asked again. I made him a cup of beef tea and toast. He drank the tea and about one mouthful of the bread. I left him and went ashore and rung up Dr Emes and got him sent on board and got Capt Sutherland, a home Man, to go off. We have all advised him to go to the Hospital, so he is to be taken ashore in the morning and of course will have to leave the ship. He has had an awful lot of trouble with his men in port, and the fact of the matter is he has been drinking and his head is full of disease, running at the ears and nose. He is four years older than me but he is too old to be from home without someone to look after him. He has got a New Mate and I just believe it's another Capt Young Case. However he will have to give up. Capt Sutherland and I have had a good talk about him so he will help him all he can. I will try to see him in the morning but have no time to do anything for him.

> Tonight I was at the Hendersons to tea. Mrs H is sending with me for Kath a silver butter dish and Mary is sending I think it's a silver egg stand, so Kath will have to write and thank them in anticipation of what is coming. Their address is 45 Military Road. [Sadly, as the consequence of events yet to be described, these gifts never reached Kathleen and Lewis.]
>
> It's a strong, fair wind today; I hope it lasts. All my bills are in. I only have to square up at Brown's office and see that they send the accounts home. Is it not strange – not a word from the Owners this Voyage but one two-or-three-lines with the Charter party and not a line or paper from Capt Kitchen. So – and not even Smith,
>
> Well my steward got clear of me. Sick [through] his own fault so he has got his money [i.e. been paid off]. I have got another steward, a Swede, a man about 30 and I think very good too, but time will show. They are a nuisance.
>
> My Old Mate is still very deaf but I think somewhat better. I have Ocnard as second and May as third. So I have the young and the old to deal with and I think they will do all right. One of our men deserted just before we left the dyck [berth] so of the old crew we only have 6 forward. The Carpenter is sticking all right.
>
> Well you can give us 60 days to fetch Callao so if this takes over 30 days to come home [to you] it will be time to write me again. I have signed on 10 of our men to be signed off in Callao. I expect to get men cheaper there. We pay £5 here and £2 bonus. Sailors on the coast here get £8. Oh I had a letter from Nellie Nicholson from Melbourne, a daughter of Bella Leask, telling me that her mother was dead.

That must have been a shock after John had been in her company only a few weeks previously. He had written then that she looked 'so old and ugly' and that 'three shoremen husbands had surely been too much for her'. He was observant if not particularly sympathetic.

> This girl's father was Jamie Nicholson, a brother of Mary that was at Olligarth. My cousin Robbie's daughter has got to Melbourne and got a place too. I am just in hopes to get a letter from you before we leave, at any rate this will have to be my sailing letter. No chance to write once we leave the buoys but I will not close it till the last thing.
>
> 2PM just going on board. Sail at 3PM may have a chance to drop a line to Mary – not so – tata. Love to all, Your Jack

The above three-page letter was embellished with a variety of additional notes written in the margins, one of which read:

> Here's where I finish up tomorrow so tata and love to all, your own loving hubby growl. Enclosed is the crew list.

A 'growl' seems to have been the word in use for a complaint. Lewis Davies used it several times in his letter.

It may be that the crew list was annotated with advances made to the crew, so that in the event of his death his estate would be able to recover from the owners the sums advanced.

John's final note[5] contained little of substance except that 'We have got Capt Thompson to the Hospital. I have been to see him and say good bye. and 3PM we are just letting go the buoys. Three steamboats taking us out, a fine, dry day and fair wind.'

1 Isbester, Captain John. Letter J27, 29.04.1913. (Isbester Collection).
2 Isbester, Captain John. Letter J28, 06.05.1913. (Isbester Collection).
3 Isbester, Captain John. Letter J29, 25.05.1913. (Isbester Collection).
4 Isbester, Captain John. Letter J30, 01.06.1913. (Isbester Collection).
5 Isbester, Captain John. Letter J31, 02.06.1913. (Isbester Collection).

22 CALLAO, PERU

In his first letter after arriving in Callao on 27 July, John Isbester is fretting, understandably, because there was no letter from Susie. As he pointed out[1]

> My Own Dear Susie,
>
> Here I am turned up again all right and no letter from you. This is now the third time since we married, both cases before it was bad news.

The first occasion was, I believe, when John Magnus, their second child, had died in June 1888 aged one year, and the second the death of their daughter Thyra, aged two, in August 1900; so John's apprehension was understandable. He continues:

> What can be the matter? I have a letter from Kath, she says nothing about anyone being ill. Her letter was written on the 8th of June. If you are well I think you have forgot about me. We had a passage of 54 days – not over good, but not too bad for us. The *Inveraven* came here a few hours after us from Melbourne, 75 days so we beat her well, and the *British Isles* that was loaded two days before us in Newcastle is not here yet. I got the Capt to hospital just the Monday that we left, so who is Capt of her I don't know. We had a very lumpy passage but got over it all right. Small damages, sails etc but all our cross trees are up. We got to anchor 8.30PM Friday so I could not get the cable sent to give you the news for Sunday. The Dr. did not come to us till nearly noon Saturday so of course I could not leave the ship and the first three days of next week are holidays. Is it not annoying, and us chartered to load nitrate at some other port on the coast for UK or Continent. So if all goes well I ought to be beside you for your birthday [11 March] if you are still alive. It wasn't much we or I could do at Rochefort and I expect it will be less next time. Kath writes bright enough but surely she is not well if there is no sign yet.

Kathleen had been married for more than a year and still no baby! Captain John was becoming impatient.

> She remarks about Arthur Sanderson's sudden death but I can't understand if it's old or young Arthur so I'll just have to wait. I hope Davies will get a boat soon. I would go Quarter Master with him.

John Isbester seems to be foreseeing that his career as a sailing ship master is coming to an end, and contemplating the possibility of getting employment as a helmsman on steamships with his son-in-law! That would be an inappropriate end to a distinguished career.

> We had very good men [for the voyage] across. They were shipped to be paid off here so they got ashore yesterday morning.

The temporary hands were paid off on arrival because they were being paid at the high rate necessary to attract men in Australia, and because while in port there was less work to be done.

> We are 14 now. The steward is not too bad, just a little liberal in some things. The other little fellow I find was a little sneak. He was paid!!

Captain Isbester does not seem to have realised that alcoholism is an illness and that the previous steward, who had been excellent when sober, appeared to have been in its clutches.

> I have three letters from the owners. Nothing much in them but the Charter parties and bear in mind do all I can to get the ship in good order. … Mr Ocnard is doing not so bad as second and May of course is third. The Old Mate is still pumping through his head but his hearing is still very bad and every time he has used the pump he goes round with cotton in his nose for an hour or two afterwards. I think losing his hearing is making him silly.
>
> I had a letter from Capt Kitchen. I sent him a PC from Newcastle. He says the reason he did not write was he thought he had offended me somehow. He wrote me twice to London and got no answer and I did not even send him a card when I was sailing. I don't remember getting his letters, and you know what time I had to write anyone when we were leaving London. I can tell by the tone of his letter that he knows that Smith and I did not get on but I don't think he has seen Smith. I think Stanhope must tell him. …
>
> I have wrote about 5 sheets to the Owners so I am just about played out. Of course I was just ashore a few hours yesterday and saw the agent etc. It's not a bad looking place as far as I have seen. Today appears to be a great day with them, lots of illuminations and fireworks etc. Kath says Norman is thin but as hard as nails. It's nice for the boys to have Kath to go to. Kath can tell Jones that lots of his slops are going but there are lots on hand yet.

Slops were clothing, oilskins, boots etc. and soap and tobacco for sale to the ship's company. It seems that on this voyage they had been supplied by a contact of Kathleen's.

> I hope the boys are getting on at School. I wonder if you got that Newcastle cheque and if Eric got his bike and if he got it strong enough. I wonder if Allan's stature is still increasing. [This sounds like a family joke, echoing Allan's schoolboy liking

for elaborate language when simpler words would do.] I suppose there is no word from Arthur St Clair or his wife. It will come yet.

This doesn't go before Tuesday Via Panama …

1.25AM!!! Monday. I am thinking of going ashore in the afternoon so will try to get this posted. This holiday is terrible. Not even the post open.

Love to all. I just hope you are all alive.

Your Loving Jack

John Isbester's next letter to Susie, written four days later[2] on 31 July, had at its head, in bold letters, 'No letters yet what on earth can be the matter JI'. He continued:

My Own Dear Susie

A week today since we arrived and no letter from you. I cannot know what to think of it. Surely something must be wrong. I wish somebody would write me. Kath's letter was the 8th June. She made no remarks of anything being wrong but lots could happen in less time. Surely the Owners would cable me if anything was wrong with you. Well, we are still at anchor in the bay, have to wait our turn to get to dock to discharge. We are nine ships in the bay now, we are the third on turn which means about a week yet. The 4 holidays are over thank goodness, but it will take the natives as many more to get over their spree so I am afraid we are not going to get much of a dispatch here. Then we are of course to ballast for some port to the southward to load nitrate for UK or Continent. So whether I get home for your birthday or not remains to be seen. I hear there is a mail in today, surely I will have a letter so I won't close this till I see. I will be at the office to see them open the doors.

Fortunately I shipped the crew in Australia to be paid off here so 16 of them have been ashore since we arrived. They are of course here yet and hard up. Some of them I expect to ship again. Wages here, I understand, is £3.10 and we were paying £5. I think my cook and steward will try to keep straight; they are afraid of being paid off. The Old Mate is just moving about and almost as deaf as a doorpost. He looks at me with such a woebegone look. When he can't hear, it just makes him silly but I don't growl much at him, the sailors do enough of that, so tata till I get ashore to hunt for letters.

Love to all, Your Own Loving Hubby Growl.

A week later on 7 August and Captain Isbester was really rattled.[3]

My Dear Susie

or somebody else, for God sake why don't somebody cable? What is the matter? Today I have cabled the owners. Whatever can be the Matter? Surely my whole family is suffocated with gas or a 1,001 other thing I imagine. For God sake give me the word. Your loving Husband.

The following day John Isbester had received a cable from the owners saying 'All well' and one from Susie with the one word 'Well', but these were no comfort to him because all his instincts told him that something was seriously wrong and it was being hidden from him. On 8 August he wrote:[4]

My Own Dear Susie

This is really terrible. I know that you are alive at all. You must be very very low and may not know that I am cabling at all. This suspense is terrible. I know you or the people around you are trying to save me some great choke[shock?]. The last cable I sent I paid three reply but got none. I then cabled to the Owners and got their reply. All Well. Your only reply was Well. That was not sufficient. A Mail is due here on Monday. If I get no letter I must insist on a reply. I think and dream of 10,000 things that might have happened. I think of the whole family being suffocated with gas or maybe a railway accident, perhaps you and the boys going to Cardiff, but it's no use accumulating on it.

I can't know nothing. All I have is the Owners 'All well' and it can't be true. I know something must be very seriously wrong with you. I wrote you a long letter last week but could not post it, because you can't be alive and conscious and you must have been ill for a long time or I would have had letters ere now. We are two weeks here now. Kaths letter the 8th June is the last word I have. Then you appeared to be all right. She was speaking about the boys coming to her for their holidays and no doubt you would go with them so what has happened I can't think. If I get no letter on Monday I must cable again and insist on a reply. I can't send this till I get some word what can be the matter. It's so terrible that no one will tell me. I may say all the world knows it but me. I can't think you will ever read this and I can't send it till I get some news. To cable me the only address is Capt *Dalgonar* Callao or any other place we may be. And any number of small words to make a sentence so long as the combined number of letters does not exceed 10_can be put as one word. I can't write. I can't think you will ever read it. Fondest love to all ,tata. No mail from here before Tuesday. We only got to dock tomorrow to commence discharging so we will be about six weeks here yet.

Two days later John was expressing his dismay and anxiety again, aware that Susie was behaving in a manner unlike anything he had known in the past 28 years.[5] It seems unlikely that the work of the ship was receiving his full attention.

My Own Dear Susie

It surely cannot be possible that you are alive. The Owners cabled to me 'All well' but that cannot be true. Of course I know that I have some terrible shock to get. Whatever it is I cannot think. I think of a 1,000 things that could have happened. If I get no letters tomorrow I must cable again. Of course I know the reason I don't get a cable, is it's too terrible to cable. I asked the owners is my wife dead. They did not answer that question. They replied 'All well' That's not true

> but of course they are holding back too till I get the news by letter. I just wonder if I will get the sad news tomorrow. Who can it be? I believe it's My Own Dear Susie. I can't write, my dreams are terrible. I am just afraid no one wrote till they heard of our arrival. If so it will nearly three weeks before I get it. I can't wait that long – I must have answer if you are alive or not. I know it's too terrible to cable to me but what must I do. What can I do if you are gone? God Grant that you are alive. Loving Hubby

Finally on 11 August John received a letter from Susie, who seems to have blamed new people in the office for failing to tell her when *Dalgona*r had sailed from Newcastle. John replied:[6]

> Well Susie Dear
>
> You have given me a gluff [Shetland dialect for fright[7]] this time. Why on earth did you not answer my cable when I sent it reply paid? Three words. I was sure you were dead and nobody would let me know how it happened till I should get the letter. Of course I had to cable to the Owners too and got their reply All well. Why you did not give me that when I paid for three words reply? At any rate you appear to have lost the run of me altogether this time. It's needless to comment on what I have thought this last 18 days. No letters and would not reply when the cable was paid for.

This is repetitive, an indication of the extreme anxiety he had been experiencing, but John had not mailed his previous letters and finally sent them along with this one, so it is only in this letter that he makes his protests to Susie for the first time.

> However your letter came today and it's all right. But I can tell you I am just about done for. I don't think I have slept 7 hours in 7 nights. This morning I was ashore at 7AM with a cable ready for The Minister [presumably of the Scottish Presbyterian church in Ilford] demanding a reply, but thank God your letter came. I could not send letters because I was sure you were dead. So send them all now.
>
> You should have written to Mr Stanhope and asked to let you know when we left Newcastle.
>
> I am well aware that the office is not as they were. But I am not going to give them any gold for brass. They can stick their ship up. I will not knuckle down to them. I will do what I think right and they can growl.

With new people in the office and *Dalgonar* to be sold, John Isbester was not a happy man and his annoyance with his instructions from the office is clear. There is no way of knowing what instruction he resented so much, but it is safe to assume that in times that were difficult for sailing ships the owners wanted more for less and that as an experienced master Captain Isbester was unwilling to comply.

> Your letter today is all grumble and money difficulties as usual.

Seamen on sailing ships were paid about half the wages received by men employed on steam ships, and the same was probably true for captains. I have found no record of my grandfather's earnings during his 28 years in command, but it is my impression is that his savings were modest and that he and his family spent without hesitation on travelling in numbers to visit the ship. They had probably helped to finance Arthur Isbester's setting up in New Zealand in 1911 when he was aged only 22 or thereabouts. Money difficulties are not the first things that spring to mind when one thinks of ships' captains, but Susie and five children would doubtless have plenty of ideas of how to spend any money that was available. At the time of John Isbester's untimely death in 1913 his estate was valued at £1,139 15s 8d.[8] The letter continues:

> Capt Shaw has brought me some tabloids [tablets] to cure my head and will post this for me so I am off to bed. Last night our rooster started crowing at 9.30 and I was sure our flag would be Half Mast today. It was all you I was thinking about. Your Jack.

John's next letter, written on 17 August, begins:

> My Own Dear Susie[9]
>
> Sunday again and we are eight days in Dock and have got about 1,000 tons discharged. Not the ¼ of our cargo. I expect to be about a month yet. The mail boat is in tonight and I expect your 2nd letter tomorrow. It's a comfort to think that you are still alive. You have given me a gluff this time but of course I will get over that and I have no wish to have anyone to manage the house or family for you.

After repeating his complaints about no letters yet again, Captain Isbester continues:

> I have had three letters [forwarded] from Newcastle, No.6.8.9. 7 appears to be missing but may come yet. You surely see now how it was, that it was a fortnight after leaving Melbourne that you heard from me. We were 13 days on the passage. We were 9 days battering about the rock in Bass Straits. So I can tell you I was tired enough when we got to Newcastle. You forget all about that sort of thing. Your letter here is a mix up. You are writing supposed to be the 6th of June and at the same time you say that Haswell wrote long ago that we sailed on the 22nd June. You are adrift in the month and I suppose you were sober. Then your next part is written on 13th July. Well the whole trouble is the owners not letting you know when we did sail. I will ask them to do so in future. I know they have changed but I don't intend to knuckle down to them in the least. Of course it will be the sack this time, ship sold or not.

Captain Isbester writes like a troubled man, still distressed by Susie's failures to communicate as expected, disturbed because he does not have a good working relationship with the new people in the office, and taking tabloids for his head. He is grizzling uncharacteristically at Susie, and ready to think the worst of his employers.

> I have been ashore every day this week except yesterday so four Captains came to the ship to know if I had kicked the bucket but I was alive and on end but had nothing to do ashore. This forenoon I was ashore about 2 hours and feel nothing the matter with me.

This rather suggests, as do the four captains calling to enquire about his health, that he half-expected to feel that something *was* the matter with him.

> So, what a lot of people married about the same time as we did are separated by death. Mrs Nicolson, Emily, Mrs Morrison, etc. So poor old Georgison has gone. Well he was about 71 when he left me. He had about £450 and I expect he will leave about £200.

Georgison was clearly a former shipmate, probably a first mate in view of his age and resources.

> So Miss Rogers had paid you a visit. She is daft of course. I am glad to hear that you had Miss Peter with you. Do you know I had her in my mind to look after our children, and another idea was to lodge Eric in London and get Kath to take the younger two and I would go on working for them for as long as I could.

John Isbester had been thinking seriously about what plans to make in the event of Susie's death. Happily, those plans could be put on hold.

> Well today we had neither cook nor steward. I paid the cook off on Wednesday and cleared the stew off last night. The cook was a little frisky and came aft making a noise with the steward. I had to speak to him. He used dirty language and the result was he wanted to be discharged. I took him at his word, paid him next day, and yesterday the mate had to be ashore seeing the coals weighed and did not get on board for tea till 10 minutes to 6. We had just finished tea. The Stew refused to give him his tea and had actually thrown it out. Of course I had to come to the rescue and demand tea for the mate or he [the steward] must get on shore. He chose the latter. None of us are sorry. He was a most disagreeable man to have about you. Today the carpenter has done the cooking of his own accord and done it the best we have had since last port. And a boy that I shipped in London [is] acting cabin boy (not the owner's boy – he deserted in Mel.) Four English ships here just now are discharging their cooks & stewards. Two cooks have been on board today but I have not decided yet. That's just to show you that I am not the only one that nobody can please. Even my wife after 30 years experience. But what I think is the matter with my wife is she is sorry that she did not get married to a foreman with £4 a week and get a hump at least every second night. However I consider I am a good judge of wives and I know that my wife is no judge of men. Now I think if you are agreeable we won't change now.

As my father Allan Isbester wrote 'As children we all knew that our parents were in love.'[10] That was what enabled them to joke so intimately and to insult each other so affectionately. Susie must have been relieved to read the last sentence!

> You never mention Arthur, likely you know nothing about him. … By the time you get this we ought to be leaving here for our next port. Tomorrow when I'm writing the owners I will ask them to let you know where we go so you can write me. I don't want to get knocked out again. You know I am not like Capt Williamson that got a wife for his money. So love to all, remember me to Auntie and tell her that I was just about wiring her. So good night, I will finish here tomorrow when I get your letter. Your Own Jack Yet Monday Night The mail has not arrived and this has to go at 8AM tomorrow so I am posting it tonight. I am getting a clean looking Chinaman [as cook] and he gets a boy with him. The Mate has been with him and says he's all right, so hope to be better than we have been. Love to all Your Own Jack

In the same post as his letter to Susie was a postcard featuring Reloj de la Darsena, a Callao harbour scene[11] for son Allan. The message read:

> Dear Allan I am pleased to hear that you have got trowsers. Look out that you don't hang them on the back of the bedroom door as Harry did. This [is] where we land with the boat from the boy [*sic*] Your loving father.

This presumably marked my father's transition from kilt to trousers. Who Harry was, and what misfortune befell him when he hung his trousers on the back of the bedroom door, we can only guess.

Some three weeks elapsed before John's next letter which, after the usual salutation, continued:[12]

> Here is Sunday night again and we are still in dock and have about 550 Tons to discharge yet. We have had lots of stoppages this week for cars to take the coals away and after tomorrow we will only be able to work with one crane. We have about 550 tons of ballast in and expect to finish ballasting before all the coals are out. I have no word yet where we are to load. I wrote Charterers on 26th ult and have no reply yet, however I expect to be all the coming week before we finish. This leaves here on Tuesday but I am not sure whether a mail comes tomorrow. Well today I have had company. Capt Evans the Deputy Dock Master and his wife and Capt – of the floating dock, his wife and daughter of 16 or thereabouts. The latter are Dundee people and very nice. They had dinner and tea with us and of course Mr Mull entertained us with his gramophone. Our China steward of course is away again, he was badly with his liver again. He had been three months in hospital with the same trouble. Our cook that left home with us is back again, spent all his money and glad to come back, and the boy I shipped in London is acting cabin boy and does remarkably well, so if I don't get a steward

> I may have to do with him. The cook has got a pull down. I think he will be not so ready to get on the high horse. My company left between 9 & 10 o'clock so all is quiet now.
>
> A week between your letters seems too long now. I weary for them. Surely it's this gloof [gluff = fright] that I have got that makes me impatient.
>
> I think I like Allan in his suit, but it's so dark a photo that you can't see it well but I have had the magnifying glass on it. He's all right. I hope he gets on well at school and will be able to do something with his head bye and bye. A dentist would be a good thing if he would only think of it and we were able to get him to that.

(Allan continued to do very well at Ilford County High School, his school reports suggesting that he would flourish at university – but following his father's untimely death,[13] the family's finances were difficult and Allan had to leave school at 16 and become a butcher's boy. He was called up for national service in 1918 and served in the Army of Occupation in Germany. As an ex-serviceman he was then able to complete a two-year teachers' training course at Goldsmiths College in London, where he made lifelong friends and was launched on a career as a teacher of English.)

John Isbester's letter ends with

> So I'll stop tonight and see what tomorrow brings forth. Love to all, your Jack
>
> I made my bed this morning myself and find I have put the blanket next to me but won't change till I see how I get on.

Oh, the problems of being without a proper steward! He probably had a rather scratchy night.

A day later John Isbester had heard again from Susie, and on 8 September he wrote:[14]

> Dear Susie
>
> Your two letters with enclosures vis Cable arrival of son Arthur Giffords and Stanhope. etc – well it's all past now, but I cannot help saying A Isbester must be a fool. How he will lose the confidence of people all around him.

From what follows in Captain John's response to Susie's letter it seems that 'Arrival of son Arthur', 'Giffords' and 'Stanhope' are three different topics. Stanhope was from the company office but no further details are provided. Dr George Gifford was an uncle of Susie's who plays no part in this account. But the reference to their eldest son, Arthur, is significant: six months previously, on 21 January 1913, in Havelock, NZ, Arthur had married Violet May Hodgman, a New Zealander.[15] Their son, Norman Gifford John St Clair Isbester, was born on 19 June.[16] Was it the fact of Arthur's misbehaviour in conceiving a child out of wedlock, or his deserting of Nellie to whom he had previously been committed,[17] or was there some other matter that caused John Isbester to write 'A Isbester must be a fool. How he will lose the confidence of people all around him'?

Captain and Mrs Isbester had for years been pillars of the Presbyterian church in Ilford and in Shetland (Fig.22.1). His own illegitimacy remained a rarely mentioned cause for embarrassment. These events, whatever their nature, seem to have caused his father more distress than Arthur's three months in gaol. Sadly grandson Norman died on 28th July 1913, of congenital heart disease, aged 39 days. There is no reason to think that John Isbester ever knew that.

His letter continues:

> Our Cook is leaving again. No Stewards to be got. I think I can get another cook so – Going to sea would be a pleasure if it were not for the low people we have to deal with.

This observation is rather more than the uninformed complaint of a captain out of sympathy with his subordinates. In the 1900s, sailing ships attracted some fine captains, officers, petty officers and apprentices, but the pay was poor and the conditions – the work, the accommodation and the food – were often grim. Some of the officers and many of the sailors were men with ill health, with little education, and addicted to drink. The temporary and arbitrary nature of their employment gave them no reason to be loyal to their employers.

Captain Isbester's letter ends with an obscure exhortation, written in the margins with a different pen. As his letter is to Susie the exhortations are addressed to her, but their purpose is unclear. 'That was one of my fears. Mull Mooning pay attention don't neglect to get advice. I can't get there to stop it –.' This presumably refers to a problem at home, mentioned in Susie's most recent letter. Reasons for worry were mounting up.

Figure 22.1 Captain John and Susie Isbester with the halfdeck in the background

John's next letter,[18] written six days later on 14 September, begins:

> Sunday night again and we are still in dock. 350 Tons to discharge yet. This last week the labourers have been three days on strike. They worked yesterday but their dispute is not settled yet so whether they work tomorrow remains to be seen. It's terrible, this delay when the ship might be doing something. I have no word where we are to load yet. I expect to be all next week in dock yet. So *Sad Jester* is gone. Well, his daughter was a bad lot. She will no doubt get her reward yet ... A new cook tomorrow again, that's the third one since weve been here. A German again. We had an English man three days and found out that his wably was wrong [he had a genital infection] so of course that would not do. I am having to look after the Stores nearly myself. The boy that's [working] in the cabin can't do [it] himself.
>
> Capts. Ladenham, Brown and I have been at church tonight again. The Dock Master always gives us a welcome but the minister is an old duffer. It's English Church so we only know the hymn book when we get the Number, and we don't kneel as they do. The congregation amounts to about 40 or 50, all of course English people. They all know us, but not many of them are sociable so we just put our shilling in the bag and come away. I just think their service all a sham.

Captain Isbester was doing his best to get *Dalgonar* ready for the threatened sale.

> We have got the tween decks all painted and hope to get the lower hold done on the passage to our loading port. Of course I am having to buy paint and oil as they were so anxious to cut down our usual supply at home for 8 Months!!! Of course it costs much more here but I don't care. I'll have it if I can see my way to get it used ...

John Isbester's next short letter,[19] written three days later on 17 September, updates the catering situation but contains little else of significance.

> We have another German cook. So far he seems all right, and the boy I shipped in London I am making cabin boy, so I will have to be steward, however I think we will get along all right. Capts Brown & Ladingham are here waiting me to go to the post so I'd better cut this short and say bye bye.

Writing on 21 September John had commercial news for Susie:[20]

> Sunday night again. Well we finished the discharging yesterday 4PM and 1000 Tons of ballast in. Still that means we have discharged 4057 Ton,s the most we have ever had, so the Owners ought to believe that I loaded down to our marks this time. Our freight is 26/- a Ton. Allan will tell you what that amounts to.

It was a nice touch for Captain John to provide a calculation for his academic son, Allan, who would have found that 4057 × 26/20 = £5,274 2s 0d, the freight earned by *Dalgonar* for transporting 4,057 tons of coal from Newcastle NSW to Callao over a period of about 160 days from departure Melbourne. That is less than £33 per day to meet all the costs of operating the ship, including various port charges, the wages of the ship's company, catering costs and equipment renewals. He continued:

> Charterers have not named the loading port yet. I wired them yesterday so will surely get it shortly. I would not be surprised if it's Taltal. If it is won't I give the Consul fits about our flags that he got and never returned, nor ever acknowledged my letters. Well tomorrow 6AM we are to move out to the bay and will likely sail on the 24th or 25th inst. I have to get ashore as early as possible to ship the men. Plenty here. The cook we had this last week was found to have a dose of lady's fever [venereal disease?] so was put ashore last night and another man arranged with to be shipped tomorrow. Well I spent the day on board doing accounts etc, went to church at 6. Capts Brown & Ladenham went up to Lima in the afternoon intending to be back to church but did not turn up even for the collection. I went to church with Mrs Capt Evans and came back with her to the house, and about half an hour later Brown and Ladenham turned up so after an hour's chat we got tea and cake. Evans, you will remember, is the deputy dockmaster. She [his wife] is a Liverpool woman and just makes us do anything she likes. Evans was out early so was too lazy to go to church and has to be out about us tomorrow too [to oversee the departure of *Dalgonar*].
>
> I was sorry to hear that Capt Summers' foot was not so well again, but it's all right ere now and he is able to dispense with the shear legs [sailor talk for crutches]. Tell Mrs Summers that I won't want to talk ship now that I am tired of them. Remember me to Auntie and Miss Rogers if she is still with you. Love to all the boys, your very own Loving Hubby

In a postscript he expressed his eagerness for Kathleen to provide a grandchild, as she and Lewis finally did in 1918:

> I hope Lewis has got over his cold and is in harness again. I think he should have a month home and see to get a shot in the locker X

Later a final page was added (Fig.22.2):

> Monday night
>
> We have got orders for Tocopilla. At 6 this morning we have towed to the bay and came to anchor and I went ashore with the tug to start the day's clearing up. Well in the first place I shipped 16 men and the cook that left home with us as cook and steward. He comes on board in the morning, nothing better to get. We are to leave here on 24th – Wednesday and if our luck is fair we ought to be not more than 20

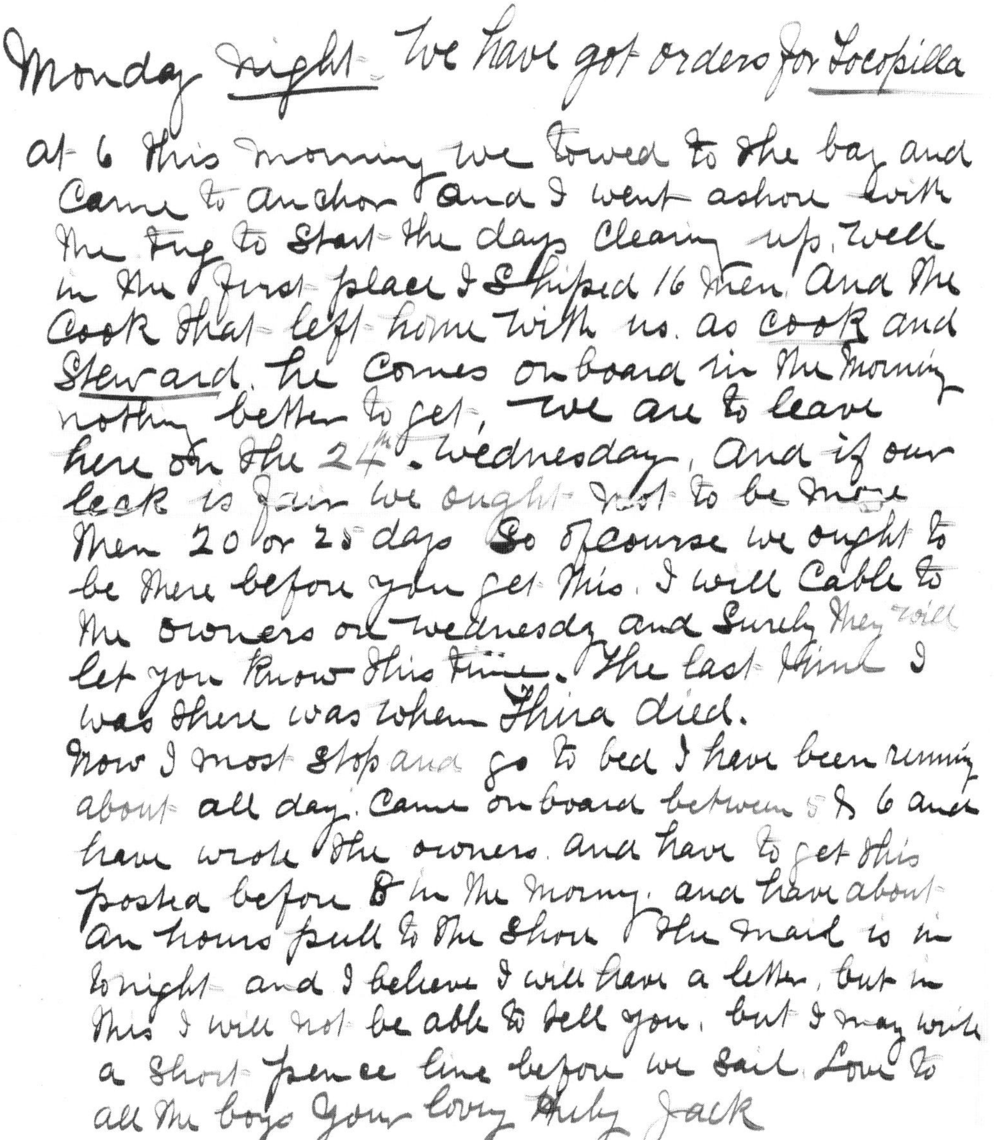

Monday night We have got orders for Tocopilla
at 6 this morning we towed to the bay and
came to anchor and I went ashore with
the tug to start the day clearing up. well
in the first place I shipped 16 men and the
cook that left home with us as cook and
steward. he comes on board in the morning
nothing better to get, we are to leave
here on the 24th. Wednesday. and if our
luck is fair we ought not to be more
than 20 or 25 days so of course we ought to
be there before you get this. I will cable to
the owners on Wednesdy and surely they will
let you know this time. The last time I
was there was when Thira died.
Now I must stop and go to bed I have been running
about all day. came on board between 5 & 6 and
have wrote the owners. and have to get this
posted before 8 in the morning. and have about
an hours pull to the shore the mail is in
tonight and I believe I will have a letter, but in
this I will not be able to tell you. but I may write
a short pencil line before we sail. Love to
all the boys Your loving Hubby Jack

Figure 22.2 The final page of John Isbester's last letter to Susie

or 25 days, so of course we ought to be there before you get this. I will cable to the owners on Wednesday and surely they will let you know this time. The last time I was there was when Thira [*sic*] died.

Now I must stop and go to bed. I have been running about all day. Came on board between 5 & 6 and have wrote the owners and have to get this posted before 8 in the morning and have about an hour's pull to the shore. The mail is in tonight

> and I believe that I will have a letter, but in this I will not be able to tell you but I may write a short pence line before we sail. Love to all the boys. Your loving Hubby Jack.

All seemed to be normal as Captain Isbester embarked on the most challenging voyage of his career.

---

1 Isbester, Captain John. Letter J32. 27.07.1913. (Isbester Collection).
2 Isbester, Captain John. Letter J33. 31.07.1913. (Isbester Collection).
3 Isbester, Captain John. Letter J34. 07.08.1913. (Isbester Collection).
4 Isbester, Captain John. Letter J35. 08.08.1913. (Isbester Collection).
5 Isbester, Captain John. Letter J36. 10.08.1913. (Isbester Collection).
6 Isbester, Captain John. Letter J37. 11.08.1913. (Isbester Collection).
7 Angus, James Stout. *A glossary of the Shetland Dialect.* Alexander Gardner, Paisley. 1914.
8 Ipswich District Probate Registry, 16.04.1914. John Isbester.
9 Isbester, Captain John. Letter J38. 17.08.1913. (Isbester Collection).
10 Isbester, Charles Allan. Note: Family history. CAI4. Undated. (Isbester Collection).
11 Isbester, Captain John. PC.CAI60, 17.08.1913. (Isbester Collection).
12 Isbester, Captain John. Letter J39. 07.09.1913. (Isbester Collection).
13 See Chapter 23.
14 Isbester, Captain John. Letter J40. 08.09.1913. (Isbester Collection).
15 New Zealand marriage certificate No.1913001747.
16 New Zealand birth certificate No.1913003632.
17 See Chapter 18.
18 Isbester, Captain John. Letter J41. 14.09.1913. (Isbester Collection).
19 Isbester, Captain John. Letter J42. 17.09.1913. (Isbester Collection).
20 Isbester, Captain John. Letter J43. 21.09.1913. (Isbester Collection).

23 THE LOSS OF THE *DALGONAR*

This account is based on the Report of the Formal Investigation[1] (Appendix 4), an impressively clear, objective and balanced document, combined with the dramatic record of events written from memory by Mr W.A.H. Mull, Chief Mate[2] (Appendix 5), while aboard the barque *Loire* in the days after the rescue, with additions taken from the account provided by Captain Michel Jaffré of the *Loire*.[3] The account of the launching of the ship's boats has been amended to take account of information provided by Captain Jaffré and by the master of the ship *Marie* who inspected the *Dalgonar* in calm conditions a fortnight after she had been abandoned. My object is to be as factually accurate as possible while including the gripping and vivid detail of the events. Discussion of the events is left to Chapter 24.

While completing the discharge of about 4,000 tons of coal at Callao, *Dalgonar* took on board 1,000 tons of shingle ballast, 660 tons in No.2 hold, and 340 tons in No.3 hold. She also had about 30 tons of coal in the forepeak. Her draught of water on sailing was 11 feet 7 inches forward and 12 feet 9 inches aft, giving a mean draught of 12 feet 2 inches. She left the dock at Callao on 21 September 1913, and was anchored in the bay in order to get her ready for sea. The deckhands who arrived at Callao in her had been paid off, and fresh crew members joined just before sailing.

The shingle ballast was trimmed and levelled down, and bulkheads of about 6 feet in height were erected at the fore and after ends of each of the two blocks of shingle. The shingle was sloped down so as to be at each end about 18 inches below the top of the bulkhead. The master sought to secure the shingle by the use in each hatchway of a diamond-shaped bin, made of wood, about 20 feet long and 3 feet deep, which was let about 18 inches into the top of the shingle, and the four corners of each bin were lashed to stanchions to keep it in position. Some centre shifting boards were put up at the fore and after ends of the ballast, but they only went about 18 inches into the ballast. The ballast was then boarded over, but the boards were not shored. All this work was done under the master's supervision. Captain Isbester is reported to have told the chief mate that the forthcoming passage was certain to be a fair weather one.

The *Dalgonar* left Callao on 24 September 1913 with a crew of 30 hands all told, bound for Taltal[4] where she was to load nitrate. On sailing, the wind was a light south-easterly and the weather was fine. All sail was set and the vessel was found to be very stiff (i.e. she rolled rapidly in the swell – an uncomfortable motion – due to the weight of the ballast concentrated in the bottom of the hold).

Heading south-west by west, the *Dalgonar* experienced fine weather until 7 October, when in latitude 29° S, longitude 84° W, the wind gradually freshened from the east and east-south-east, and some canvas was reduced. On 8 October, the wind was still freshening and the weather was squally. At noon all hands wore ship, putting the vessel on the starboard tack heading north-east to north-north-east. At 1900 the fore upper topsail was taken in, and at 2300 the main and mizzen upper topsails were taken in. The vessel was put under three lower topsails and foresail.[5] At 0830 on 9 October, the vessel was running north-east and it was blowing a moderate gale from east-south-east with high seas running from the south-east. The captain sent the first mate and carpenter down into the hold to see if the ballast was all right, and a few of the hatch covers were taken off to allow some light into the hold. The mate stated that when they got below and were standing on the ceiling (i.e. the base of the hold) forward of the ballast in No.2 hold, the ballast was found to be all right. At that moment the force of the wind carried away the fore topsail and the watch went up aloft to pick up the remains. At the same time, the ship gave a heavy lurch to port and the shingle in No.2 hold shifted bodily from underneath the bin. The shift of ballast in No.2 hold caused the vessel to have a list to port of about 20 degrees. The master ordered all hands below to trim back the ballast, and with considerable difficulty they succeeded in getting her nearly upright by 1130. The planks and hatch covers were replaced on top of the ballast, which was then for the first time shored down from the tween deck beams. The position at noon was latitude 31°45 S, longitude 85°27 W, and it 'was blowing a very hard gale with a terrific high sea and heavy rain squalls every half hour'.

Attempts were afterwards made by the men of the starboard watch to shore down the shingle in No.3 hold in a similar manner, but this was not completed before the disaster occurred at about 2 30 pm, when a very heavy squall struck the vessel accompanied by a very high sea, throwing her nearly over on her beam ends, with heavy spray flying over the vessel 'like steam', with the result that the shingle in Nos. 2 and 3 holds again shifted bodily to port, the shores gave way and the vessel acquired a heavy list. Some of the crew working in the hold had their legs trapped by the shifting shingle and had great difficulty in freeing themselves. All hands were again called on deck, some of the port watch arriving almost naked, and the carpenter was ordered to batten down the hatches.

Captain Isbester then attempted to wear the ship, to bring the wind to port which would tend to push her upright. The main and crossjack yards were squared, the sails were shivered and the helm was put hard over. When, after turning only from north-east to north-north-east she would go no further, Captain Isbester ordered the mate to hoist the inner and outer jibs with sheets to windward. While this was being done the fore sheet, new only recently, carried away and she lay in the trough; a few moments later another heavy sea struck her so that with a still further and final shifting of the shingle, she was brought right over to port on her beam ends, with the main and mizzen topsail yard-arms in the water (Fig.23.1). Captain Isbester and the carpenter rushed into the cabin to get the axes from the store room, and the captain then ordered the two boats on the port side to be cut away – the extreme list made it impossible to launch the boats stowed on the starboard side. The carpenter asked the captain to leave the main deck and come up on to the poop, but he insisted on remaining where he was.

The port boat on skids amidships was first got into the water all right, and six or seven hands jumped into it – but try as they would they could not get it away clear of the ship on account of the backwash and the ship's rolling; the boat was sucked alongside and crushed against the ship. The men who were in the boat managed to scramble back safely on board.

The port lifeboat was then launched, and Mr May (third mate), Hugo Unger (cook), H.J. Cousins (sailmaker), R. Jones (cabin boy), A. Confrere (AB) and two or three more jumped into it, and it was got into the water – but the forward davit head came down on the cook, who

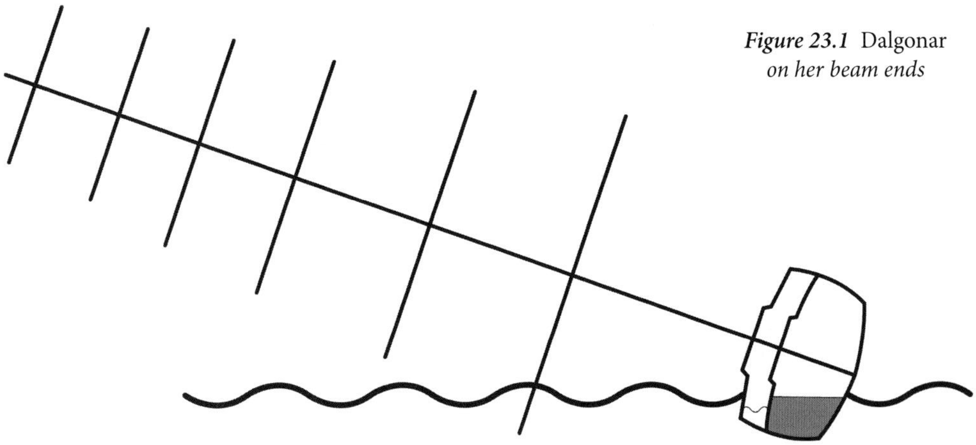

Figure 23.1 Dalgonar *on her beam ends*

"The vessel on her beam ends over to port with her main and mizzen topsail yardarms in the water ... The sea was washing half-way up to the hatches ... The ballast was rolling about like marbles with the rolling of the vessel ... They also found water fore and aft in the tweendecks but they kept that quiet from all the men as it might have caused a panic." Mr Mull

was in the bow of the boat, and crushed both him and the bow of the boat. The boat turned over twice, throwing all the men into the sea. They all managed to get back on board again with the exception of the sailmaker and the cook, who were drowned. Unfortunately, however, Arthur Confrere, one of the men who had scrambled back on board, got entangled in the braces and hung there in the gear which was washing about under the main rail, on the main deck.

Captain Isbester, who was at this time holding on amidships in front of the cabin, on seeing Confrere's perilous position, let go with the evident idea of trying to save him, but was himself at once thrown to leeward and struck his head against the lee rails, and was stunned. He was washed overboard and drowned before any assistance could be given to him. At this time the carpenter had been playing a leading role with the launching of the boats, while the chief mate, who had been forward with several men to set the jibs, was working his perilous way aft along the outside of the ship, as the decks were nearly vertical.

Under the dangerous circumstances in which they were placed, it was not possible for anyone to render any assistance to Confrere, and his body remained entangled amongst the ropes for two days before the sea finally washed it away piece by piece.

After the captain was washed overboard the mate gave orders to cut away the rigging, to allow the masts to fall overboard. The carpenter, second mate and one man cut away the mizzen rigging, and several men were sent forward to get axes out of the carpenter's shop, into which they managed to climb with the help of ropes. These men started to cut away the fore backstays and lower rigging. The vessel was fitted with screw lanyards, and the crew were unable to get at the lee lanyards, so they were limited to cutting the weather rigging. The mizzen mast went first, breaking about 10 feet above the deck, and breaking again just outside the rail. The main mast was the next to go, cut away by the second mate, the carpenter and some of the men. It also broke about 8 or 10 feet above the deck and again outside the lee rail. Then the foremast the same way, but with the rolling of the ship the head of the foremast lifted up about 10 feet and came down repeatedly with terrific force on the keel.[6] Every time it came down it shook the ship terribly. If it had once missed the keel it would certainly have gone through the ship's shell. In about 40 mins the three masts were over the side and all to leeward. The lee rigging could not be reached to cut it away, as it was all below the water – the sea was washing half way up to the hatches. Every moment the survivors were expecting the spars to poke a hole through the ship's side, and fearing that the ship would turn over altogether. All this weight of masts and rigging hung onto the vessel until the screw lanyards ultimately broke away, thus relieving her considerably, after which the lee rail came out of the water.

It was now about 2000 and the gale still continued with violent rain squalls and a fearful high sea. The survivors mustered outside the rail, on the half-round. The decks were near vertical, so they had to stand on the ship's side. The second and third mates, with some of the men, went through the skylight on the poop, down through the charthouse and into the saloon with the aid of ropes. They then placed the chief mate, who was aged 60 or more, in a chair and lowered him into the saloon and out of the weather. They were all wringing wet and cold, but managed to get some dry clothes from the slop chest, and some biscuits. All the rooms on the lee side of the cabin were full of water, which broke up everything which was in them. The survivors settled for the night in the saloon and the charthouse, each of them having a lifeline around him to enable him to get up on deck again. They had little hope of rescue or even of survival, but the mate posted one officer and two men on watch, maintaining that nothing is impossible for God.

At midnight the gale was raging heavily with a very high sea and heavy rain squalls, the vessel rolling heavily with the decks sometimes perpendicular. The survivors feared that she would turn over at any moment. A little more than three hours later, at 0330 on 10 October the green light of a sailing vessel was sighted by Mr May and the men on watch with him. Rockets and blue lights were quickly taken from the charthouse and one rocket after another, and one blue light after another was fired, but no more than two or three rockets had been fired when the other ship answered with a blue light and the survivors rejoiced that their prayers had been answered. At dawn the other vessel came close and the survivors could see that she was the French four-masted barque *Loire* of Dunkerque, flying the signal 'Do you wish to abandon?' which was answered in the affirmative.

As dawn broke Captain Jaffré, Master of the *Loire*, saw

> A ship lying completely on its port side with its three masts shorn off at deck level;
> I steered astern and as I passed astern I saw it was the *Dalgonar*, out of Liverpool.
> From time to time the keel emerged from the water as the waters surged.

The *Loire* sailed round the crippled *Dalgonar* four times on 10 October, but could not render any assistance because of the fearful gale and the high sea that was raging at the time. Several of the men that could swim wanted to jump overboard when the vessel was close to the *Dalgonar*, but the chief mate persuaded them that they would never reach the *Loire* and they took his advice.

At daybreak on 11 October there was no sign of the *Loire*. It was found that all three of the *Dalgonar*'s masts had broken off and gone, taking with them the jibboom. The survivors were cheered by this – it would improve the buoyancy of the wreck.

The tracing of an unlabelled sketch, presumably done by someone aboard the *Loire*, shows *Dalgonar* from the port side, with tiny figures waving from the poop (Fig.23.2).[7]

The carpenter and several men volunteered to go forward and cut away the port anchor, which was lashed on the forecastle head. They were successful, and this lightened the ship a little. They then lowered themselves into the hold by way of the fore hatch, and found that the ballast was as far as possible in the port side of the hold, right up against the tweendeck beams. The ballast was 'rolling about like marbles' and they concluded that absolutely nothing could be done to improve the situation. They also found water fore and aft in the tweendecks, a fact that they kept to themselves for fear of causing panic amongst the rest of the crew.

When at 1000 the French barque hove in sight, the gale was still blowing with great force accompanied by high seas. The survivors were all wearing their lifejackets and 'prepared for the worst'. During the course of the day the Frenchman hoisted a signal reading 'Wait until the weather moderates', which increased the confidence of the survivors that he would not leave them but would save them or see the last of them.

At 1500, realising that they would not be rescued that day, the survivors found dry clothes and biscuits for themselves and also with great difficulty they succeeded in getting some water from the tanks, which fortunately had held in position, notwithstanding that the vessel was lying on her beam ends. They found that the fresh water pump was working all right and were thankful for water, as they had been getting very thirsty.

At 1600 the *Loire* came close for the last time that day; her captain begged the survivors to be cool and patient, and assured them that he would stand by them, an assurance that the survivors greeted with three cheers. They then settled for another night of discomfort and peril.

That night the weather and seas remained as adverse as ever – no boat could live in it. Something could be heard 'giving way' down below: it would go off like a gun, and the vessel was shaking and trembling terribly.

On the morning of 12 October the gale still continued with high seas. Visibility was poor as a consequence of the squally conditions, with heavy showers of rain. The chief mate calculated that the ship was drifting north-north-west at about 2.5 knots and this was subsequently confirmed by the *Loire*. At about 0900 a funeral service was held for the four men who had lost their lives, the service being conducted by Mr May, third officer, who being a clergyman's son was thought

Figure 23.2 Dalgonar *from port side, as seen from* Loire. *Masts gone, seas breaking on deck, men on the starboard side of the poop*

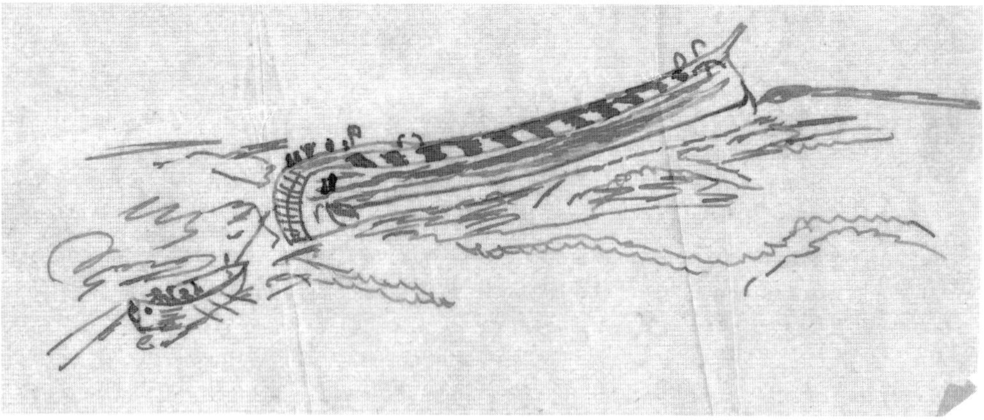

Figure 23.3 The rescue as seen from Loire. *The whaler is close astern of the* Dalgonar *with men on the poop*

most appropriate. One of the crew produced a bible and prayer book from his pocket, hymns were sung and God was thanked for bringing the *Loire* to save them. She was the first ship they had sighted since leaving Callao, 16 days previously. The survivors were all shaking like leaves, soaking wet all the time from the spray and rain.

The *Loire* remained in sight all day, and when night came the two ships kept in touch with flare up lights at intervals. At midnight the gale abated a little and the sea went down considerably.

On the morning of 13 October the wind started to freshen again but the sea had gone down a good deal. The *Loire* was hove to on the weather beam of *Dalgonar* under topsail and foresail, and flying the signal 'I am coming to your assistance'. A whaler was launched with chief mate Yves Cadic in charge, assisted by bosun Hamet and seamen Cochard, Poulhaër, Pesnel, Brochen, Kerné and Le Vay, and it approached the weather quarter of *Dalgonar* despite the fact that the wind was again increasing and the sea rising. Captain Jaffré had decided to use one of his whalers in preference to a lifeboat, as he considered the former were more seaworthy and suitable for the task. He put a man on watch up in the mizzen top to report on the slightest moves by the whaler, and moved to a position close to leeward of the wreck to minimise the return journey for the boat.

A 2-inch rope bent on to a lifebuoy was floated to the whaler, which could not approach closer than 120 yards/metres because of the high seas. The rope was then used to pass a 3½-inch rope, which was made fast in the stern of the boat, the other end being fastened aboard the ship. The boat also had a sea anchor out with 15 fathoms (30 yards/metres) of line forward to prevent the boat from being thrown end-over-end by the sea. Next, the end of the *Dalgonar's* deep sea leadline (with lead removed) was floated down to the whaler. A bowline was tied in the middle of the leadline, a sailor stepped into it and was lowered by leadline into the water where the mate and bosun in the whaler hauled him to, and into, the whaler. Then 12 more men were hauled across, the old and the injured first, Mr Mull, the chief mate, being included in that number. Remarkably he had with him the ship's papers, but had been unable to save his chief mate's log book because his cabin had been flooded.

A tracing of a sketch of the rescue as seen from the *Loire* is at Fig.23.3.

When the first boatload of 13 survivors was returning to the *Loire*, having left the leadline and the 3½-inch line tied to the floating lifebuoy, second mate Mr Oonard, still aboard the *Dalgonar*, hoisted the R flag on a short pole to inform the *Loire* that their whaler was returning. Aboard the *Loire* Captain Jaffré rigged a lifeline, spread some oil on the water and stationed men at the ship's side to help pull them in. The whaler came alongside safely and the first group of survivors jumped aboard the *Loire* when the decks were level and when crew members were ready to catch them.

Mr Cadic and his crew returned immediately to the *Dalgonar* to rescue the remaining 13 men, the stalwart carpenter being the last to leave. All were brought safely aboard the *Loire*, where the survivors helped to hoist the whaler quickly aboard to prevent it getting damaged against the ship's side. All were safe aboard by noon in latitude 28°58 S, longitude 87°04 W. The wind was south and rapidly increasing to a strong gale. The yards were trimmed, and the vessel was steered by the wind, on the port tack.

The survivors were given dry clothes, something to eat and drink, and were treated with the utmost kindness. Each man was given a bunk; wood shavings were created to serve as mattresses and two good sails were cut up to make blankets. Conditions were very clean, warm and dry. Injured survivors were treated by Michel Jaffré, the captain, and Mr Mull. R. Jones, ship's boy, had an arm that was terribly swollen from shoulder to fingertips, but the bone was not broken. The captain bandaged him up and gave him a berth in the quarterdeck house. The carpenter was badly bruised about the hip and knee, and had a sore and cut foot too. He was bandaged up and given quarters with the carpenter from the *Loire*. E. Maganske, Charles Ellison, James Kavanagh, Mitchell Singer and B.A. Mullaney, all ABs, were all bruised about the arms and legs, and received daily treatment.

There were 26 survivors from the *Dalgonar* and the crew of the *Loire* were 33 all told. With a total of 59 on board it was necessary to put all on half rations, and the crew of the *Loire* accepted this willingly. During the homeward passage to Dunkerque Mr Mull and Mr Cadic, the heroic chief mate of the *Loire*, both had periods of ill health.

Six of the *Dalgonar* survivors were transferred during the voyage to the three-masted *La Fontaine*, and landed in Falmouth. The remainder were carried to Dunkerque, where they arrived in early January 1914. The *Loire* passed Beachy Head on 4 January 1914, and signalled that she was short of provisions and required a tug from Dover immediately.

Commenting on his fellow survivors, Mr Mull wrote:

> I am very proud to say that Mr Oxnard [*sic*] 2nd officer and Mr May 3rd Officer have done their duty like true British seamen and carried out my orders to the letter and at all times cool and collected and great praise is due to them. Our carpenter Mr Dunker behaved like a hero and stuck to his work like a man, cheering up the men who were working with him in cutting away the masts and I must say that he is worthy of great praise. Praise is also due to all the men; they all kept very cool and collected and carried out orders like noble British seamen. May God bless them all and protect them.

H. Dunker, a 24-year-old German from Bremen, who had signed Articles as carpenter and donkeyman and had been aboard throughout the voyage, does indeed seem to have been a tower of strength, mentioned in connection with almost every vigorous activity contained in Mr Mull's report. The men behaved like noble British seamen but there is an irony here. Two-thirds of the ship's company were actually American, German and Scandinavian, and had been aboard this British ship for only a fortnight. In Newcastle Captain Isbester had written of his officers:[8]

> My Old Mate is still very deaf but I think somewhat better. I have Ocnard as second and May as third. So I have the young and the old to deal with and I think they will do all right.

He would have been pleased that his assessment was correct, even in such exceptional circumstances.

The remarkable level of commitment, skill and competence displayed by Captain Jaffré and his crew in the rescue of the *Dalgonar* survivors was recognised by King George V: on the advice of the President of the Board of Trade, he presented each of the 8 members of the rescue whaler with a silver medal for gallantry and each of the remaining 22 members of the *Loire*'s ship's company with a silver medal for saving the lives of British subjects. In addition, the Board of Trade presented Captain Jaffré with a gold watch, Mr Cadic with 'a piece of plate', the second and third mates with 'binocular glasses', the sum of £4 to each member of the rescue boat crew and the sum of £2 to each remaining crew member, two pounds being roughly equivalent to a fortnight's wages for a seaman.[9] By March 1914 the *Loire*, with Captain Jaffré still in command, was in North Shields Albert Edward Dock loading her next cargo, and the opportunity was taken to present Captain Jaffré and his two senior officers each with a silver medal and an illuminated vote of thanks provided by the Liverpool Shipwreck and Humane Society. Also presented to Captain Jaffré was 'a massive silver salver' from Messrs Gracie Beasley and Co., managers of *Dalgonar*, and two other pieces were handed to the North of England representative of A. D. Bordes & Sons of Paris, the owners of *Loire*, for delivery to Messrs Cadic and Boullet.[10]

The French authorities seem, with good reason, to have valued the rescue equally highly.[11] Captain Jaffré was presented by the Société Centrale de Sauvetage des Naufragés with the Émile Robin prize and a gold medal (first class), while Mr Cadic, chief mate, was also awarded a gold medal (first class) and shared with the rescue boat crew the prize awarded by the Baron and Baronne Léopold Davillier. The members of the crew of the rescue boat also received bronze medals (first class). In addition the rescue boat crew shared the Henri Durand de Blois prize of 2,000 French francs, Mr Cadic being awarded 1,000FF, the bosun receiving 160FF and the remainder 140FF each.

Tragically, Mr Cadic, as a consequence of his unselfish efforts in charge of the rescue lifeboat, died of bronchitis a few weeks after arriving in Dunkerque, so the generous recognition that he received was mostly posthumous. He died aged 29 on 14 March 1914 leaving a wife and a 14-month-old son. As Captain Jaffré put it dramatically:

> It was lieutenant Cadic who died. He was a Breton and when a sailor from the Côtes-du-Nord dies from exhaustion at sea, you can judge what he must have suffered. Those 4 days of saving lives put death into his blood. After disembarking from the *Loire*, his next vessel was a coffin.[12]

1 Formal Investigation No7640: *Dalgonar*, 1913. http://www.plimsoll.org/images/85024_tcm4-329265.pdf.

2 Mull, W.A.H, Chief Officer. Log and Record of the wreck of the ship *Dalgonar*. 14.10.1913 (Isbester Collection).

3 Jaffré, Michel. Master, barque *Loire*. Quoted in 'Braves Gens de France'. *Paris Soir*, 17.09.1934. Translation by Allen Martin. (Isbester Collection).

4 Mr Mull says the destination was Taltal. In Captain Isbester's final letter he names Tocopilla, 200 miles nearer on the coast of Chile. The charterers presumably changed the loading port at the last moment. The position at the time of the casualty suggests that they were navigating towards Taltal, going well offshore and well south to allow for the northerly set of the Humboldt current near to the coast, and this destination appears to have been unchallenged at the subsequent formal investigation.

5 Formal Investigation No. 7640: *Dalgonar*, 1913, Op cit. This document says that *Dalgonar* was also carrying the foretopmast staysail at this point, but the *Dalgonar* sail plan (Fig.16.6) shows no such sail. It could, perhaps, be otherwise known as the Inner Jib. However Mr. Mull was later sent to set the inner and outer jibs, which suggests that no headsails were being carried at this time.

6 Mr Mull's report says 'keelson', a feature inside the ship. He must mean keel.

7 *Dalgonar*, derelict, port side. Tracings 2 views of derelict. Unsigned, uncaptioned. (Isbester collection).

8 Isbester, Captain John. Letter J30, 01.06.1913. (Isbester Collection).

9 Gallantry at Sea. *Liverpool Echo*. 26.03.1914.

10 Heroism at Sea. *Newcastle Daily Journal*. 11.03.1914.

11 French internet forum at: https://www.google.fr/url?sa=t&rct=j&q=&esrc=s&source=web&cd=6&cad=rja&uact=8&ved=0ahUKEwiUudL_x-nMAhUDchQKHWX4BUgQFghAMAU&url=http%3A%2F%2F pp.14-18.mesdiscussions.net%2Fpages1418%2FForum-Pages-d-Histoire-aviation-marine%2Fmarine-1914-1918%2Farmement-antoine-dominique-sujet_3583_1.htm&usg=AFQjCNEExVFVxw5r5wlK9aMkUtrFXGi7ag

12 Jaffré, Michel. Op cit.

24 THE BACKGROUND TO THE TRAGIC LOSS

The attempt to wear ship: In normal conditions 'wearing ship' is the way of turning a square-rigged ship from having the wind on the starboard side to having it on the port side, or vice versa. When wearing, the turn is always made in the direction that will put the wind astern. Captain Isbester wanted to turn to port from his heading of about north-east, with the wind on the starboard beam, to south-west, with the wind on the port beam, so that the wind would then tend to push the ship upright. Before this last desperate manoeuvre was attempted, *Dalgonar* was carrying foresail, main lower topsail and mizzen lower topsail (Fig.24.1).The topsails, being set towards the stern of the ship, would resist a turn to port. That resistance was minimised by squaring the yards and shivering the sails. The wind would then be blowing parallel to the sails rather into them. The helm was put hard over, but the effect of that could only be small because the ship must only have been moving slowly, and it is likely that because of the list much of the rudder was out of the water. The inner and outer jibs were set and sheeted home to windward to maximise their turning effect (Fig.24.2) but when the foresail sheet parted, spilling the wind from the foresail, the headsails proved insufficient to turn the ship further against the resistance of the swell and the attempt had to be abandoned. The swell was from the south-east and, responding to its effect, the ship would tend to lie aligned north-east–south-west, and would resist attempts to turn her across the swell (Fig.24.3).

The track chart: Throughout the period when the *Loire* was standing by the *Dalgonar*, Captain Jaffré maintained a track chart for both vessels, and a copy of Mr Mull's tracing of this

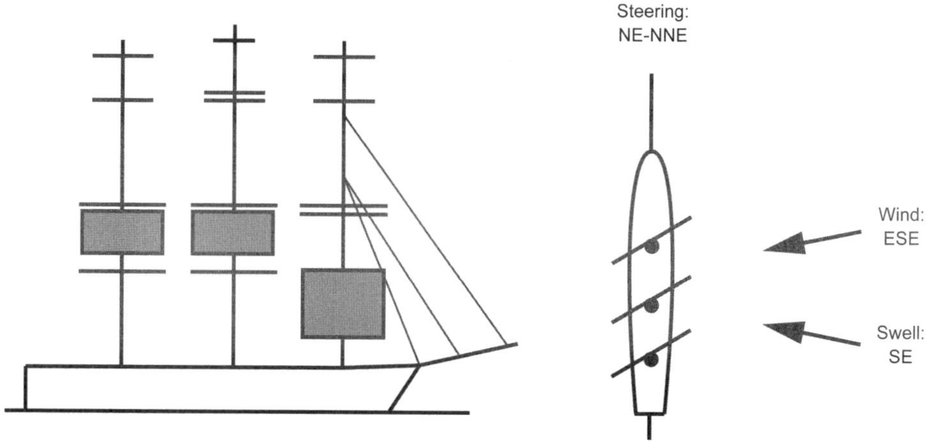

***Figure 24.1** The sail plan before attempting to wear ship*

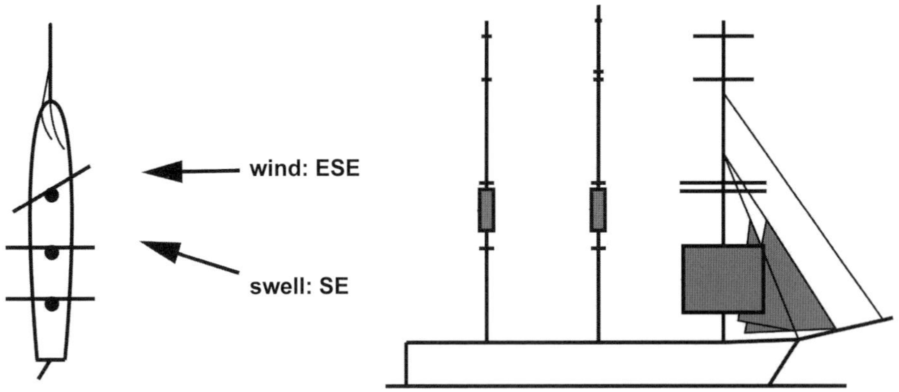

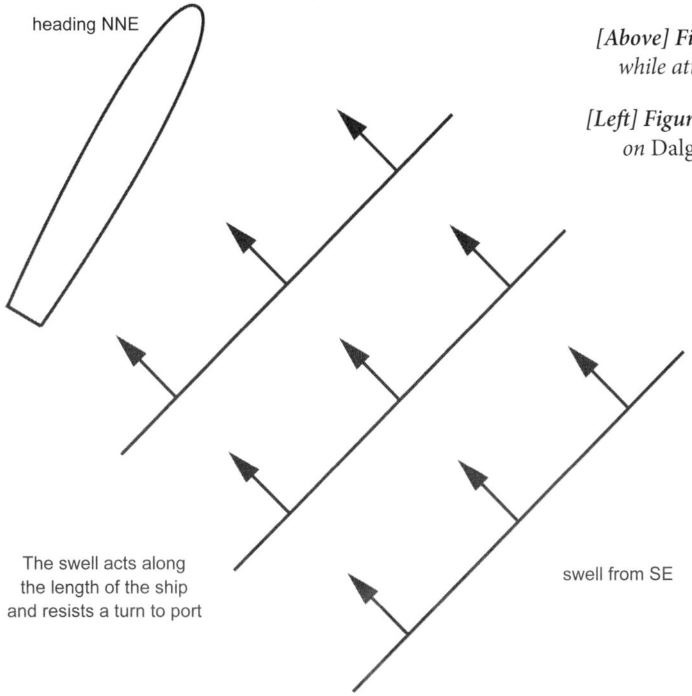

*[Above] **Figure 24.2** The sail plan while attempting to wear ship*

*[Left] **Figure 24.3** The effect of swell on* Dalgonar*'s ability to turn*

is at Fig.24.4.[1] It shows *Dalgonar* drifting north-north-west at a rate of about 2 knots, and *Loire* passing close to *Dalgonar* by day and prudently keeping further away by night. The complexity of the *Loire*'s track chart gives an indication of the skill with which *Loire* was navigated over an intense period of four nights and days, and the physical demands of the associated sail handling. An identical track chart, with captions in French, can be seen on the internet.[2]

The launching of the lifeboats: The official account of how the *Dalgonar* was lost is that issued by the official inquiry following their taking of evidence at the end of March 1914 from Mr Mull, Mr Ocnard, Mr May, Mr Dunker and others[3] (Appendix 4). That account accepts Mr Mull's log of the launching of the boats and concludes that the port lifeboat was launched and wrecked,

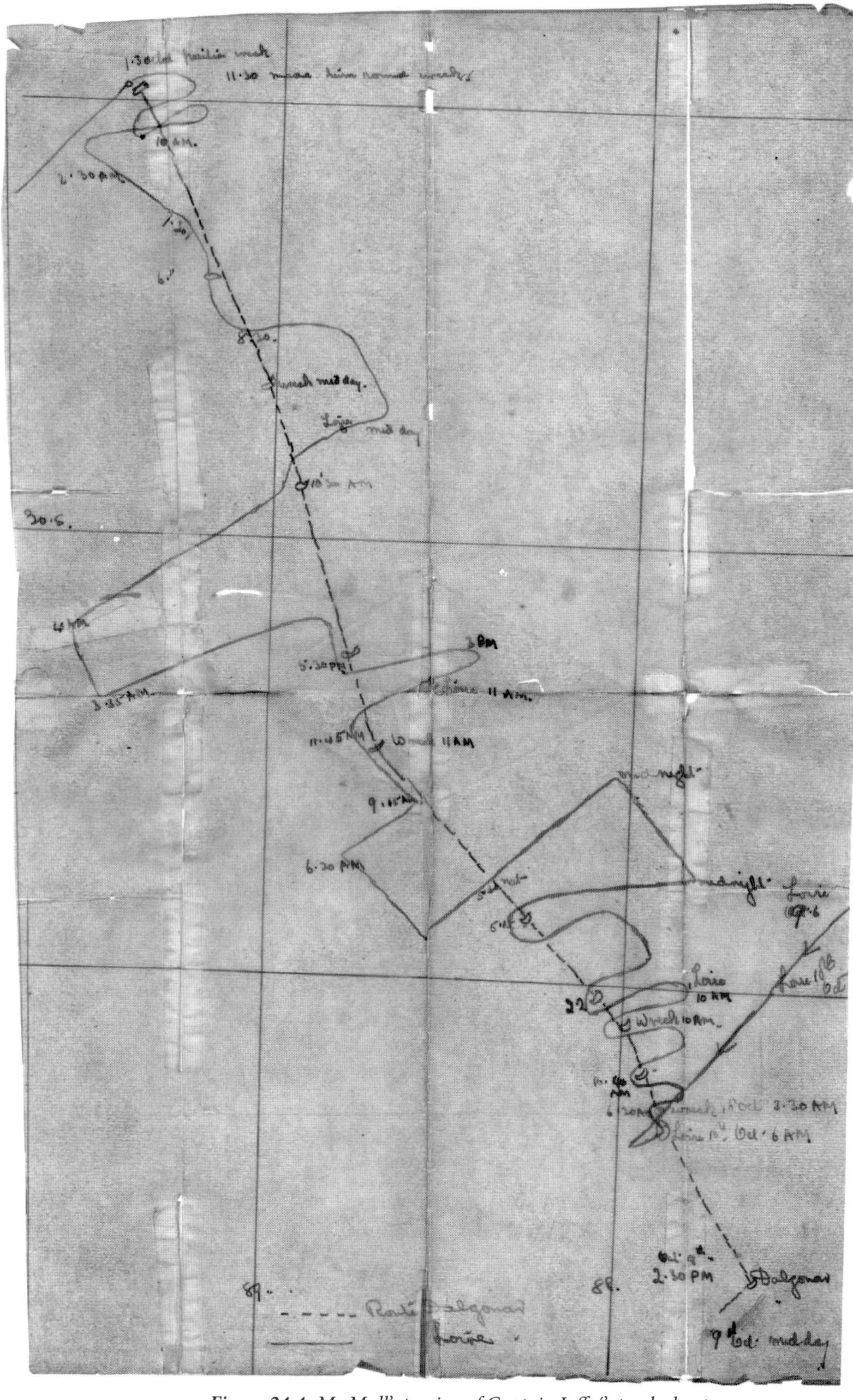

Figure 24.4 Mr Mull's tracing of Captain Jaffré's track chart

[Above] ***Figure 24.5*** *The lifeboat stowage, on a platform beneath radial davits, immediately forward of the poop*

[Below] ***Figure 24.6*** *View looking forward from the poop. Captain Isbester on the 'fore and aft bridge' which gave access from the poop to the lifeboat and gig stowages. The gig chocks between Captain Isbester and the starboard lifeboat are empty – the gig was presumably in use*

Figure 24.7 *Launching a lifeboat with radial davits*

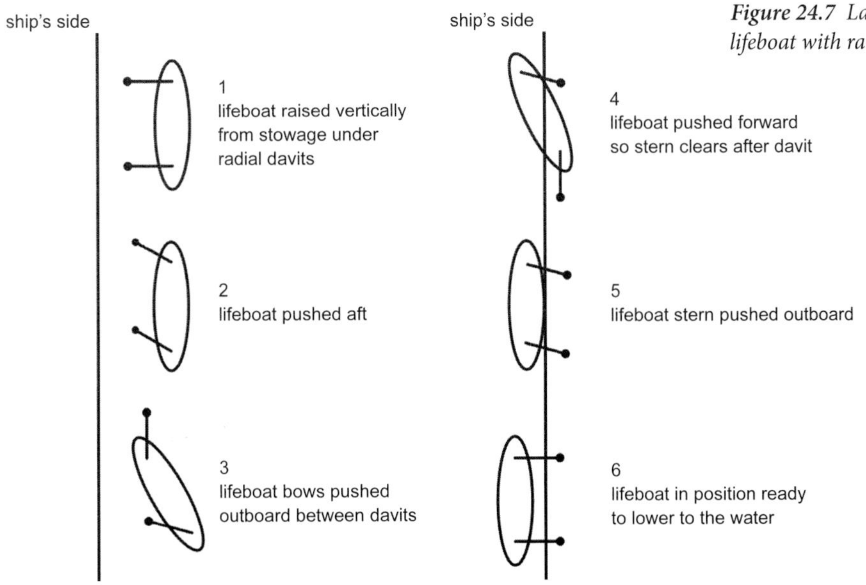

[Letf] ***Figure 24.8*** *Launching a lifeboat, Step 3 (this lifeboat was carried by* Rossdhu*)*

[Right] ***Figure 24.9*** *Lifeboat outboard and almost ready for lowering: Step 6*

followed by the starboard lifeboat which was launched and wrecked with loss of life. This account has always seemed most unlikely to me. The lifeboats were stowed under radial davits on platforms immediately forward of, and level with, the poop deck (Figs 24.5 & 24.6). Launching involved first raising the boat, next manoeuvring it between the davits (Figs 24.7–24.9) before lowering it over the ship's side. Launching the starboard boat when the ship was listing 60–70 degrees to port would have been impossible. It would have involved pushing the lifeboat almost vertically upwards while standing on a very steeply sloping and narrow platform. Additionally, the falls (the ropes by which the boat was suspended) provided for the starboard boat would not have been long enough to reach the water when the ship was in ballast and listed 60–70 degrees to port. Finally, the assertion that when the starboard boat was destroyed the men 'managed to get back onto the vessel' with one getting 'entangled in the gear which was washing about' clearly describes a reboarding on the low port side, not the starboard side, where the deck would have been 25 feet or more above the water.

Captain Jaffré reported that when first sighted 'I see that he has only a large lifeboat aft and a skiff forward'[4] and the facts are put beyond doubt in the report[5] of F. Moricet of the French vessel *Marie*, which sighted and inspected the wrecked *Dalgonar* on 28 October 1913 and reported 'Two boats gone. Two boats remain on starboard side.'

(To digress for a moment, the boarding party from the *Marie* also found a black cat aboard *Dalgonar* and presumably rescued it. We can only hope that the three other cats with which the voyage commenced had deserted in one of the ports *Dalgonar* had visited.)

What very probably happened is that the pinnace, stowed on skids on the port side, was the first boat to be launched and destroyed, but the men were able to scramble back aboard. The port lifeboat would have been more of a struggle but was next put into the water when a vicious blow from the davit, driven by the heavily rolling ship, killed the cook right in front of his shipmates' shocked eyes and destroyed the bows of the lifeboat. With the sailmaker and AB also drowning and with no more launchable boats, any further thoughts of abandoning ship were forgotten.

How did Mr Mull get this wrong? It is possible that he thought that he might be criticised for failing to launch the starboard boat and deliberately embellished his account, but I think it

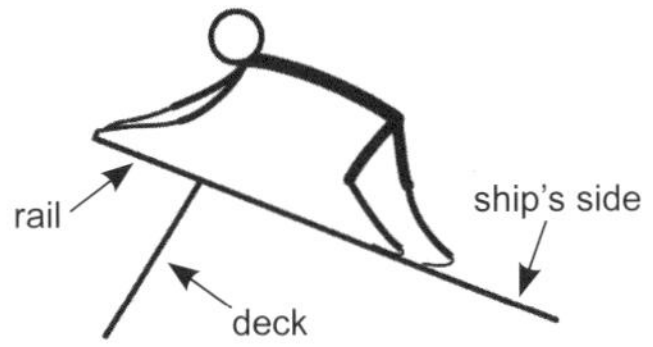

Figure 24.10 *Mr Mull clambering along the ship's side listed to 70 degrees*

more likely that he did not see these events himself, because he was making his slow and precarious way aft along the outside of the ship's hull (Fig.24.10) from the forecastle head where he had been tending the headsails. He relied on accounts from his shipmates, who probably merely spoke of the first boat and the second boat. While on the poop during the final few days his eyes would have lit upon the starboard boat, but it was a familiar part of the scenery and his mind would have been on other things.

Captain Isbester's death: Mr Mull's account of the captain's death is:

> When our poor captain saw the starboard [*sic*] lifeboat being crushed he evidently felt that he must go and help for he lost his hold and went with his head up against the after davit which must have fractured his skull. He never spoke or moved and the backwash took him away and we saw him no more. I was scrambling along on the outside of the ship with the men I had with me to set the jibs, when I saw the poor captain go over the side.

The account provided by the inquiry also associates Captain Isbester's death with the launching of the starboard lifeboat. It seems likely that for this, too, Mr Mull relied upon what he thought he had been told rather than what he saw.

The procedure for the rescue of the survivors: The transfer of the survivors from the poop of *Dalgonar* to the *Loire*'s whaler appears to have been a carefully planned and seamanlike set of operations. Captain Jaffré and his officers had had, of course, several days in which to discuss how best to carry out the transfer, but the understanding and assistance of the survivors was needed too. They had to provide a lifebuoy, a suitable rope to act as painter (i.e. mooring rope for the whaler) and a strong, light rope (the deep sea leadline) with which to transfer the survivors. Communication had to overcome distance, noise of the wind and sea, and language, but previous experience may have helped. When the four-masted barque *Kelton* of Glasgow was foundering in the Western Approaches on 25 April 1894,[6] 'The men were then lowered into the water with life-belts on, and were pulled to the life-boat with a line and taken to the *Europe*' in a rescue not described in detail but which nevertheless has echoes of the *Dalgonar* rescue. Rescues of this sort may have been part of the shared experience of sailors at the end of the 19th century, discussed and passed on as common lore.

Similar vessels lost: Three other large sailing vessels were lost in the eastern Pacific in similar circumstances to those of the *Dalgonar*, and at about the same time. The British barque *Dunreggan* sailed from Callao four days after the *Dalgonar*. Like *Dalgonar* she was heading south, for Iquique in her case, and was ballasted with shingle.[7] A week later the ship *Inveravon* left Callao bound north for Portland, Oregon, also in ballast. Evidence was given that she too would have met severe storms off the coast of Oregon in November, though not the same gales as those met by *Dalgonar*.[8] Basil Lubbock also lists the *Marechal Gontaut* (actually the French barque *Maréchal de Gontaut*, 2,240 tons register) as another vessel lost in similar circumstances in the same area at the same time.[9] None of these three vessels was ever heard of again.

The exceptional weather: Between 1874 and 1913 Captain Isbester had sailed through the waters off Chile some 30 times, and most of those transits would have taken weeks rather than days. He knew those waters well. His passage from Callao to Taltal would be through a usually benign south-east trade wind zone. He reportedly told the chief mate that 'they were certain to have a fine weather passage'[10] and the evidence suggests that this is what he believed. There is no record of what pilot books and nautical publications he had aboard, but they might well have included a contemporary commercial publication such as *Findlay's South Pacific Ocean*,[11] which describes the trade wind zone off Chile as one of the least uncertain climates on the face of the globe, but goes on to predict occasional storms between May and August. *Dalgonar* was to depart late in September.

Confronted with the anticipated south-east trade winds and the Humboldt current setting north along the coast of Chile, Captain Isbester took a south-south-westerly course out into the Pacific (Fig.24.11) until on 8 October 1913 he wore ship to bring her onto the starboard tack, steering north-east. Throughout the passage the winds had been south-easterly as expected, and they continued to blow from this general direction throughout the five days of storm. There is no obvious explanation for this unwelcome and unseasonal storm, but it is tempting to wonder whether in the waters off Chile it was an El Niño effect.

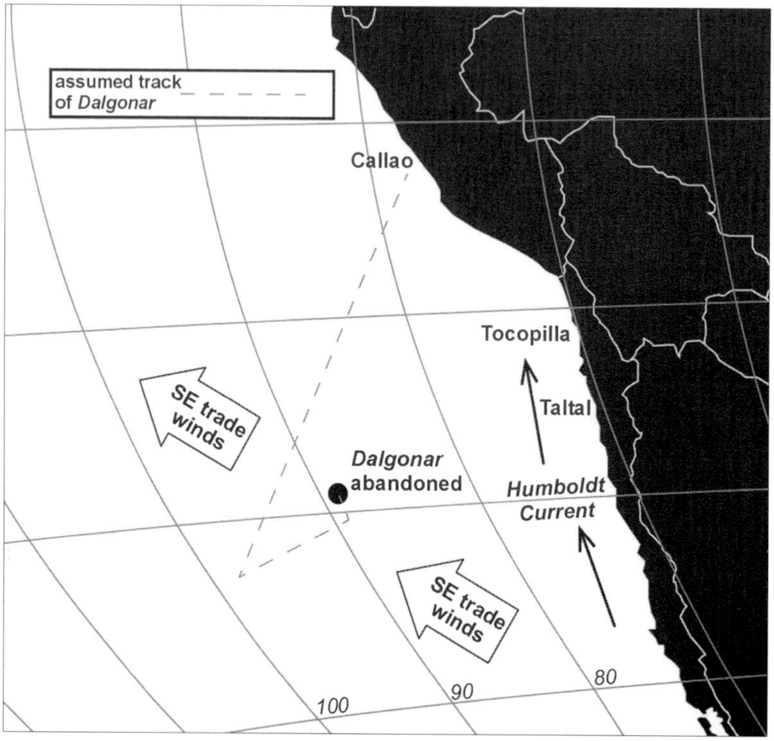

Figure 24.11
Dalgonar's *final passage*

Joseph Conrad's comments: When Mr Mull's log of the disaster was published[12] in 1921, Conrad wrote to the *London Mercury* to draw attention to several errors which had crept into the text. Having attempted to clarify some inconsistencies regarding the sails which had been taken in, he continued:

> Thus at 11 p.m., [on 8 October] the ship was reduced down to her foresail and the fore and main lower topsails, which was a possible and seamanlike canvas for her to carry in the then state of the weather.

With the benefit of a typewritten copy of Mr Mull's report (Appendix 5),[13] the document on which the *London Mercury* article with its various errors is based, it can be seen that in reality it is likely that the ship was actually reduced down to her foresail and the fore, main 'and mizzen' lower topsails.[14]

Joseph Conrad continues:

> I cannot, however, defend myself from the impression conveyed by the narrative and also from what happened afterwards, that the foresail was carried on her too long. That large piece of canvas must have had the effect (at least at times) of forcing the ship one and a half or perhaps two knots through the water-for no object that I can see. And **there** was the danger.[15]

In making this comment he discounts several possible reasons for sailing slowly onward: steering would be assisted and the destination was ahead. John Isbester was making his way to Taltal to load the next cargo. Conrad's next words show sensible caution: 'But it is easy to be wise after the event.' In conclusion Joseph Conrad wrote:

> I agree with all my heart with the editorial note heading the story [which says that Mr Mull's account was not written for publication but that no justification is needed for the publication of such a fine, simple account so powerfully told]. There can be nothing finer or more simple. The crew of the *Dalgonar* behaved as well as I have ever seen the crew of a British merchant ship behave in a critical situation and they deserve fully the encomiums and blessings Mr Mull, the chief officer, gives to them in his report written on board the *Loire*. A tribute of admiration is due, too, to the captain of the French ship for his humane determination to save those men, and for the display of seamanlike resolution and skill in maintaining his ship in position for so long in such desperate weather. Nobody but a seaman can appreciate the risks and the difficulty of the task, and the severe strain put on the endurance of the crew and officers of the *Loire* in sheer physical exertions, in unremitting vigilance and plucky seamanship, which enabled them to remain by and finally to take off the crew of the *Dalgonar*.

The securing of the ballast: I believe that there can be no doubt that the inquiry was correct to conclude that the ballast was inadequately secured. Indeed the only person to claim otherwise was Mr Mull, who was contradicted by the second mate, the carpenter, and the account of what actually happened. The shifting boards, the bins and the shoring from the deckhead were, it appears, all inadequate or non-existent. Even Mr Mull in his evidence to the inquiry said that:

> Having regard to his experience in the vessel on her last voyage, if he were again securing such ballast, he would have three rows of shifting boards instead of two and would have them from 18 inches to 2 feet from the bottom and bedded in the shingle, as on the occasion in question. There were plenty of boards on the vessel if more security had been thought necessary.[16]

The *Board of Trade Safeguards* for securing ballast: Thirteen years before the tragic loss of the *Dalgonar* two ships, the barque *Limache*[17] and the four-masted barque *Cape Wrath*,[18] sailed from Callao in ballast and were lost without trace. The Report of the Inquiry into the loss of the latter vessel included the following passage:

> The ballast shipped at Callao is shingle and very liable to shift. Accordingly, with such a dangerous description of ballast as this, special measures should be taken to secure it. Centre shifting boards should invariably be used, also wing shifting boards where practicable. All shifting boards should be thoroughly well secured in position. Further bulkheads should be built at the forward and after ends of the ballast and brought up to the same height as the ballast in order to prevent the ballast moving forward or aft. Finally the ballast should be securely tommed down.

This advice is identified in a 1914 Inquiry Report as 'Safeguards recommended by the Board of Trade'.[19] His Britannic Majesty's Consulate General in Callao had in 1901 issued a printed notice on the securing of Callao ballast, but precisely what it said and whether in 1913 it was still being distributed is not known. Captain James Learmont of the four-masted barque *Bengairn* visited Callao in 1907. He claimed that the ballast provided was 13 per cent under weight until he insisted on receiving the balance, and pointed out that a shortage of ballast would cause a ship to roll more heavily. He further asserted that a notice was displayed in the British Consulate in Callao which read:

> Shipmasters are herewith warned that in consequence of so many ships being lost after leaving Callao they must use every endeavour to see, first, that they receive the weight of ballast they require and then that it is properly secured by shifting boards in the hold.[20]

This text is clearly inadequate to reflect the exceptional requirements for securing Callao shingle but although Captain Learmont is writing about events in 1907, it is clear from a reference to the *Dalgonar* that he makes later in the passage that he was writing some years after the event. For the text of the notice displayed in the Callao consulate he may have been relying upon an imperfect memory.

How effective were the Board of Trade Safeguards as a means of preventing ballast from shifting, and how well were they understood? The bulkheads (i.e. fencing) at the forward and after ends of each pile of ballast would have to be higher than the pile, and would have to be

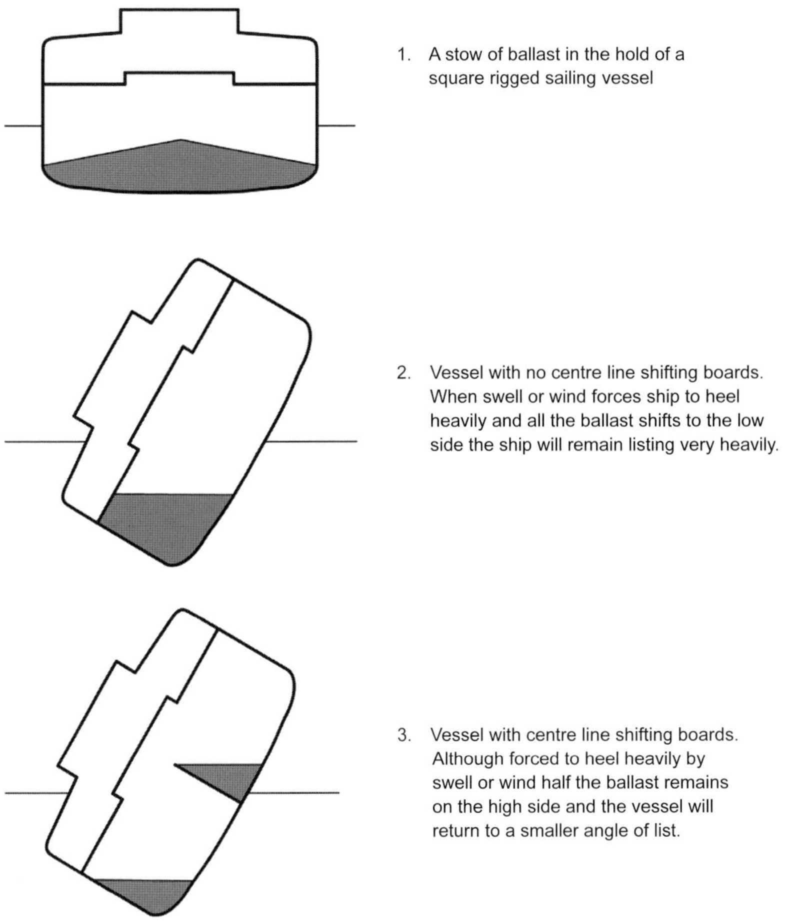

Figure 24.12 *The value of centreline shifting boards*

constructed early in the ballast loading process to allow the ballast to be stacked level against the bulkheads. If loading two separate stows of ballast as *Dalgonar* did, four fences each about 2.0 metres high and 12.0 metres wide would be required – a substantial challenge to position correctly before the ballast was loaded and a substantial task to construct, but the requirement was uncomplicated.

The shifting boards (Fig.24.12) were another challenge. Their purpose was to ensure that the cargo or ballast on the starboard side of the ship could not slide to port of the centreline and vice versa when the ship was inclined by waves, wind or other force, thus minimising any list of the ship caused by shift of cargo. At their best, when shifting boards were fitted before the cargo or ballast was loaded and were continuous from the bottom of the hold upwards, when they were continuous from forward to aft throughout the length of the stow, when boards were secured on both port and starboard sides of the centre line pillars, when the timber used was robust and consistent, and when the completed array of shifting boards contained no significant gaps, the arrangement would be very effective in achieving its purpose. These requirements were challenging. The evidence is limited, but occasionally Board of Trade Wreck Reports include a detailed discussion of how the cargo or ballast was secured, and in a number of these cases the fitting of shifting boards was clearly inadequate. Some masters used no shifting boards.[21,22] Sometimes tweendeck hatchboards[23,24,25] or spar ceiling[26] (portable timbers normally fitted at the vessel's sides to prevent the cargo from making contact with the steel hull) were used as shifting boards, which must have resulted in a less than perfect fit. Shifting boards were not always fitted for the full depth of the stow. The *Dalgonar* Inquiry[27] referred to this:

> it appears to be the practice among some masters when carrying ballast to use shifting boards which only extend from a foot or two above the ballast to about the same distance into it. This is a most dangerous practice as shown in this case. All shifting boards should extend from the bottom of the hold to well above the top of the ballast and should be properly secured. It would be well if steps were taken to enforce this.

Mr Mull, speaking with the benefit of hindsight in his evidence quoted earlier,[28] spoke of three rows of shifting boards 'starting eighteen inches or two feet from the bottom' as being desirable. He still did not recognise the value of complete and total separation between the port and starboard sides of the hold.

There were problems, too, with the recommendation that 'the ballast should be securely tommed down'. Tomming down involved first levelling the ballast, next covering it with boards, then cutting toms (i.e. timbers) exactly to length, and hammering them into near vertical positions between the boards and the tweendeck beams some 3 or 4 metres above. Wooden wedges might be used to achieve a tight fit, and toms might be nailed to the boards, but if the ship's structure or the toms flexed during heavy pitching and rolling, or if the shingle settled in the slightest, the toms would fall out and become ineffective. The large number of boards and the great number of toms required to secure the top of the stow entirely would have presented another problem. By the time, in 1914, that the court had considered the losses of *Dalgonar, Dunreggan* and *Inveravon*, the limitations of tomming down had been recognised and the court proposed that the Board of Trade's Safeguards be modified

> because experience shows that this shingle ballast settles down while the vessel is at sea, and there is the possibility if not the probability of the toms falling out of position and thereby becoming useless.[29]

It may well be that the limitations of tomming down were evident to Captain Isbester, and this explains his lack of enthusiasm for ensuring that it had been done.

The modification proposed a year after the loss of the *Dalgonar* called for the addition of a timber frame or raft to be placed over the ballast and secured with wire or chain to six or eight fixing points at the ship's sides.[30]

The securing of the Callao ballast aboard *Dalgonar*: In the decades before the First World War British shipping was not tightly regulated, and shipmasters had much more freedom than in recent times to decide, in collaboration with the services of the port and taking note of advice from their owners, how to load, stow and secure their ballast or cargo. A vivid picture of the confused circumstances in which world shipping operated can be gained from the minutes of a meeting held in Newcastle, NSW, to discuss the safest way to carry a cargo of coal.[31] The shipmasters, owners, coal shippers, stevedores, trimmers and agents who participated in discussions which extended over several days were split between those who thought that well-filled and trimmed holds were all that was necessary, and the larger number who considered that bulkheads or shifting boards were required. However, the latter group split between those who thought that the boards were needed only at the ends of the hold, those who would fit them only in the mid-body of the hold and those who were not specific and would, perhaps, fit them for the full length of the hold!

Captain Isbester chose an unconventional way to secure the Callao ballast aboard *Dalgonar* (Fig.24.13). For the very first time during his 28 years in command he had no apprentices in circumstances where he had been accustomed to having six or eight, though he would not have hesitated to use his newly promoted second and third mates to assist the carpenter in securing the ballast. It is not obvious that the absence of apprentices during the final days of loading the ballast influenced the thoroughness with which the ballast was secured, though it seems to me that it may have done.

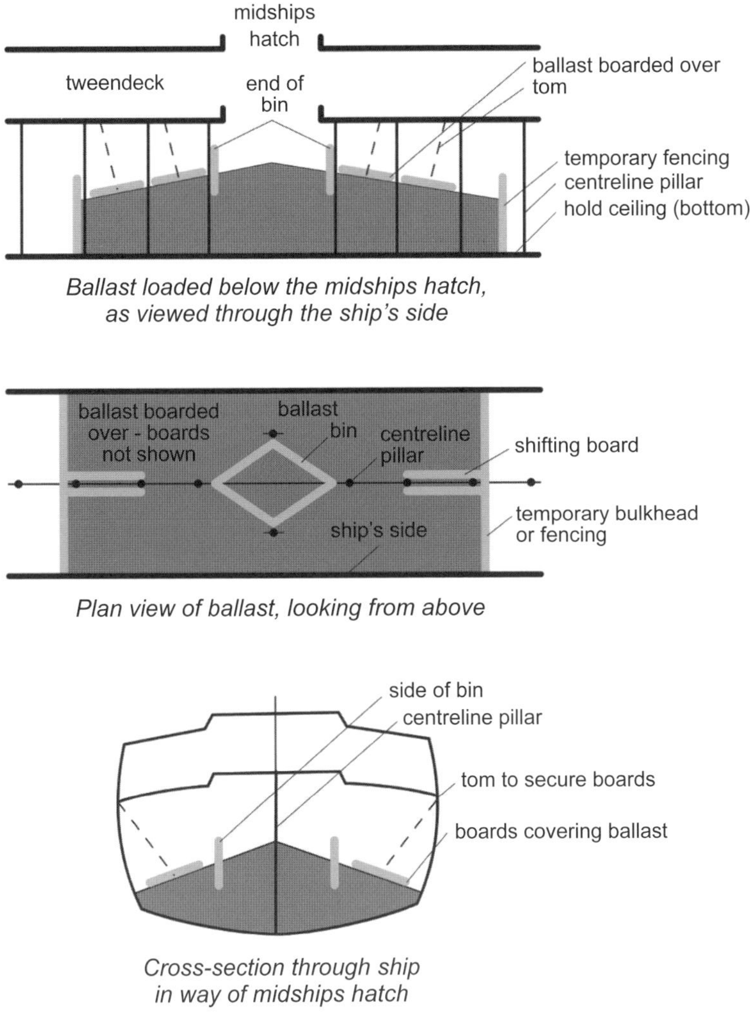

***Figure 24.13** Intended securing of the Callao ballast aboard Dalgonar*

The reason which he gave for constructing diamond-shaped bins in the centre of each ballast heap was to raise the centre of gravity of the ballast. This was a valid and interesting objective. If the centre of gravity of the ballast was higher the ship would be less stiff and would roll less violently, which would be safer for the ballast and more comfortable for the ship's company. However, this objective was poorly implemented, with the bins sitting on the ballast rather than embedded deeply in it. The carpenter may have come to this task late because of the time required to construct the four bulkheads.

It is clear from his Callao letters that John Isbester at this time had health problems and a variety of worries. He was taking 'tabloids for his head', and when one morning he failed to meet his fellow captains ashore, four of them came aboard to find whether he had 'kicked the bucket', which suggests that they were concerned about him. Over his head was hanging the prospect of losing his job at the end of the voyage, and he was experiencing the uneasiness of working with new people in the owners' office, whose ways were unfamiliar and unsettling. In addition, the exceptional absence of letters from his beloved Susie had shaken him profoundly, as would have the news about his son Arthur that had precipitated his disapproval.

Where ships in ballast have been lost and survivors have lived to tell the tale[32,,33,34] the triggering of the shift of ballast has usually been a single, exceptional swell or gust of wind. Ships and ships' captains can go for a lifetime and never experience such an exceptional event. A year after the loss of the *Dalgonar* the Board of Trade's Safeguards for ships sailing from Callao were recognised as inadequate and recommendations for their amendment were submitted. It could be that even if Captain Isbester, like (the evidence suggests) his colleagues aboard *Dunreggan* and *Inveravon* had complied with the Board of Trade's Safeguards, the inadequacies of that system would have been exposed by an exceptional swell, and *Dalgonar*, like the others, would still have been lost.

To summarise the foregoing, the system of securing the ballast was inadequate because the shifting boards, where fitted, were not continuous for the full depth and length of the stow, the bins were unorthodox and inadequate, and nothing was done to hold down the top of the stow. The absence of apprentices to do the securing may have delayed the work, but it was done to Captain Isbester's orders, and at the last his health and his personal problems may have distracted him, and his judgement and experience may have let him down. For once, the waters off the coast of Chile in October were not placid.

John Isbester was a kindly man who cared for the men under his command. His shipmates believed that his final act was to try to help a drowning man, and that was how he would like to have been remembered. He would have found it difficult to live with the knowledge that three of his crew had died and his beloved *Dalgonar* had been lost while under his command.

---

1 Track chart, *Loire* & *Dalgonar*, 9–13.10.1913, tracing. (Isbester collection).

2 Track chart with French captions. http://pages14-18.mesdiscussions.net/pages1418/Forum-Pages-d-Histoire-aviation-marine/marine-1914-1918/armement-antoine-dominique-sujet_3583_1.htm.

3 Formal Investigation No.7640 *Dalgonar*, 1913. http://www.plimsoll.org/images/85024_tcm4-329265.pdf.

4 Jaffré, Michel. Master, four-masted barque *Loire*. Quoted in 'Braves Gens de France'. *Paris Soir*, 17.09.1934. Translation by Allen Martin. (Isbester Collection).

5 Moricet, F. *Dalgonar*. Manuscript note. 28.10.1913. Isbester Collection).

6 Formal Investigation No. 4936 *Kelton*, 1894. http://www.plimsoll.org/images/16405_tcm4-219241.pdf.
7 Formal Investigation No.7662 *Dunreggan*, 1913. http://www.plimsoll.org/images/85038_tcm4-329281.pdf.
8 Formal Investigation No.7663 *Inveravon*, 1913. http://www.plimsoll.org/images/85039_tcm4-329282.pdf.
9 Lubbock, Basil. *The Last of the Windjammers*, Vol. 1. Brown, Son & Ferguson, Ltd, Glasgow.1954. P.18.
10 Formal Investigation No.7640 *Dalgonar*, 1913. Op cit.
11 South Pacific Ocean. 5th Edition 1884 with 1900 Addendum. Findlay, Alexander George, FRGS, quoting Captain FitzRoy. pp.1081–2.
12 Mull, W.A.H. *A True Story*. The London Mercury. Vol.IV, No.23. 01.09.1921. p.482.
13 Mull, W.A.H. Log and Record of the Wreck of the Ship *Dalgonar.* 14.10.1913. Isbester Collection.
14 The typescript read 'At 7 *P.M.* wind and sea were increasing and we took in the (Mizzen) fore upper topsail'. I believe that the typist in Dunkerque, working from Mr. Mull's manuscript document, found the word Mizzen weakly deleted and, being uncertain what was intended, cautiously included it, but within brackets. The typewritten transcript continues: 'At 11 P.M. wind and sea still increasing took the mizzen and main upper topsails'. The *London Mercury* transcribed this as reporting that the mizzen upper topsail had been twice taken in. Joseph Conrad recognised that this was a nonsense and deduced, without the benefit of the original typed version, that the mizzen *upper* and *lower* topsails had been taken in.
15 Conrad, J. *Last Essays.* J M Dent & Sons Ltd. 1926. p.118.
16 The *Dalgonar* Disaster. *Daily Commercial News & Shipping List*, Sydney. 11.05.1914.
17 Formal Investigation No.6260 *Limache*, 1900. http://www.plimsoll.org/images/71037_tcm4-304248.pdf.
18 Formal Investigation No.6259 *Cape Wrath*, 1900. http://www.plimsoll.org/images/71040_tcm4-304251.pdf.
19 Formal Investigation No.7663 *Inveravon*, 1913. Op cit.
20 Learmont, Captain James S. *Master in Sail.* Percival Marshall & Co. Ltd. London. 1954. pp. 153–155.
21 Formal Investigation No. 6160 *Moel Tryvan*, 1901. http://www.plimsoll.org/images/71029_tcm4-304240.pdf.
22 Formal Investigation No 5882, *Midas*, 1898. http://www.plimsoll.org/images/69026_tcm4-295313.pdf.
23 Formal Investigation No. 7290 *Toxteth,* 1909. http://www.plimsoll.org/images/80034_tcm4-323263.pdf.
24 Formal Investigation No. 4936 *Kelton,* 1894. http://www.plimsoll.org/images/16405_tcm4-219241.pdf.
25 Inquiry No.145 *Clan Macpherson,* 1909. http://www.plimsoll.org/images/82074a_tcm4-326722.pdf.
26 Formal Investigation No.5600 *Lord Dufferin*, 1896. http://www.plimsoll.org/images/67075_tcm4-288097.pdf.
27 Formal Investigation No.7640 *Dalgonar*, 1913. Op cit.
28 The *Dalgonar* Disaster. Op cit.
29 Formal Investigation No.7662 *Dunreggan*, 1913. Op cit.
30 Formal Investigation No.7662 *Dunreggan*, 1913. Op cit.
31 Newcastle Chamber of Commerce meeting Minutes, 8–10.10.1894. http://www.plimsoll.org/images/65124_tcm4-278566.pdf.
32 Formal Investigation No.7640 *Dalgonar*, 1913. Op cit.
33 Formal Investigation No.6827 *Eulomene*, 1905. http://www.plimsoll.org/images/75039_tcm4-313074.pdf.
34 Formal Investigation No.6802 *County of Anglesea*, 1905. http://www.plimsoll.org/images/75036_tcm4-313071.pdf

25 THE AFTERMATH

The *Dalgonar* had been expected to arrive at Tocopilla – or was it Taltal? – about the middle of October, and a cable to the owners announcing her arrival would have been immediate. Normal mail would have reached London by mid-November, so as the weeks went by and no news was received everyone hoped for the best but feared the worst. Susie and the children all knew that shipping casualties were all too frequent. At that period about 100 ships a year were being lost to foundering, fire, collision or stranding, and every family with seafaring members had heard of the loss of friends. There must have been times in the past when the family had been worried, when a voyage took five months when it should have taken four; but this time it was a short trip and the possibility of a safe outcome was becoming increasingly remote.

Fifty years later my father, Allan Isbester, still had vivid recollections of how the dreaded news reached them – it was in the newspapers before any of the family had been told.[1]

Nellie Thompson, a friend who had typed the McJannet Log of the *Dalgonar*[2] saw the news and hurried round in distress to see if Mrs Isbester had been informed. At that time she had not. Mrs Isbester was very fond of Nellie's playing and singing – she often came to the house to practise on the piano so she asked her to come into the parlour and play and sing to Mrs Sandison and her daughter Emmie, old Shetland friends who were staying with her at the time. She was distraught but wanted to preserve the proprieties. She said afterwards that she never knew how she managed to.

My father's sister Kathleen was living in Cardiff. The owners were in touch with her, and notified her that news of her father's death was in the newspapers. She wired the news to a neighbour of her mother's living in Ilford and ending 'Coming home. Tell mother.' The husband of the neighbour took the instructions to himself and arrived, and without preamble handed Mrs Isbester the evening paper to read. As she shaded her eyes with one hand to read by gas light he said, 'No need to believe the bit about the captain and three men.' She replied, 'I don't see why it should not all be true.' The item read:

> Disaster to English Ship
>
> A Lloyds Paris message says:- Information received from Dakar by wireless states the vessel *Loire* spoken in 6.17N.29W reports that she has on board twenty-six men of the English ship *Dalgonar* of Liverpool since October 9. The English captain and three of the men were dead.[3]

My father writes:

> I had gone to a big local Sunday school choir practice, – and one of the boys in the choir told me what he had seen in the paper. I began to cry, I was 13, and the choir

> master who had also seen the paper sent me home – where my little brother was crying, and whispered the news to me. Kathleen had arrived and taken my Mother to her bedroom from where we could hear her sobs. She'd kept quite calm until she and Kathleen were alone together.

My grandmother survived my grandfather for 20 years, remaining in Ilford where she was cherished by family and friends but suffered from declining health.

The *Dalgonar* and the events associated with her loss remained news reported worldwide for months and has been regularly resurrected over the last 100 years. First it was the details of the casualty, frequently misreported,[4,5] that made the news. Next it was the honours heaped on the heroic master and crew of the *Loire*, and then, in Liverpool, the official inquiry into the loss. Later the disaster was discussed in Parliament, where the findings of the Court of Inquiry that the ballast had shifted were confirmed and, rather feebly, the intention to issue a notice to shipowners and shipmasters was confirmed.[6]

Dalgonar herself lived on as a hulk for far longer than expected. The French ship *Marie* from Nantes, owned by Société Nouvelle d'Armement, came across her on 28 October 1913 in position lat.27° S, long.95°47 W. Captain F. Moricet reported that two boats were gone and that two boats remained on the starboard side. The ship's port side was damaged and her keel was out of the water. The deck on the port side was just touching the water and all the masts had been cut off. There were plenty of provisions on board. There was no damage except in the places where the masts had fallen overboard. The vessel was in ballast, which had shifted to the port side. One cat was aboard and the red ensign was flying from the stern.[7]

The hulk was next reported on 4 February 1914 in lat. 26°33 S, long. 122°41 W when she was boarded by Captain Rasmusson from the schooner *Inca*, who made a cursory examination and reported the hull in good condition.[8] He removed the captain's sextant, two chronometers and the compass and binnacle.[9]

Dalgonar's travels ended when she grounded on a coral reef near Maupihua island in lat. 16°30 S, long. 154°0 W, after drifting some 5,000 miles, a sad end for such a fine ship.[10]

---

1 Isbester, Charles Allan. Note CAI 5. About 1969. (Isbester collection).
2 Chapters 16 and 17.
3 'Disaster to English Ship'. Local Ilford newspaper. 06.12.1913. (Isbester collection).
4 Lubbock, B, *The Last of the Windjammers,* Vol.I, pp.16–18.
5 'Atlantic Ocean. Captain and three men killed by falling mast.' Newspaper cutting. (Isbester collection).
6 Terrell, Mr George. *Movable ballast.* HC Deb 21 May 1914 Vol 62 cc2160-1W.
7 Moricet, Captain F. Manuscript notes. (Isbester collection).
8 Woollard, Commander Claude L.A., RN, FRGS. 'Career of the Dalgonar'. *Sea Breezes.* Feb. 1965, p.144.
9 Thomson, Captain J.P, OBE ExC. *Captain John Isbester's Career at Sea,* p.25. Unpublished manuscript. (Isbester Collection).
10 Woollard, Commander Claude L.A., RN, FRGS. Op cit, p.144. Feb. 1965.

APPENDIX 1 CARGO WORK FOR A TYPICAL *CENTAUR* VOYAGE

Centaur's voyages between the UK and San Francisco usually involved carrying coal on the outward passage and wheat on the homeward passage (Fig.26.1). Captain Isbester, like any other master, would have been fully involved in a supervisory role, directing the chief mate, the stevedores (known in Australia as wharfies or in the USA as longshoremen) and the trimmers, in all the processes involved in carrying the cargo safely and efficiently. When arriving in the loading port *Centaur* would have been carrying a quantity, perhaps 600 or 700 tons, of ballast, consisting of sand, gravel or rubble, some of which had to be retained aboard until some of the cargo had been loaded. As mentioned in the story, if the holds contained no cargo and no ballast, the ship, as a result of her tall masts, spars and rigging, would be unstable and would list heavily or even capsize. The quantity of ballast needed while the vessel was in port, perhaps 60 per cent

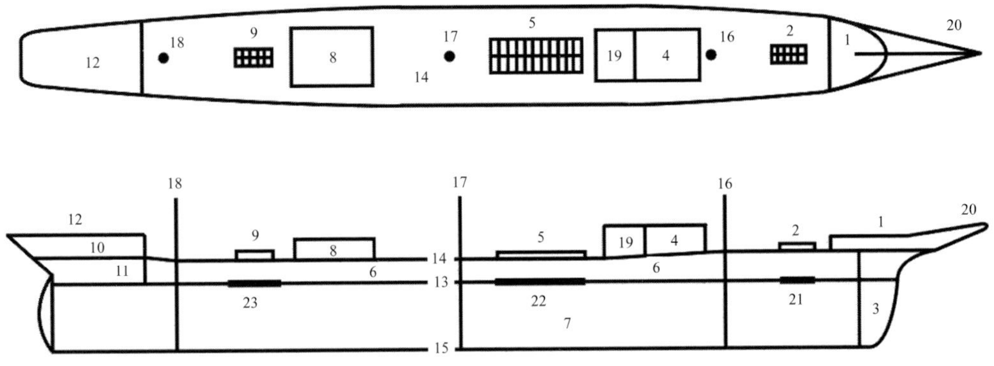

Key

1. Forecastle store
2. Forward hatch
3. Forepeak
4. Crew's forecastle
5. Main hatch
6. Tweendeck
7. Hold, extending from forepeak to stern
8. Apprentices' half deck
9. After hatch
10. Captain and officers' quarters
11. Storerooms, sail locker
12. Poop
13. Main deck
14. Upper deck
15. Keel
16. Fore mast
17. Main mast
18. Mizzen mast
19. Galley and donkey boiler
20. Bowsprit and jibboom
21. Forward tweendeck hatch
22. Main tweendeck hatch
23. After tweendeck hatch

Figure 26.1 *Figure of a generic three-masted square-rigged sailing ship* of that required in a seaway when the ship was exposed to rolling, was given a different name, the 'stiffening'.

Discharge of ballast and hold preparation

Before the loading of coal could commence through the main hatch, it would have been necessary to have discharged any ballast from the mid-length of the hold and to have swept the area clean, retaining sufficient ballast below the forward and after hatches to provide the necessary stiffening. In the 1890s the discharge of loose bulk material such as ballast from the ship was probably achieved by first filling wooden tubs, shovelful by shovelful, with perhaps a ton of ballast. Each tub would then be hoisted out of the hold and delivered over the ship's side using a 'yard and stay' system, with one block fastened to a rigging stay located above the open hatch and a second secured to the lowest yardarm, which would be projecting over the ship's side.[1] Ropes rove through both blocks would be hooked onto a tub, with the other end of each rope led to a convenient capstan or warping end. With this arrangement the tub could be raised out of the hold by hauling on the rope from the block secured on the stay. To swing the load outboard the yard rope was hauled while the stay rope was slacked as necessary. When the tub was over the quay both ropes were slacked to lower the tub to a position over the horse-drawn wagon or whatever vehicle was to receive the contents. Finally the tub would be tipped over and emptied by some mechanical means. In principle this arrangement was exactly the same as the 'union purchase' rig used aboard power-driven general cargo ships equipped with derricks. The power for the hoisting would be provided by the ship's steam-powered donkey engine, if she had one, or by a donkey engine on the quay. *Centaur* was not equipped with a donkey engine, but John Isbester's later command, *Dalgonar*, did have one.

An alternative system for disposing of ballast, used at Wallaroo in the Australian Spencer Gulf, was for the ship to anchor three miles off the port, shovel the ballast into canvas bags, hoist them out of the hold, swing them to the ship's side, attach another hook to an eye on the underside of the canvas bag and lower away, thus capsizing the bag and emptying the ballast into the sea.[2]

Rigging shifting boards

In addition to sweeping the holds before loading coal it was necessary to rig shifting boards in the hold and tweendeck. Shifting boards were necessary for bulk cargoes like coal and ore, and for grain whether in bags or loose, and also for ballast. Shifting boards were intended to form a wooden wall extending along the centreline for the full length of the hold and tweendeck. The purpose of the boards was to ensure that when the ship was rolling heavily in a seaway cargo could not shift from one side of the hold and come to rest on the other side, causing a heavy list or even a capsize. Sailing ships were constructed with iron or steel pillars on the centreline spaced about 5 feet apart and extending the full length of their hold and tweendeck. Most of the pillars were permanent, but those in way of the hatches were portable and could be removed when cargo or ballast was being loaded or discharged.

Lengths of planking could be lashed to the pillars, and when the materials were adequate and the work was competently done the shifting boards could be very effective. Most of the evidence of the manner in which shifting boards were assembled at the end of the 19th century is to be found in the Wreck Reports of ships which were lost or abandoned and is therefore unlikely to represent best practice, but the impression gained is that the fitting of shifting boards was poorly enforced by the authorities and that when fitted they were often inadequate.[3]

Loading the coal

The easiest way to load the coal would be simply to lift it aboard tub by tub, one or two tons at a time, and to tip it through the hatchway into the hold where it would form a cone-shaped pile, the hoisting and tipping being done in the same manner as the ballast was handled. This process would not deliver the coal to the areas between the hatches, nor to the tweendeck wings. To place coal in these areas chutes would be used, but the trimmers, working in the gloom of the unlit holds and breathing the dust generated by the cargo, would have the task of delivering coal to all the spaces served by the chutes and beyond the cones of coal below each of the three hatches.

Coal was a hazardous cargo. If it shifted it could cause the ship to capsize, and besides that it could go on fire and it could release gases which would explode. None of these hazards was easily prevented, and towards the end of the 19th century the loss of coal-laden ships was far too common.

Discharging the coal

Those who survived the five-month voyage from Europe to San Francisco as, happily, John Isbester always did, had next to see their cargo discharged. A San Francisco historian writes:

> The usual unloading method was to shovel the bulk coal into wooden ballast tubs, round and about five feet across and three feet deep. The ship's mainyard was rigged like a crane overhanging the pier, and using either the ship's own donkey engine or a donkey on the pier, the tub was lifted out of the hold, shifted to a runner from the yardarm to swing it over the pier, lowered a bit, and then tipped into a funnel-shaped hopper on the pier. The hopper was in turn emptied into a single horse cart, which was positioned under the funnel like machine.[4]

The historian continues:

> Cleaning the holds before grain
>
> Cleaning out the holds after a coal cargo … would likely have been done by crews from one of the stevedore companies, probably with the help of any remaining ship's crew, to save money. I believe that the workers in the shore crews were hired by the day, through a shape-up. Would have included bums and drunks, as well as sailors between ships. No doubt some very skilled foremen to insure that the job was done correctly. Part of the preparation for a grain cargo was to fully line the interior of the hold and the tweendeck with fresh fir planking, covered with old sails or burlap. It was considered essential to keep the bags from coming into contact with the iron or steel of the ship's hull. This would have led both to wetting from the condensation on the plates, and to chaffe [chafing], which would wear through the bags. The bags were considered essential in order to keep the grain from shifting. The wooden lining meant that the odd bit of coal wedged behind

> a frame would not have been a big deal, although they no doubt tried to get the holds as clean as possible.[5]

Cleaning holds sufficiently well to avoid contaminating grain could be an even more demanding process when previous cargoes had been smelly. An Australian reminisces:

> The ballast being gone it was necessary to clean out the hold, which was by no means a clean job. There was guano and such like in all the cracks. When guano is wet the smell would knock one flat ... While we were at anchor we cleaned the bilges. This was a dirty job. I had to get down underneath the water tanks and bale out the stinking water ... All the deck supports and ironwork [in the hold] had to be bound with sacking.[6]

In San Francisco stiffening was loaded or discharged at a jetty or directly from another ship lying alongside.[7]

Loading grain

The San Francisco historian writes:

> As to loading grain, all of this work would have been done by stevedore gangs, essentially longshoremen hired by the stevedore companies. Deepwater crews never handled cargo, although they might work on preparing the holds. At San Francisco, the grain would have come aboard by the sling load, perhaps twelve bags or so at a time, using the ship's yards and her own donkey [steam engine] or one on the pier. The bags would be dropped on the main deck, and then slid down into the holds on wooden chutes. The loading in the hold was done by a very small, highly-skilled crew. Maybe four men would see to the packing of the entire cargo. The bags would be lifted, one by one, by one man, who would carry them into position to be added to the piles. It was essential to get this right, in order to prevent shifting and to maximize the use of the space. At Port Costa, where the majority of California grain was loaded after the late 1870s, the warehouses were set up so that train cars could be unloaded at a second story level, allowing the bags to be slid down chutes to the main deck of the ship. Loading was then by chute and manhandling.[8]

Stowing grain

The Wreck Report for the *County of Denbigh* in 1880[9] concluded on the basis of reports received from her loading port, Astoria in Oregon, that she had been loaded in accordance with the strict regulations of the port of San Francisco and that the cargo had been properly stowed. The evidence was that double rows of shifting boards were rigged, lashed to the stanchions in the centre, and that the full cargo of 1,636 tons of wheat was in bags which were in very good condition. The bags would have been centals, 100lb bags, as required by Liverpool merchants.[10] Amidships the bags were arranged in longers (i.e. with their axes laid fore and aft) and in the wings they were stowed a-burton (with axes athwartships).

1 Kennerley, Dr. Alston. Personal letter dated 23.05.2013.

2 Carter, Robert. *Windjammers, the final story.* Rosenberg Publishing Pty Ltd, 2004, p.195.

3 For a coal cargo loaded in Shields in 1886 shifting boards were fitted to a barque of about 1,200 tons register by a master rigger assisted by the mate. The evidence of the master rigger was: 'The shifting boards consisted of planks two inches thick and about seven inches wide ... lashed to the stanchions in the tweendecks from two feet below the main deck beams to the upper deck beams, about six inches apart, so in my opinion the cargo could not have shifted.' [*Cumeria* Wreck Report. 27.12.1888 http://www.plimsoll.org/images/15388_tcm4-192527.pdf] Shifting boards spaced six inches apart would be ineffective in preventing coal, even though it was described as 'large', from seeping through the gaps in the shifting boards when, for example, the ship ran for a number of days with a constant wind, keeping the ship heeled to the same side but still continuing to pitch and roll. It was reported that the hold was filled with coal right up close to the deck, but it must be remembered that while the coal was probably delivered to the hold by chute, which would place it in the required area, the final trimming was done by men with shovels who would have to deliver each shovelful to a position at head height and would be tempted to build the coal high at the front of the stow to conceal the fact that it was lower further back.

4 Canright, Stephen. Park Historian, San Francisco NHP. Email dated 02.11.15 from gina_bardi@nps.gov (Isbester Collection).

5 Canright, Stephen. Park Historian, San Francisco NHP. ibid.

6 Carter, Robert. Op cit., p.195.

7 Bardi, Gina. Email dated 02.11.15 from gina_bardi@nps.gov (Isbester Collection).

8 Canright, Stephen. Park Historian, San Francisco NHP. Op cit.

9 U K Formal Investigation No782 County of Denbigh. http://www.plimsoll.org/images/14425_tcm4-161628.pdf.

10 Paul, Rodman W. 'The Wheat Trade Between California and the United Kingdom' *The Mississippi Valley Historical Review* 45.3 (1958): 381–412.

APPENDIX 2 WORKING OUT THE DEAD HORSE

Account written by Arnold Franz McJannet:[1]

> In these days of steam, when the sailor is fast disappearing, the old usages pertaining to the sea life are also vanishing. Steam, short voyages, and the absence of the necessity for seamanship, all tend towards this consummation. I have now found out how the custom of working out the dead horse should be observed accurately. Very few of those now at sea have ever witnessed the performance, and at best it is, and was on board here, a perfunctory performance to afford an excuse for a libation of grog. As it was an old custom now rapidly dying out, I shall endeavour to describe it for your benefit.
>
> The end of the month since signing on has arrived, and the Ship being in the N.E. trade, there is fine quiet weather with a fair wind, preparations have been going on forward for some days, which have been kept strictly private. At 8 o'clock a flourish of a Concertina is heard in the foc-sel [fo'c'sle/forecastle], then lamps appear and by their light a procession begins to wend its way aft. As the procession reaches the foot of the poop we see what it is. A rough platform has been knocked together which travels on the wheels of the carronage carriage, which have been taken off for that purpose. Upon this moving platform is erected a rough (very rough) figure of a horse, made of canvass and stuffed with shavings and straw. Upon this animal sits the scallywag of the crew, with a battered tall hat on his head and wielding a long whip, and now the men who drag this conveyance haul to the regulation song -
>
> *They say, old man, your horse will die,*
> (chorus) *And they say so,*
> *And they hope so,*
> *They say, old man, your horse will die,*
> *O – poor – old – horse.*
> *And if he dies I'll tan his hide,*
> *And if he lives I'll ride him again.*

Arriving at the quarter deck the procession halts, the rider dismounts, and, striking an attitude, apostrophises his ragged animal -

Old horse, old horse, what brought you here,
After carrying stone for many a year
From Skibbereen to Ballyhack,
Where you fell down and broke your back?
And after years of this abuse
They salt you down for Sailors' use;
Then tan your hide and burn your bones
And send you down to Davy Jones.

After this he mounts his steed again and to the tune,

And they say so,
And they hope so, &c.

the old horse is dragged to the lee gangway.

A whip and line have been fixed on the main yard-arm; to this line the old horse is bent on, one of the men sitting across his shoulders, and the two – horse and man – are run up to the yard-arm. The fellow clambers up on the yard, cuts the old horse down and fires a blue light. As the carcass drops over-board a lighted tar-barrel, which has been got ready on the foc-sel, is dropped also. Three cheers are given, and the Skipper calls out -

Splice the main brace!

and grog is served out as it was in those happy days.

---

1 McJannet, Arnold Franz. *The Log of the Dalgonar*, 02.07.1908. (Isbester Collection)

APPENDIX 3 CROSSING THE LINE CEREMONY

Account written by Arnold Franz McJannet[1]

As I have already said the old customs of the sea are dying out, and they are more honoured in the breach than in the observance. Captain Isbester has, from the first, disapproved of the barbarous and enmity provoking old habit of shaving with tar and dipping into a sheet filled with water that used to welcome the aspirant to Neptune's Court on crossing the line, and he instituted a more humane and civilised procedure, which was, at the same time, laughter provoking, but not at the expense of physical pain or extreme discomfort on the part of the initiant.

I shall endeavour shortly to describe the ceremony as it was held to-day. The for-ard end of the Fore Hatch was draped with flags, and a bench and seats placed on the Hatch preparatory for the arrival of Mr. and Mrs Neptune and their Satellites. Over all was placed a sail, which was spread over the scene and thus made a cosy tent in which tea was partaken of, and thereafter a sing-song held. Neptune – a tall elderly sailor with a deep hoarse voice – was dressed in an oil-skin coat, long thick whiteish stockings covering his nether limbs and feet. A tin crown having Father Neptune in red painted on it and a long flowing beard made of yarn completed his facial adornments. A three-pronged trident and winter gloves gave him an imposing appearance. His wife, Nancy – whose feet were rather noticeable – wore a long flowing wig of the same material as adorned her liege and master done up into a straggling knot, with the ends over both shoulders. Her costume consisted of a red counterpane and a checked blouse. Her proportions were ample, and, I may say, to put it delicately, that she was much inclined to embonpoint. The parts were fairly well taken, the female being a young stoutly built man – a Minister's son by the way. The Doctor – a comical little Irishman – bearing the patronymic of Murphy – had a battered old felt round hat, dilapidated as to the brims and in appearance, and an Overcoat reaching to his heels. He carried a dressing case and a large enigmatical smile. Among the retinue were – a Barber with an enormous wooden razor, and the Bosun as Policeman, wearing a Souwester with a tin plate badge, three stripes on the arm of an Apprentice's brass buttoned tunic, and a considerably thick truncheon.

At four in the afternoon Neptune came on board over the bow, and proceeded aft in a Motor Car, with his wife seated beside him, and followed by the Band, the doctor, Policeman and others being in close attendance. They were met by the Captain, and, after shaking hands, in which the matronly Mrs Neptune joined with much effusiveness and *bonne humeur*, Neptune was informed that he (the Captain) had two gentlemen on board who did not desire to follow the occupation of the sea, and therefore would not join the holy extraordinary ordinary Order, but they undertook to be worthy and loyal advocates for His Majesty when on shore. They were willing to pay their dues and wished Father Neptune a continued long life of prosperity. This explanation having been accepted and the dues – in the shape of a couple of bottles of grog – paid and consumed, the Captain was appointed Examiner in Chief.

He presented five Apprentices for initiation. They had been brought forward, tied hand to hand in single file by the Policeman, who had some little difficulty in keeping order. The name, age, and sex of the first applicant having been ascertained, the test of the senses was proceeded with. First, for example – sense of taste – Having been blindfolded he was told to open his mouth and a piece of sugar was popped in, the Captain saying at the same time that we all knew this was sugar. On being asked what the article was, the Apprentice replied 'Sugar! Wonderful.' Next a piece of cheese was tried, all being informed that it was cheese. The blindfolded boy replied 'Cheddar cheese! Marvellous.' Then when that was consumed a piece of bread. 'Bread!!' The reply was again accurate. General consternation. Liquids were now resorted to. Tea, Coffee and Water in turn with the same formula that, of course, we knew that this was tea, that coffee, and that water. The answer in each particular case was absolutely correct.

Excitement now at fever heat. A Stethoscope, in the shape of an old sounding trumpet, was now applied to the chest, and the pronouncement made that he had two hearts, but that his other organs seemed in order. Lung testing was then resorted to. A cautious nip did not produce much lung power, but a loud roar soon testified that the lungs were in perfect working order. He was measured for height and breadth – the measurements each way being absolutely abnormal. His toes were now counted and again counted and again, but always the same number – 11 – was made. The Examiner stated to His Majesty that perhaps he had made an error in calculation, but the two big toes being together rather confused him. The boy then had to cross his feet so that the two little toes were alongside, but counting proved difficult as he could not remain stationary long enough.

He was then put under the X Rays to ascertain what he had for Breakfast. The Breakfast had disappeared, but it was announced that he had had pork for the previous day's dinner. These, to put it shortly, were some of the tests each had to go through, and, His Majesty being informed that they had duly satisfied them and the Examiner, they kissed the Holy-stone, and were admitted by Neptune and his wife to the freedom of the seas. The latter's greeting being characterised by much warmth, so much, indeed, as to excite the jealousy of her noble lord. Thereafter tea was partaken of, and song and sentiment finished the ceremony at 8 bells.

---

1 McJannet, Arnold Franz. *The Log of the Dalgonar*, 04.07.1908. (Isbester Collection)

APPENDIX 4 REPORT OF *DALGONAR* FORMAL INVESTIGATION

(No.7640).

DALGONAR.

The Merchant Shipping Act, 1894

In the matter of a Formal Investigation held at Liverpool on the 27th and 30th days of March and the 1st day of April 1914, before STUART DEACON, Esquire, Stipendiary Magistrate, assisted by Vice Admiral A.G. TAIT, and Captain David Davies, into the circumstances attending the abandonment of the British sailing ship DALGONAR in the Pacific Ocean on or about the 13th October 1913, and the loss of life which occurred.

Report of Court

The Court having carefully inquired into the circumstances attending the above mentioned shipping casualty, finds for the reasons stated in the Annex hereto, that the British sailing ship DALGONAR, of Liverpool, was abandoned by her crew on the 13th October 1913 in about latitude 28° 58 S, and longitude 87 4 W., and that the immediate cause of such abandonment was that the shingle ballast, which the vessel had taken on board at Callao, had not been properly secured, with the result that it shifted in the course of a heavy storm which broke over the vessel on the 9th of October and which caused the vessel to take such a heavy list to port that by about 2.30 p.m. on the afternoon of the last-mentioned day she was thrown over to port nearly on her beam ends, and could not, thereafter, be uprighted.

The master, Mr. Isbister (*sic*), and three of the crew unhappily lost their lives in the course of the storm before mentioned, and the rest of the crew, after undergoing terrible privation and suffering, were ultimately rescued by the French barque *Loire* on 13 October and to the captain and crew of this latter vessel the thanks of the Court and all concerned are due for the assistance which they rendered and the kindness which they afterwards showed to the crew of the DALGONAR,

Dated this 1st day of April 1914.

STUART DEACON, judge.

We concur with the above Report

A.G TATE, Assessor
DAVID DAVIES, Assessor

The inquiry was held in the Magistrates' Room, Dale Street, Liverpool, on the 27th and 30th days of March and the 1st day of April 1914. Mr Paxton (Messrs. Avison, Morton and Paxton) appeared on behalf of the Board of Trade, Mr A. H. Maxwell (instructed by Messrs. Hill, Dickinson & Co.) watched the proceedings on behalf of Messrs. Gracie, Beasley and Co., and Mr L. S. Holmes (Messrs. Miller, Taylor and Holmes) watched the proceedings on behalf of the chief officer, Mr W. H. Mull.

The *Dalgonar*, official number 99367, was a sailing vessel built of steel at Southampton in 1892, by the Southampton Naval Works, Limited, and was completed by Messrs. Gracie, Beasley and Co., of Liverpool. She was registered at the port of Liverpool.

Her length over all was 296 feet, her breadth 42.3 feet, and her depth of hold 25.2 feet; her registered tonnage being 2565.15 tons. She had a forecastle and poop, the master and officers were berthed in the latter, the seamen and petty officers were berthed in a deckhouse forward, and the apprentices in a deckhouse aft. She carried a donkey boiler and winch in the after end of the forward deck house, and she had three masts and was rigged as a full-rigged ship. She carried two life-boats on skids under davits aft, also a dinghy, a pinnace and a gig, which were carried on skids on top of the forward deck-house. They were all in good order and fully equipped. She had six life-buoys and a full complement of life-jackets, the latter being kept in the sail locker on the poop, and quite handy to get at when required. She carried rockets and blue lights, which were kept in the chart-house on the poop; and the ship seemed to have been well found in every respect. She was owned jointly by Mr. William Gracie and Mr. Edwin Arthur Beazley, both of 25, Water Street, Liverpool, Mr. William Gracie being, by and on behalf of the owners, by advice under the seal of the sailing ship Dalgonar Co., Limited., received 8 February 1892.

The *Dalgonar* left the Thames in November 1912 with a full cargo of cement in barrels for Melbourne, after the discharge of which she took on board 1,000 tons of sand ballast for Newcastle, N.S.W. This was stowed in Nos. 2 and 3 holds, her mean draught of water on leaving Melbourne being 12 feet. Shifting boards were used on this occasion, a temporary stanchion being put up in the middle of No.2 hatchway to support them. This ballast was carried safely, and did not shift. At Newcastle she loaded a full cargo of coal for Callao, shifting-boards being used with this cargo, which carried all right.

After the discharge of this cargo at Callao, she took on board 1,000 tons of shingle ballast, her draught of water being 11 feet 7 inches forward and 12 feet 9 inches aft, giving a mean draught of 12 feet 2 inches. This was 2 inches more than when she left Melbourne, and the Court is satisfied that she took her full weight of 1,000 tons on board in Callao.

Mr Beasley, one of the owners, stated that on a previous voyage on the West Coast of South America the vessel had only 850 tons of ballast aboard, but further explained that on that occasion she was going from a southern to a northern port along the land, with favourable prevailing winds.

She left the dock at Callao on 21 September 1913 and anchored in the bay, in order to get her ready for sea. The seamen, who arrived in her at Callao, were paid off, and the fresh crew joined just before sailing.

Mr Mull, the chief mate, stated that the shingle ballast was trimmed and levelled down, and that bulkheads had been erected at the fore and aft ends of the same to keep it from spreading fore and aft. He also stated that diamond shaped bins were constructed in the hatchways, the corners of which were securely lashed to the stanchions, and that all this work was done under the master's supervision.

The mate, who had had previous experience of Callao shingle ballast, had a conversation with the master with regard to the securing of this ballast with shifting boards. The master told him that he was adopting the system of bins in lieu of shifting boards in the hatchways for the purpose of raising the weight as much as possible in the centre of the vessel, at the same time saying that it would be all right, as they were certain to have a fine weather passage.

The mate further stated that the ballast in Nos.2 and 3 holds was boarded over, and a few shores put up, but he did not recollect how many. He, however, said that at the time he was satisfied with the way in which the ballast was secured, seeing that the master was satisfied.

Herman Dunker, the carpenter, stated that he put up some centre shifting-boards at the fore and after ends of the ballast but that they only went about 18 inches into it. He also described the bins which he constructed by the master's orders, and stated that he remarked to the master that they would not be of any use to keep the ballast from shifting, and that the master told him to go ahead with the work and mind his own business. This witness further stated that after the ballast had been levelled down, some loose boards were spread over it, but that no shores had been put up before leaving Callao.

Mr Joseph Oxnard [*sic*], the second mate, who held no certificate, was formerly an apprentice, but had been promoted during this voyage. He corroborated the statement of the carpenter with regard to the method the master adopted to secure the ballast from shifting, and also stated that the ballast was not shored down before leaving port.

According to the owners' statement in Court the *Dalgonar* left Callao on 24 September 1913 with a crew of 30 hands all told, bound for Taltal where she was to load nitrate.

The *Dalgonar* experienced fine weather until 7 October, when the wind gradually freshened from the East and E.S.E., and some canvas was reduced. On 8 October, the wind still freshening, at 7 p.m. she was put under three lower topsails, foresail and fore topmast staysail. At 8 30 a.m. on 9 October, it was blowing a moderate gale with high seas running. The captain sent the first mate and carpenter down into the hold to see if the ballast was all right, and a few of the hatch covers were taken off to allow some light into the holds. The mate stated that when they got below and were standing on the ceiling, fore part of ballast in No.2 hold, the ballast was found to be all right. He, however, stated that at that time a heavy squall struck the vessel and carried away the fore lower topsail, and at the same time she took a heavy lurch, when the ballast was observed to be moving bodily to leeward. The lower portion of the ballast seemed to be moving bodily underneath the bins. This caused the vessel to have a list to port of about 20 degrees. The master ordered all hands below to trim back the ballast and they succeeded in getting her nearly upright by 11.30 a.m. The planks and hatch covers were replaced on top of the ballast, which was then shored down from the tween deck beams.

The crew were engaged in retrimming the ballast in No.3 hold, about 2 30 p.m. the same day, when a heavy sea struck the vessel, throwing her nearly over on her beam ends, and causing the ballast to shift again, this bringing all the shores down. The crew were ordered to come up on deck, and an attempt was made to wear the ship. The main and cross jackyards were squared, and the jibs hoisted with sheets to windward. The sheets however carried away when she had only payed off a couple of points, and the vessel lay in the trough of the sea and was thrown on her beam ends. The master ordered the life-boats to be got out. The port life-boat was successfully got into the water but she was immediately swamped and the men who were in her managed to get back on board again. This part of the narrative is fully described in answer to Question 4, the captain and three of the crew losing their lives, and the starboard lifeboat being swamped.

After the captain was washed overboard, as stated in Answer No. 4, the mate gave orders to cut away the rigging, to allow the masts to fall overboard. The vessel was fitted with screw lanyards, and the crew were unable to get at the lee lanyards, so they cut the weather rigging and all the masts fell over to leeward. All this weight hung onto the vessel until the screw lanyards ultimately broke away, thus relieving her considerably, after which the lee rail came out of the water. The crew afterwards managed to get on the poop, and eventually into the cabin, through the chart-house, where they managed to get some food, and also with great difficulty they succeeded in getting some water from the tanks, which fortunately had held in position, notwithstanding that the vessel was lying on her beam ends. At 3 30 a.m. of the 10 October the green light of a sailing vessel was sighted, and rockets were fired and blue lights burnt. These were soon responded to, and the other vessel, which proved to be the French barque *Loire* came and stood by, but owing to the heavy weather and high sea, it was impossible to render any assistance until the 13th, by which time the weather had somewhat moderated. The *Loire* sent a boat which, however, could not get nearer than about 60 fathoms to the wreck, and communication had to be established by lines. By these means the crew were drawn through the water to the boat without any further casualty. The crew of the *Dalgonar* lost all their effects, and the log books and other documents were also lost, and the vessel was abandoned in Latitude 28°58 N (*sic*) and longitude 87°4W.

The *Loire* was on her homeward passage, and eventually landed the survivors at Dunkerque, with the exception of six who had been transferred to La Fontaine, and landed at Falmouth.

The following is a list of those who lost their lives in this disaster:- John Isbister (*sic*) master; Hugo Unger, cook; H.J. Cousins, sailmaker; Arthur Confrere, A.B.

Arising out of this Inquiry, it appears to be the practice among some masters when carrying ballast to use shifting-boards which only extend from a foot or two above the top of the ballast to about the same distance into it. This is a most dangerous practice, as shown in this case. All shifting boards should extend from the bottom of the hold to well above the top of the ballast, and should be properly secured. It would be well if steps were taken to enforce this.

At the conclusion of the evidence Mr Paxton, on behalf of the Board of Trade, submitted the following questions for the opinion of the Court:

1. What was the cost of the vessel to her owners? What was her value when she sailed on her last voyage? What insurances were effected upon and in connection with her?
2. What amount and description of ballast was shipped on the vessel at Callao in about September 1913? Was it sufficient in quantity and was it properly stowed and secured from shifting?
3. What was the cause of the ballast shifting and the vessel listing to port at or about 8 30 a.m. and 2 30 p.m. on the 9 October last? Was every possible effort made to trim the ballast back into position and to get the ship upright?
4. What were the circumstances in which the master and three members of the crew lost their lives?

5. When and where was the Dalgonar abandoned? What was the cause of the abandonment of the vessel.

The Court returned the following answers to the questions of the Board of Trade:-

1. The cost of the vessel to her owners was £23,262 7s 1d. Her value, when she left on her last voyage, was stated by her owners to be fully £11,000. She was insured for £10,250, and her freight was insured for £5,580. There was no insurance on disbursements. The captain's effects were insured by him, through the owners, for £150.
2. The vessel shipped at Callao 1,000 tons of shingle ballast, and she also had about 30 tons of coal in the fore-peak. In the opinion of the Court the ballast was sufficient in quantity and was properly stowed, but was not properly secured from shifting. The evidence shows that the master sought to secure the shingle by the use in each hatchway of a diamond shaped bin, made of wood, about 20 feet long and 3 feet deep, which was let into the top of the shingle about 18 inches, and the four corners of each bin were lashed to stanchions to keep it in position. Each bin was about 1 foot 6 inches above the top of the ballast. Bulkheads of about 6 feet in height were erected at the fore and after ends of the shingle which was sloped down so as to be at each end about 18 inches below the top of the bulkhead. The amount of shingle placed in the No.2 hold was 660 tons, and in No.3 hold 340 tons. The Court having regard to the dangerous description of the ballast, such as shingle has always proved itself to be, can only repeat and emphasise the recommendations which were made by a Court of Inquiry sitting in Liverpool as long ago as the year 1901 in a similar case to this, namely, that of the ship *Limache*, which meet with this Court's entire approval, and were in these words:- The ballast shipped in Callao is shingle, and with such a dangerous description of ballast as this, centre shifting boards should invariably be used, and also wing shifting boards where practicable. Further, bulkheads should be built at the forward and after ends of the ballast and brought up to the same height to prevent the ballast running forward or aft. Finally the ballast should be securely tommed down.
3. The cause of the ballast shifting, and the vessel listing to port, at about 8 30 a.m. on 9 October last, was the fact that at the time a gale was blowing from the ESE and a heavy sea was running from the SE, while the vessel was heading NE, when the force of the wind carried away the fore topsail. At the same time the ship gave a heavy lurch to port and the shingle in No.2 hold shifted bodily from underneath the bin. The captain at once ordered all hands to go below and secure the shingle which was retrimmed and (for the first time) shored down, an operation which was taken to be satisfactorily accomplished, although with considerable difficulty, by 12 noon. Attempts were afterwards made to shore down the shingle in No.3 hold in a similar manner, but were not completed before the disaster occurred.

At 2 30 p.m., while the crew were still at work in No.3 hold, a heavy squall caught the vessel and threw her nearly on her beam ends, with the result that the shingle in No.2 and 3 holds again shifted bodily to port, and the shores gave way and the vessel acquired a heavy list. The captain at once called all hands to wear the ship, but she only paid off two points and then lay in the trough of the sea, and a few moments later another heavy sea struck the vessel so that with a still further and final shifting of shingle, she was brought right over to port on her beam ends.

Under the before-mentioned circumstances, the Court is satisfied that every effort was made to trim the ballast back into position, and to get the ship upright.

4. The circumstances under which the master and three members of the crew lost their lives were as follows:- After the vessel had been thrown over to port on her beam ends, as detailed in the answer to the preceding question, the port life-boat was lowered into the water and some of the crew got into it but the boat was sucked alongside at once, and one of the davits, owing to the heavy list of the vessel, crushed into the fore part of the boat. The men who were in the boat managed to scramble back safe on board. The starboard lifeboat was next got into the water, but she was also immediately damaged and swamped, with the result that the crew were thrown into the sea, and the sailmaker (named H. J. Cousins) and the cook (whose name was Hugo Unger) were drowned, while the others managed to get back onto the vessel. Unfortunately, however, one of these last-mentioned men (Arthur Confrere, A.B.) got entangled in the gear which was washing about, and was drowned. The master (Mr. John Isbister (sic)) who was at this time holding on amidships in front of the cabin, on seeing Confrere's perilous position let go with the evident idea of trying to save him, but he was at once thrown to leeward and struck his head against the lee rails, and was evidently stunned, washed overboard, and drowned before any assistance could be given to him. Under the dangerous circumstances in which they were placed it was not possible for anyone to render any assistance to the man Confrere, and in fact his body remained entangled amongst the ropes for two days before the sea finally washed it away.

6. (sic) The vessel was abandoned on 13 October 1913, in latitude 25°58 South, longitude 87°4 West. She was not prematurely abandoned. The immediate cause of the abandonment was the fact that it had been found necessary to cut away the masts of the vessel in the hopes of righting her and this did not prove effectual.

STUART DEACON, Judge

We concur with the above Report
A. G. TATE, Assessor
David Davies, Assessor

Liverpool, 2nd April 1914
(Issued in London by the Board of Trade on the 28th day of April 1914)

APPENDIX 5 MR MULL'S LOG OF THE CASUALTY

Barque "Loire",

Dunkerque,

October, 14th, 1913

Log and Record of the Wreck of the Ship "Dalgonar" of Liverpool bound from Callao to Taltal.

[Transcript of the original typescript based on Mr Mull's manuscript document]

We left Callao Dock Sept.20th at about 1 P.M. Ship's draught water 12'9" aft and 11'7" forward, main (sic) draught 12'2" and anchored in the Bay. Crew down in the Hold levelling down the ballast in both Hatches, shifting boards all up and well lashed, having also diamond shaped shifting bens (sic) in the square of each hatch, all well lashed and the ballast covered fore and aft and shored down from between deck beams. We had also bulkheads at the ends of each lot of ballast, 660 English tons in No. 2 Hatch and 340 tons in No. 3 Hatch and the ship was fumigated fore and aft and in the hold.

Sept. 23rd at 4 P.M. we left Callao, 30 hands on board all told, for Taltal, light S. E. wind and fine weather. Set all sail and found the vessel very stiff and steering by the wind on the port tack. Heading S.W. by W. moderate and fine weather continued until we reached the Lat. 29° S and Long. 84° W.

Oct. 7th as well as can be remembered the wind gradually increased and we reduced sail accordingly.

Oct. 8th A.M. we experienced strong east wind and squally weather. We were under the topsails and foresails I had a look down below and all was well. At noon all hands wore ship, put the Vessel on the Starboard tack heading N.E. and N.N.E. At 7 P.M. wind and sea were increasing and we took in the (Mizzen) fore upper topsail. At 11 P.M. wind and sea still increasing took the Mizzen and main upper topsails.

Oct. 9th A.M. Hard gale and high increasing sea and very showery. The Vessel was labouring and straining heavily. At 6 A.M. the 2nd. Officer, Mr. Oxnard (sic), went down the hold to see if the ballast was all right and he reported everything was well down below. 8 A.M. the wind moderated a little, but a terrific high sea from the S.E. Ship's head N.E. and N.N.E. At 8.30 A.M. Captain Isbester told me to go down with the Carpenter and see that the ballast was all right. We found everything well when we came down, but while we were standing looking at the ballast a squall struck the Vessel and the fore lower topsail carried away. The Watch went up aloft to pick up the remains. At the same time the Vessel made an extra heavy roll and the ballast shifted a little on the lee-side; we called all hands on deck and down below trimmed the ballast back again, covered it well, and shored it down well. At noon the starboard watch came down the hold and relieved the port watch, putting up extra shores and the port watch went down below. Lat. At noon 31^{0}-45. S, Long. 85^{0}-27.W.

It was blowing a very hard gale with a terrific high sea, and heavy rain squalls every half hour. At 2.30 P.M. a terrific squall struck the Vessel and at the same time a fearful high sea struck her on the starboard beam and heavy sprays flying over the Vessel like steam, and threw the ship nearly on her beam-ends, carrying away all the shores and throwing the ballast clean over into the port wing. Some of the men in the starboard watch got their legs buried in the ballast and had great difficulty in clearing themselves. They all scrambled up on deck; the port watch was immediately on deck, some of them almost naked.

The Captain ordered the carpenter to batten down the hatches; he then gave orders to put the ship on the port tack. The helm was put hard over and we squared-in the main and crosjack yards and shivered the sails. Ship's head was N.E. when we put the helm up and she paid off to N.N.E. but would not go any further. The Captain ordered me to hoist up the inner and outer jibs to help to pay her off, and when doing this the fore sheet, which was brand new only recently made, carried away and with a terrific lurch the Vessel was thrown on her beam ends, with the main and mizzen topsail yard-arms in the water.

Captain Isbester and the carpenter rushed into the cabin, and told the carpenter to get the axes out of the store room and stand by. The Captain went into his room for something and they both came out on the main deck. The carpenter asked Captain Isbester to come up on the poop but he refused to come. He ordered the port life-boat to be cut away which was done, and got into the water all right: 6 or 7 hands jumped into her, but she was immediately crushed by the davits, and the men managed to scramble back on board again.

The Captain then gave orders for the starboard life-boat to be cut away, which was immediately done, and Mr. May 3rd Officer the Cook, sailmaker, R. Jones (Cabin-boy), A. Confrere A.B. and 2 or 3 men more jumped into her, got her into the water all right, but try as they would, they could not get her away clear of the ship on account of the back-wash and the rolling of the Vessel. The forward davit head came down on the cook, who was in the bow of the boat, and crushed him and the bow of the boat also. The remaining part of the boat turned over twice throwing all the men into the sea; they all managed to get back on board again with the exception of the cook, who was crushed, the sailmaker, who was drowned, and A. Confrere, A.B. managed to get back inboard again but got entangled in the braces and hung there under the main rail for the two days after. We could not get any where near him and he was washed away piece by piece.

When our poor Captain saw the starboard life-boat being crushed he evidently felt that he must go and help for he lost his hold and went with his head up against the after davit which must have fractured his skull. He never spoke or moved and the backwash took him away and we saw him no more. I was scrambling along on the outside of the ship with the men I had with me to set the jibs, when I saw the poor Captain go over the side.

I immediately ordered the masts to be cut away and the carpenter, Mr. Oxnard, 2nd Officer, and one man cut away the mizzen rigging and I sent 3 or 4 men forward to try and get axes out of the carpenter's shop and they managed to get them by the aid of ropes, started to cut away the fore backstays and lower rigging. The mizzen mast went first; it broke about 10 feet above the deck and broke again just outside the rail. Cheered our gallant officers and men up all I could to give them courage at their work, and in about 40 minutes the three masts were over the side. The main mast was the next cut away by Mr. Oxnard, the carpenter and some of the men; it also broke about 8 or 10 feet above the deck and again outside the rail. Then the foremast the same way, but with the rolling of the ship the head of the foremast lifted up about 10 ft. and came down with a terrific force on the Keelson; if it had missed once it certainly would have gone through the ship's bottom. Every time it came down it shook the ship terribly and we did not expect to see many hours more, but any way after the masts were cut away it made her lower rail visible once more. We could not get at the lee rigging to cut away as the sea was washing half way up to the hatches and all the rooms in the Cabin on the lee-side were full of water, and it broke up everything that was in them. It was utterly impossible to get into them: every moment we were expecting the spars to poke a hole through her side or else turn over altogether.

I cheered up everybody and told them to trust in God, and He would help us all. It was now about 8 P.M. and the gale still continued with violent rain squalls and a fearful high sea. We all mustered outside the rail on the halfround. Mr. Oxnard and Mr. May with some of the men went down into the saloon by the aid of ropes through the skylight and down through the chart house and they secured a chair in the saloon and lowered me down out of the weather. We were all wringing wet and cold but we managed to get some dry clothes from the slop chest and some biscuits. After this we resigned ourselves to God Almighty and as we did not expect to see another day dawn on us, we were too far South and not far enough West for any homeward bounders to fall across us, but anyway I set one Officer and two men on watch as there is nothing impossible for God. The rest took shelter in the charthouse and in the saloon by my side but everyone of us had a life-line round us to enable us to get up on deck again. I sat all night in my chair praying to God with all my heart and soul and I have no doubt they were all doing the same.

At midnight the gale was raging heavily with a very high sea and heavy rain squalls, the Vessel rolling heavily, sometimes the decks being perpendicular, and we were expecting her to turn over at any moment.

Oct. 10th, Mr. May and his two men on watch say a green light on the port bow. We quickly got some rockets and blue light out of the charthouse and we fired one rocket after rocket and blue light after blue light, but we had not fired more than two or three when the ship answered with a blue light. Oh! how we all cheered and thanked God:. No tongue can tell. The Lord had heard our prayer and sent this ship to our rescue and at day-break we saw her coming down on us with square yards, on our starboard quarter: she came close round our stern and under our lee and everybody that was capable joined in with the three cheers. The Vessel's name was "Loire" of Dunkerque, and she flew the French Ensign with the signal "Do you wish to abandon", which we answered in the affirmative. She sailed round us four times this day but could not render assistance owing to the fearful gale and high sea that was raging at the time. Several of the men that could swim wanted to jump overboard when the vessel was close to us, but I managed to persuade them not to try it, as I felt sure they would never reach the ship and they took my advice.

At daylight we found that all three masts had gone and broken off just outside of the Rail and taken with them the jib-boom. It had broken off just outside of the inner jib stay band and the screws had carried away just below the boxes. It made our hearts feel a little lighter when we saw this. There is one thing I wish I could mention about my good Officers and men; I am very proud to say that Mr. Oxnard 2nd Officer and Mr. May 3rd Officer Have done their duty like true British seamen and carried out my orders to the letter and at all time cool and collected and great praise is due to them. Our carpenter Mr. Dunker behaved like a hero and stuck to his work like a man, cheering up the men who were working with him cutting away the masts and I must say he is worthy of great praise. Praise is also due to all the men; they all kept very cool and collected and carried out orders like noble British seamen. May God bless them all and protect them.

At 3 P.M. when we found it impossible to be rescued this day we tried to get some biscuits and water and put on dry clothes and were successful in getting them, by the aid of ropes. We found the fresh water pump working all right and we were very glad of that as we were getting very thirsty.

At 4 P.M. our companion the four-masted barque "Loire" sailed round us the fourth and last time this day and went close under our stern. The Captain waved his hand and begged us to be cool and patient and he hoisted the signal that he would stand by us and we joined in with three cheers again which he returned. This cheered us up considerably. We then prepared for the night as before having flare up lights for a stand-by in case of emergency and then resigned ourselves to God to protect us against the perils of the deep.

Oct. 11th. At daylight we were a little disheartened at not seeing the French Vessel. Our hero carpenter and three or four men volunteered to go forward and cut away the port anchor, which was lashed on the forecastle-head and they were successful in doing so which lightened the Vessel a little; then they volunteered to be lowered down the hold from the fore-hatch to ascertain if anything could be done with the ballast, but when down there they found all the ballast over on the port-side and up under the tween-deck beams, and utterly impossible to do anything to such a ballast as we had: it was rolling about like marbles with the rolling of the Vessel. They also found water fore and aft in the between-decks, but they kept that quiet from all the men as it might have caused panic.

At 10. A.M. the French barque have in sight again on our starboard quarter and in a few minutes we could see her bearing down on us with square yards. No one but those who have experienced such a terrible situation know how the sight of her lightened our hearts and we once more knew that our prayers had been heard by our great Creator. The gale was still blowing with great force and high sea. We all had our life-belts on and prepared for the worst. Our merciful friend sailed around us twice this day and the second time he hoisted the signal saying "Wait until the weather moderates". Oh! how we cheered and thanked him. We now felt sure that he would not leave us but see the last of us and save us. Then we resigned ourselves to God for another night, and kept a keen watch. At midnight it was still blowing very hard and a mountain of a sea. No boat could live in it and every now and again we could hear some-thing giving away below; it would go off like a gun and the Vessel was shaking and trembling terribly.

Oct. 12th. A.M. The gale still continued with a high sea and as near as I could judge, the Vessel was drifting in the N.N.W. direction at about 2½ miles an hour; which proved pretty correct when we were safe on board our good ship "Loire". At day-light the good ship was not in sight but we could not see very far as it was very squally, with heavy showers of rain. At about 9,A.M we got a Bible and Prayer Book which one of the men had in his pocket and we held a funeral service for poor Captain Isbester, and H. Unger (cook & steward), H. J. Cousin (sailmaker), and Arthur Confrere (A.B), who had lost their lives. The service was conducted by Mr. A. L. May, 3rd Officer, him being a clergyman's son and the most suitable for the occasion, singing hymns and thanking God for his most wonderful mercy in sending this vessel to our rescue; we had not seen a single ship since we left Callao. After the service was over our friend hove in sight again and came close round our stern and under our lee but still impossible to put out a life-boat, the gale was still raging with violent rain squalls. We were all shaking like leaves, soaking wet all the time with the spray and rain. This day our friend kept within sight all the time and when night came on we kept a flare-up light going at intervals, which she answered. At midnight the gale abated a little and the sea went down considerably.

Oct. 13th. At daylight the wind started to freshen again but the sea had gone down a good deal. Our friend the four-masted barque was hove to on our weather-beam under the topsail and fore-sail. She had a two flag signal saying "I am coming to you assistance" and in a few minutes we saw them launching a life-boat and coming to our weather quarter, - the Chief Officer, Mr. Yves Cadic was in charge - at the risk of their lives for the wind was rapidly increasing again with a very heavy sea. We had a 2" rope bent to a lifebuoy and floated to them as they could not come any nearer than 60 fathoms on account of the high sea. They picked this up and we bent a 3½" rope to it and they hauled it in and made it fast in the stern of the boat; they also had a sea anchor out with 15 fathoms of line forward to prevent the boat from being thrown end over end to the sea. Then we took our new deep sea lead line which we had on the poop and bent it on to another buoy and floated it to them; then we made a bowline in the middle of the lead line. The carpenter took a turn with the lead line round the rail and one A.B. went in the bowline. The carpenter then lowered away into the water and the Chief Officer and his boson sat in the stern of the boat and hauled away and got the man safe in the life-boat and so everyone hauled in, all the old men and invalids first, until they got 13 of us in the boat. I was in the life-boat and had with me the ship's papers but my Log Book is lost. I tried to get it out of my room after our first night's outing on the halfround, but my room was full of water and everything broken messed up. They then made the life-boat fast to the line again and let them go and rowed away for the ship. Mr. Oxnard hoisted up a little pole the letter "R" according to our Captain friend's instructions to his officer to let him know that the boat was coming back again.

We got alongside safe and stood by to jump when the boat was level with the ship's rail and her crew were ready to catch us. 13 of us got all safe on board and the Chief Officer, Mr. Cadic did not wait one moment with his gallant crew but gallantly pulled back again at the risk of their lives to save the rest of our shipmates and they were successful in doing so. The carpenter was the last man to leave the wreck. The letter "R" was flying and he lowered himself down and when in the sea he let go the line and they hauled him safe into the life-boat and she got safe alongside and all on board in the same manner as before. They then hooked on the life-boat and we all helped to run her up quick in order to prevent her from getting smashed up and landing her on deck. We all went on the quarter-deck and thanked God, the Captain, officers and his crew and gave them all three hearty cheers for saving our lives at the risk of their own.

They had the second life-boat ready in tackles to put out in case anything happened to us in the first; they had also very large bags full of oil hanging over the bow and stern which prevented the heavy rollers from breaking and swamping the boat. When the first boat-load were safe on deck I saw the Captain standing on the bridge and crying like a child and I rushed up to him and thanked him. He then told me that he would have never left us if he had to stand-by us for thirty days; he would see the last of us or save us. We were all safe on board at noon on Lat. 28° 58 S. and Long. 87°4 W. the wind south and rapidly increasing again to a strong gale.

They trimmed the yards and steered by the wind on the port tack and the Captain, Officers and crew gave us dry clothes and something to eat and drink; they treated us with the utmost kindness. The men all got a bunk each down in the fore peak and the Carpenter and some men were making shavings to serve as beds and the Captain sacrificed two good sails, cut them up and made blankets for them all. It was very clean, nice and warm down the fore peak and the men were all very comfortable. The Captain and myself attended to all those who were hurt and gave them quarters. R. Jones was the first attended to; his arm was swollen to a terrible size from the shoulder to the finger ends but the bone was not fractured. The Captain bandaged him up and gave him a room in the quarter-deck House. Our Carpenter got badly bruised about the hip and knee; also his foot got hurt and cut and the Captain bandaged him up also, and gave him quarters with the Ship's Carpenter E. Maganske. Charles Ellison, James Kavanagh, Mitchell, Singer A.B. and B. Mullaney all got more or less bruised about the arms and legs but the Captain attended to them regularly every day. Mr. Oxnard and myself got a room in the Saloon and Mr. May got quarters with the 3rd Officer of the "Loire" and so everybody was made very comfortable.

There were 26 of us saved and the ship's crew all told is 33; total 59 lives on board which made it absolutely necessary to put all hands on half rations. The Ship's crew were willing to do so for our sake and I hope they will all be highly rewarded on our arrival home and may God bless and protect our rescuers where-ever they go.

Great praise is due to Captain Michel Jaffré master of the good ship "Loire" for his heroic action in standing by us for four days working his vessel all the time. He never had his foot off the Deck from the time he saw our rockets until we were saved and also to the Chief Officer Mr. Yves Cadic who was in charge of the Boat and his crew for the seaman like manner in which he handled the lifeboat at the risk of their lives to save ours; also to the 2nd Officer Mr. Paul Boulet and crew for their smartness in handling their vessel in order to save our lives.

I hope that God, Our Heavenly Father will bless and protect them all and highly reward them all for their heroic action.

November 11th. The third day after we were saved my head began to swell terribly and I was very ill for a week and the Chief Officer, Mr. Cadic was also laid up through exposure in the Lifeboat, with a heavy cold and was off duty for one week but he is not well yet and has been under the Captain's medical care all the time; the rest of us are all well at present, thank God.

(Signed) W. A. H. Mull.

Chief Officer.

BIBLIOGRAPHY

Abrams, Lynn. *Myth and Materiality in a Woman's World - Shetland 1800–2000.* Manchester University Press. 2005

Angus, James Stout. *A Glossary of the Shetland Dialect.* Alexander Gardner, Paisley. 1914.

Carter, Robert. *Windjammers, the Final Story.* Rosenberg Publishing Pty Ltd, Australia. 2004.

Clunes, A.T. (ed). *The Shetland Book.* The Shetland Times Ltd, Lerwick. 1967.

Conrad, J. *Last Essays.* J.M. Dent & Sons Ltd., London. 1926.

Findlay, A.G. FRGS, *Directory for the Navigation of the South Pacific Ocean.* Fifth Edn. Richard Holmes Laurie. 1884

Halcrow, Captain A. *The Sail Fishermen of Shetland.* The Shetland Times Ltd, Lerwick. 1994.

Harland, John. *Seamanship in the Age of Sail,* Bloomsbury Publishing plc, London. 2015.

Jamieson, Robert. *Shetland - A Love Story.* The Shetland Times Ltd, Lerwick. 2010.

Johnson, J. Laughton. *A Kist of Emigrants.* The Shetland Times Ltd, Lerwick. 2010.

Kihlberg, Bengt, (ed.). *The Lore of Ships.* Tre Tryckare, Cagner & Co, New York. 1963.

Learmont, Captain James. *Master in Sail.* Percival Marshall & Co Ltd, London. 1954.

Lubbock, Basil. *The Last of the Windjammers,* Vol.1. Brown, Son & Ferguson Ltd, Glasgow. 1927.

Lubbock, Basil. *The Last of the Windjammer,* Vol.II. Brown, Son & Ferguson Ltd, Glasgow. 1929.

Sandison, Charles. *The Sixareen and her Racing Descendants.* The Shetland Times Ltd, Lerwick. 2005.

Thompson, Paul. *Living the Fishing.* Routledge & Kegan Paul, city?. 1981.

Thompson, Paul. *The Edwardians.* Weidenfeld & Nicolson, London. 1975.

Williams, James H. *Blow the Man Down.* E.P. Dutton & Co. Inc, New York. 1959.

Underhill, Harold A. *Deep Water Sail.* Brown, Son & Ferguson Ltd, Glasgow. 1963.

Woollard, Commander C. L. A., RN (ed.). *The Last of the Cape Horners.* Arthur H. Stockwell, Ltd, Ilfracombe. 1967.

INDEX